BEST SEAT IN THE HOUSE

BEST SEAT IN THE HOUSE

Love Letters to a Profession

WINSTON WEBBER

sh.
SUTHERLAND HOUSE

TORONTO, 2026

Sutherland House
416 Moore Ave., Suite 304
Toronto, ON M4G 1C9

First edition, November 2026

If you are interested in inviting one of our authors to a live event or media appearance, please contact sranasinghe@sutherlandhousebooks.com and visit our website at sutherlandhousebooks.com for more information about our authors and their schedules.

We acknowledge the support of the Government of Canada.

Manufactured in China
Cover designed by Leah Ciani and Jordan Lunn
Book composed by Karl Hunt

Credit for "Di rayze aheym" from *Her Birth and Later Years: New and Collected Poems, 1971-2021* © 2022 by Irena Klepfisz. Published by Wesleyan University Press. Used with permission.

Library and Archives Canada Cataloguing in Publication
Title: Best seat in the house : love letters to a profession / Winston Webber.
Names: Webber, Winston, author
Identifiers: Canadiana (print) 2026020143X | Canadiana (ebook) 20260204870 | ISBN 9781990823718 (softcover) | ISBN 9781990823725 (EPUB)
Subjects: LCSH: Webber, Winston. | LCSH: Violinists—Canada—Biography.
Classification: LCC ML418.W285 A3 2026 | DDC 787.2092—dc23

ISBN 978-1-990823-71-8
eBook 978-1-990823-72-5

For Walter

Can you live without music?

If you can live without music, thank the Lord and goodbye.

—Nadia Boulanger

Contents

Introduction

THE BRIGHT SIDE

Via viatores quaerit

(The way seeks those who would walk it)

THIS BOOK IS A LOVE letter, a book-length love letter to classical music, an imprecise term of art carrying more than a whiff of stuffiness but what can you do? It is for anyone curious about the seemingly remote but astonishing world this great art lives in, a world at once hermetic and narrow, yet open to the broadest of skies.

I played assistant principal second violin in a big-league professional orchestra for almost forty years, sitting at the exact focal point of the sound, front and centre, where your shoes damn well better be polished. At that location, the sheer acoustic power of the orchestra going at full tilt is beyond belief. It's the best seat in the house.

The flip side, of course, is that "playing second fiddle" is seen as a fate worse than death, as the cliché goes. And a job title as eye-catchingly long as mine, with "second" right in the middle, would seem to make it even worse, but no. My chair is in the absolute centre of the musical action. Professionals know that the difference between a good orchestra and a great one is the quality of its inner voices. The "seconds" enrich the sound, support the first violins in their stratospheric pyrotechnics, and create the musical pulse that everyone else depends on. Unfortunately, that's hard to explain at parties.

Like so many others, I spent the COVID lockdown behind a computer keyboard, in my case posting on Facebook a sort of glorified daily blog about music and musicians, written for my locked-down colleagues and friends. Every day I challenged the copyright censors on Soundcloud and posted a recording of something I loved, shamelessly ripped off from a favourite CD or LP or a live broadcast recording from my chaotic but cherished tape collection, accompanied by an essay about it. With a pretty picture. They're still there.

But it wasn't just a labour of distraction. To paraphrase the physicist Jeremy Bernstein, performers like me live to share with you the infinite astonishments of music, and the great minds, great personalities, and great souls who enable us to create it. When the pandemic prevented us from doing that in the usual professional way, onstage, we found other ways. I did this.

The excellent journalist Paul Wells liked my essays enough to get me in touch with the excellent publisher Ken Whyte of Sutherland House, who actually read them. And here they are.

But the story isn't about me. I love music like life itself, you'll see, but I'm not famous, so who would care? This is about everything else. My experiences have been pretty universal for a classical musician who had enough talent to make the risk of trying for a professional career not totally crazy, but not nearly enough talent to make it easy. Ha, of course; it's never easy.

I've been playing in professional orchestras now for fifty years. A long time. And I'm still in love. That permanent infatuation may have prevented a career in engineering or medicine (early ambitions in the imagination of my heart) and could easily have caused a career catastrophe if devoting my entire higher education to practicing the violin hadn't resulted in my winning an audition for a fine orchestra . . . and full employment. The Toronto Symphony heard 120 candidates before I was offered the one available position. The amount of luck involved in that success makes my blood run cold. I look back now at the risks I took and it scares the daylights out of me. Was it worth it? As everyone in love says, "Yes! Yes! A thousand times, yes!"

That wonderful insanity is what this book is about.

THE LESS BRIGHT SIDE

Performing musicians—great ones, decent ones and poor ones—come and go: even the best of them leave a mark which quickly fades . . .

—Harvey Sachs, *Toscanini*

This grim assessment of the musical life appears in the last pages of a doorstop of a book by Mr. Sachs, full of excellent writing and deep research that is still, after nearly fifty years, the definitive biography of the most famous conductor of all time. Sachs goes on:

> [I]t seems absurd that a highly gifted human being like Toscanini should have lavished his vital energies on trying to realize this or that melodic figure in one way instead of another. The most amazing thing about Toscanini, however, was that his struggle to

> achieve a beautiful performance was absolutely a matter of life and death . . .

As you see, Harvey Sachs is an admirer. Sachs's mentor, the distinguished music critic Bernard Haggin, whose dense, severe prose I quote at length later in this book, was also an admirer of the great maestro and so am I. But, with the greatest respect to Mr. Sachs, a writer of abilities and accomplishments far surpassing my own, Toscanini's existential devotion to his art was not unique to him. There are many performers who see giving their best onstage as a matter of life and death. I am privileged to know some of them. On my better days, I am one of them myself. If you think this is an exaggeration, you haven't seen a performing artist at work up close.

On a hot night, any fine orchestra, working with a fine conductor (or, more and more these days, without one) will be putting out megawatts of life-or-death energy. I write about a powerful example of this in "Kiss Me as If It Were the Last Time." I have experienced that kind of musical nuclear fusion onstage many times. After one such performance, a dear friend came backstage, tears in her eyes. "That was life-changing!" And indeed it was, for all of us. *That's why we do it.*

A great solo pianist, alone on a big stage, can levitate an audience for an entire evening. To make a career of doing that a hundred times a year for decades is simply superhuman. With an orchestra, the most astonishing co-operative operation in the history of the performing arts (except for opera, but that's a whole other beast), the music can be Mahler, digging down into the darkest recesses of . . . somewhere, it can be John Williams making bicycles fly, it can be Johann Sebastian Bach writing about Judas betraying the Son of God, or it can be a young composer just learning the craft and discovering a gift for creating something beautiful out of nothing. Getting all this together at eight o'clock in the evening, on a date planned two or three years in advance, usually in the winter, is not nearly as easy as we make it look.

Indeed, this book is about "yes, yes, a thousand times yes." That's what makes the musical world go 'round. But it's also about Churchill's "blood, toil, tears, and sweat," the kind of work necessary to create the miracle you can see onstage, live, right in front of you, just for the price of a ticket.

Dramatis Personae

OTTAWA

The beautiful capital city of Canada, one of the world's great parliamentary democracies, which we appreciate more and more every day. We're located at the confluence of two ancient rivers of commerce—the Ottawa, from the Algonquin word *adawe*, meaning "to trade," and the Gatineau, used until recently to transport logs from the forests of La Belle Province—so we were multicultural from the word go. You'll find us on the map approximately four hundred miles northwest of New York City, but it's easier to get to Disney World.

NATIONAL ARTS CENTRE

A large, imposing—huge, actually—performing arts complex, built on prime real estate overlooking Parliament Hill to commemorate the centennial of the founding of Canada, no less. The NAC, as it's always abbreviated, was the crowning achievement of the National Capital Arts Alliance, originally endorsed by Canada's fourteenth prime minister,

Lester B. Pearson, of airport fame. Construction wasn't finished until two years after the centennial, partly because the parking garage was dug right next to the picturesque, historic—and wet—Rideau Canal. The project also went massively (some said intentionally) over budget, but the eventual result was a beautiful structure of imperishable quality with three performing halls second to none anywhere in the world. Boasted Prime Minister Pearson's successor, the one and only Pierre Elliot Trudeau, "In a country often accused of a complex of inferiority, there is nothing inferior about this complex." That's because the project was spearheaded by G. Hamilton Southam, a patrician scion of a wealthy newspaper family, war hero, diplomat, and gentleman after the grand manner who wouldn't take no for an answer. For that we are eternally grateful.

NATIONAL ARTS CENTRE ORCHESTRA

The best orchestra nobody's ever heard of, at least outside Canada. Inside Canada, *everybody* knows who we are, admires our playing and envies our government funding, leaving aside the eggs-in-one-basket thing. Originally a large chamber orchestra of forty-four members, NACO, as it's always abbreviated (pronounced *nackoh*, not *knackered*), was created as the resident ensemble of the NAC and modelled on the virtuoso Mannheim Orchestra, the greatest orchestra of Mozart's time. We're now considerably larger (like most things) and play everything from Monteverdi to Lutoslawski, but Mannheim is in our DNA. We still play the pants off Mozart.

ME

Born in Detroit, "the Motor City," back when cars for the world rolled off its assembly lines by the thousands, just a few years after tanks and bombers rolled off its assembly lines by the thousands and saved the free world. Really, it did, look it up. Detroit back then was full of great expat musicians with names like Mischakoff, Zerounian, and Bistritsky, so I learned to respect the music of Beethoven and Brahms as much as they did. Of course they respected it. Beethoven and Brahms saved their lives.

PART I

Conductors: What do they *really* do?

All and sundry don't have the faintest idea about conductors, including yours sincerely.

—Carlos Kleiber

The Most Beautiful Music Ever Written by Anybody, Anytime

Never look encouragingly at the brass.

—Richard Strauss

PROFESSIONAL ORCHESTRA MUSICIANS AGREE ON only three things: J. S. Bach was the greatest composer ever, Carlos Kleiber was the greatest conductor ever, and the last twenty minutes of Richard Strauss's opera *Der Rosenkavalier* is the most beautiful music ever written by anybody, anytime. God knows how this middle-class, card-playing German sat down in front of a blank piece of paper and came up with music that makes you not care if you die, so long as this is the music you die to.

The supremacy of Bach is really too obvious to need much discussion. He wrote a staggering amount of music of huge heart, sincere faith, and overwhelming intellect. He was a virtuoso organist—"his feet flew over the pedals as if they had wings"—he knew everything about organ building, and he taught a generation of fine composers, some of whom were his sons. He also trained and conducted one of the most famous choirs in Europe, the Thomanerchor in Leipzig, founded eight hundred years ago (you read that right), and still had energy left over to be a tireless pain in the ass, especially to those who deserved it. But Carlos Kleiber was supreme at a more elusive art.

We orchestra musicians are a conflicted lot. We put in the apocryphal ten thousand hours to master absurdly difficult classical instruments, we band together in a group almost as large as a military battalion, big enough to intimidate anybody, but then subjugate ourselves to people called conductors who don't play a note, often celebrities who are hugely well-paid to not play a note.

It's complicated.

To be honest, most conductors are not very good. If they played an instrument like they conduct, they would have applied to medical school years ago. Worse, we know this upside-down state of affairs is our own fault, because orchestras have become so expert that we play well no matter what's going on in front of us. But here's the thing: we'll be the first to admit that the rare conductor who is truly gifted has the keys to the kingdom. We worship the ground they walk on. Again, it's complicated.

When the great Russian conductor Gennady Rozhdestvensky (yes, I had to look it up) was asked what made a good conductor, he dryly replied, "the radiation." Leaving aside the *frisson* from hearing the word "radiation" with a Russian accent, he was right on the money. It's undefinable, it's personal, and it can't be taught. You either have it or you don't.

This is my son Carlos. Totally unmusical.

—Erich Kleiber

Erich Kleiber was one of the most famous conductors in pre-war Germany until he left the country in disgust after the rise of the Nazi party. His cruelly untrue statement about his obviously gifted son was meant to protect young Carlos, born Karl Ludwig Bonifacius Kleiber (poor kid) from the cut-throat politics of music. Obviously not thinking ahead, he thought chemistry would be just the thing. In fact, his "totally unmusical" son had music in every cell of his body. When the family fled to Buenos Aires in 1935, young Karl Ludwig Bonifacius became Carlos. That probably helped.

> "For him to conduct was a religious act, something extremely deep that required a lot of honesty, and most of the time . . . he felt always that he was too inferior to the music that he had to conduct. Yet he was the greatest." —Riccardo Muti

> "He looked for perfection, for the absolute, in living, in art, in music, that one never finds. The failure of Kleiber is the failure of the artist." —Ioan Holender

> "And then he called me the previous night and said, I hope you know that I am more expensive since yesterday." —Wolfgang Sawallisch

> "Kleiber wasn't for every day. Once or twice a week is nice, but *Rosenkavalier* three times a week? You could've killed him with a tomahawk." —Kai Bernhöft

Leaving aside the tasteless threat, doubtless rhetorical, Carlos Kleiber was all those things. Only six years after Kleiber's death, *BBC Music Magazine* announced with trumpets and drums that "Carlos Kleiber has today been crowned the greatest conductor of all time by a selection of 100 of today's finest maestros." Yes, such a headline is an insult to the art, but the stunt actually had some value. If, with a roll of the eyes, we accept the premise of such an exercise, like *The New York Times* music critic Anthony Tommasini with composers (see "Chaconne") the real challenge turns out to be deciding who was the *second* greatest conductor. Now we're onto something. When, in a field of stellar accomplishment, one artist stands out so far above the others as to be beyond debate, there is something to learn.

When you read down past the carelessly written headline, you learn that the question asked of the "100 leading conductors" was actually to name the conductor who most *inspired* them. And to that more interesting question, the one hundred conductors (who did, in fact, include some serious names like Sir Colin Davis, Gustavo Dudamel, Valery Gergiev, and Mariss Jansons) voted Carlos Kleiber number one. So, not necessarily "the greatest," but rather the most inspiring to his professional peers. That's different. And better.

Said the former president of the Federal Republic of Germany, Richard von Weizsäcker, "The unforgotten, unforgettable Carlos Kleiber was the great 'unknown' among the rare, great fixed stars in the conducting firmament. . . . In his feelings, he bore the imperfection of the world with an infinite burden. He was constantly searching for the flawless, the ideal, the perfect—that is what makes him special . . . he conducted . . . in a way that always overwhelms everyone anew, literally leaving us listeners breathless."

So Carlos Kleiber actually was the greatest *and* the most inspiring (and the most exhausting) conductor of all time. So say his distinguished colleagues, so say the musicians who worked with him, so says his ever expanding and awe-struck audience, so says the former president of the Federal Republic of Germany. That settles it.

All right, all right . . . The second-greatest conductor of all time was Leonard Bernstein, who conducted more orchestra concerts in a year than Kleiber conducted in his whole lifetime. Bernstein was also a fine pianist, a pioneer in music education, and a fantastically successful, one-in-a-million composer who wrote classical, Broadway, and jazz. Quite a number two. Then follow Claudio Abbado, Herbert von Karajan (fourth! love it), Nikolaus Harnoncourt, Sir Simon Rattle, Wilhelm Furtwängler, Arturo Toscanini, Pierre Boulez, Carlo Maria Giulini, Sir John Eliot Gardiner, Sir John Barbirolli, Ferenc Fricsay, George Szell, Bernard Haitink, Pierre Monteux, Yevgeny Mravinsky, Sir Colin Davis, Sir Thomas Beecham, and Sir Charles Mackerras. What a list, great talents all. A few were even nice people. And yes, Furtwängler rated above Toscanini. That will start a new culture war right there.

Another conductor who also "had it" on the same lofty scale was the less well-known German-born Franz-Paul Decker. People often ask, "What does the conductor *really* do?" (you can tell they're already suspicious). So what did Franz-Paul Decker *really* do? Well, among other things, he absolutely radiated Richard Strauss.

Decker—I never heard a musician call him Franz-Paul, it was always DECKER—loved to repeat the Viennese joke: "If Richard, Strauss. If Strauss, Johann." It was a facetious way of dumping on both Richard Wagner and Richard Strauss, huge composers, of course, but neither even remotely Viennese. Which is to say, Richard Strauss is not to be confused with Johann Strauss of all the lovely Viennese waltzes, but either are to be preferred to that *awful* Richard Wagner.

All that aside, Richard Strauss wrote indescribably beautiful music that holds a unique place in the affections of musicians because he was such a master of both his art and his craft. The simple, subtle opening phrase of "Morgen!" brings tears, the magnificently orchestrated first chord of "Im Abendrot" is a vision of eternity, the archly caricatured "Das Diner" from *Le bourgeois gentilhomme* (Strauss having his languages both ways) has some of the funniest music outside Mozart, and then there's the last twenty minutes of *Der Rosenkavalier*, the deepest, most complex evocation of human affection outside novels too heavy to pick up. And Strauss knew it. As the eighty-one-year-old composer said imperiously to the American soldiers who knocked on his door in 1945: "I am STRAUSS, composer of *Elektra*, *Salome*, and *Rosenkavalier*." They bid him good day and left him alone. Wouldn't you?

Franz-Paul Decker began his career that same historic year, at age twenty-two, conducting at the Cologne Opera. Yes. The National Arts Centre Orchestra worked with Decker countless times, but I was too stupid to ask him how in the world opera happened in Cologne while the Americans and the Canadians and Bomber Harris were doing their best to level the city. After the war, because he was so gifted (and because he survived), Decker was invited to sit in on Richard Strauss's beloved after-concert card games. It's how the great man unwound. So young Franz-Paul Decker was a big talent, conducted opera between Allied bombing raids, and played cards with the last great German romantic composer. I was too intimidated by all that to ask who won.

To be fair, not everyone at every time in Franz-Paul Decker's long career had the luminous experiences we had with him. As artistic director of l'Orchestre symphonique de Montréal, his changes in personnel "made both friends and foes," as one careful writer put it. But for us he was a favourite guest who never let us down. He came so often that we developed a sort of ritual of re-acquaintance each time. At the first rehearsal he'd ascend the podium and sit down on a bar stool swiped from the café, wearing his trademark brown corduroys and black turtleneck. He'd look down his aquiline nose at us inscrutably through his thick glasses and things would get quiet. Then, from my seat right in front, I would ask, "How are you?" And it was off to the races.

We could never tell what would come back, usually something on politics or the *terrrrible* state of the world: "I am so grateful that I will not have to endure this *ridiculous* state of affairs as long as my dear daughters." Or about his most recent encounter with Ida Haendel, the superlative, diminutive and colourful violinist of the snakeskin boots (see "Ida! Don't Do That to Me!"). We really had no idea what Decker would say, but it was our little dance that sealed our special relationship with him, an artistic partnership we treasured beyond words.

More years ago than I like to think, I was sitting right in front of Decker when we did an absolutely incandescent suite from *Der Rosenkavalier*. The suite was put together by another famous conductor, Artur Rodziński, who was so disliked that he that carried a gun to rehearsals, but that's neither here nor there. Decker's great gift was that he simply stood there and this fabulous sound happened. *Strauss* happened. God knows how he did it. We loved him so much he didn't need a gun.

Actually, I know how he did it. We all know how he did it. There are certain conductors for whom musicians have such respect that somehow, with them, the orchestra's pulse quickens, its collective intelligence develops more neurons, its internal radar goes on high power. It would be an insult to the art to give less than everything in the presence of such a musician, so we take the risk of engaging our whole hearts, not something one does with just anyone, in music or anything else.

The peerless pre-war timpanist of the Berlin Philharmonic, Werner Thärichen, was also a composer. Timpanists have long stretches of time when they don't play, sometimes whole movements, so Thärichen always had a score with him, which he would study while the orchestra played. One afternoon, Thärichen was watching his score while a, let's say, less-than-ideal conductor was slogging his way through something (yes, even in Berlin) when Thärichen noticed a change. He looked up. Everything seemed the same, but there was a new clarity and resonance, a special energy in the sound. Suddenly there was *music*. Then he noticed. Wilhelm Furtwängler had walked in the back of the hall.

That's a great conductor.

Decker was a great conductor in that way, too, and Strauss wasn't the only thing we loved him for. He was a hugely cultured musician but also gently and charmingly eccentric, which meant his rehearsals and programming and choice of soloists could also lean towards the gently and charmingly eccentric. I very much doubt I'll ever play another concerto for castanets. And he had a laconic way of setting off one section of the orchestra against another, just for fun. "Madame principal *vioooola.* Your section is not bowing the same as the first violins. *They* go up, *you* go down. Why is that?" He knew very well why, we all knew why. Sitting on opposite sides of the stage, twenty-five feet apart, the violins and the violas had become two solitudes, like a relativistic distortion in the musical space-time continuum. That sometimes happened late in the day. It would be fine tomorrow and he knew that, he just wanted to stir the pot a little. Not for nothing he was sometimes affectionately known as "Crazy Decker."

He also made life gently and charmingly difficult for the terrible management we had back then. Things are different now, but in those dark days "terrible" was a polite word for the psychopaths who occupied a hallway of offices upstairs we called Death Row.

The Canadian Encyclopedia says this: "The music program of the Centre was singularly successful during its first decade, particularly through the extraordinary distinction and tireless activity of the resident National Arts Centre Orchestra." That wasn't just PR, it was true. In the NAC's early days there were attempts to create other resident companies—English and French theatre companies, a dance company—but the only one that flew was the orchestra. And did it ever: a recording contract with RCA Red Seal, a wildly successful New York debut with music director Mario Bernardi as both conductor and featured piano soloist, a tour to the Soviet Union, a performance for the General Assembly of the United Nations (not sure in what order), and stellar lineups of international soloists. The city, the whole country, was proud of its new orchestra, dubbed by the press as "the jewel in the crown" of the National Arts Centre. But that title came back to haunt us. A decade later, that jewel in the crown went through holy hell.

Pierre Elliott Trudeau's Liberals, after fifteen years in power, were succeeded by a Progressive Conservative government that wasted no time commissioning a study that recommended privatizing the National Arts Centre Corporation and eliminating the orchestra's budget. Why is it always conservatives who seem most interested in un-conserving things? The upside to government support is, well, government support. The downside is what can happen with the stroke of a partisan pen.

In the middle of all this, Trevor Pinnock, one of the most accomplished musicians in the world and top-selling recording artist for Deutsche Grammophon, was appointed our artistic director. The actual process to engage him was even more like 3-D chess than usual (I know, I was on the search committee), but Trevor was our final choice and it was a good one. Unfortunately, the unhelpful political environment of the time and our unhelpful management (they were related) soon sabotaged his best efforts. For the gory details, visit "Figure Out Which One You Are and Please Don't Do That."

Among other unhappy things, Trevor had been asked to stop engaging our beloved, brilliant, gently eccentric Franz-Paul Decker. Decker was thought to be "too difficult." Trevor, already stressed beyond reason, went along, and we noticed. The orchestra met with him about several issues (there were always issues) and, during a lull, I piped up and told him we were disappointed not to see Decker on the coming season. I tried to be diplomatic, really I did, but the remark embarrassed the hell out of Trevor because he knew why I said it. He could see by our faces that I was not the only one who felt that way, so he re-engaged our favourite guest for several programs and so, among other good things, we were able to do that spectacular performance of music from *Der Rosenkavalier*. The concert was broadcast live on the CBC but the master tape seems to have gone wherever master tapes go at the CBC, so I can't give you a link to listen to. You'll have to make do with Carlos Kleiber.

Last Week Was Unacceptable!

That's one of life's most difficult problems,
what to give for a birthday or anniversary
to a person you don't particularly like.

—Dmitri Shostakovich

AT THE UNIVERSITÄT FÜR MUSIK und darstellende Kunst Wien (University of Music and Performing Arts Vienna), one of the best music schools in the world, conducting students must be able to play full scores at sight on the piano, reading all the different clefs and transposing instruments, a stratospheric skill. But the revered Czech conductor Karel Ančerl was a percussionist. He took another route, paying his way through the Prague Conservatory by playing in jazz bands. I'm sure he had the keyboard skills the lofty Viennese school would demand, but his real instrument was, well, anything you could hit. Beautifully, of course.

At the conservatory it became obvious that young Karel Ančerl was a born conductor but, a decade later, that great gift didn't stop the Nazis from deporting him and his family to Theresienstadt. Likely, in fact, they were sent there precisely because of his gifts. The town of Theresienstadt was being transformed by the Nazis into a propaganda tool, a "model ghetto" (what a horrible euphemism). Many of the Jews imprisoned there were artists, writers, intellectuals, and musicians. Despite unspeakable conditions, the prisoners created a cultural life to help themselves survive. This Nazi-promoted "cultural showcase" was exploited, among other ways, in a propaganda film known under the skin-crawling title *Der Führer schenkt den Juden eine Stadt* (The Führer gives the Jews a city). Ančerl appears in the film, conducting an orchestra of prisoners playing a composition by another prisoner, Pavel Haas. The film shows Ančerl in a well-tailored suit, the "audience" also in jackets and ties. The edge of the stage was even decorated with flowering plants. The plants certainly beautified the scene for the cameras, but the real reason was to block the view of the prisoners' feet. That was because they had no shoes.

Immediately after the production of the film, all the musicians, including Ančerl, were sent in cattle cars to Auschwitz.

Take a breath.

OK. One of the most powerful recordings ever made of *Le sacre du printemps* (*The Rite of Spring*), Stravinsky's famous *succès de scandale*, is by Karel Ančerl and the high-octane Czech Philharmonic. Recorded eighteen years after the war, the superb Supraphon recording is in vivid, spacious stereo sound, helped by the matchless acoustics of the Rudolfinum's Dvořák Hall in Prague. All great orchestras have great percussion sections, by definition, but there is something even greater about this one. I'm sure Ančerl didn't micromanage their incredible playing on this recording, that's not where playing like this comes from. I like to think they knew that their work was appreciated by their fellow percussionist on the podium, that they had a mutual understanding. It sure sounds like it.

Like my unforgettable experiences with Helmuth Rilling, which I talk about in the chapter about him with the ridiculously long but accurate title, my single year playing for Karel Ančerl in the Toronto Symphony looms larger in memory than that limited time would suggest. It should have been many more years. But near the end of that season, on a hot evening in July, the death of our revered Czech music director was announced to us at the intermission of an outdoor concert. The sun had just set. Nobody remembers anything after that.

I was just a kid out of school in Ann Arbor when I won an audition for the Toronto Symphony. They'd had several rounds of international auditions that season without hiring anyone. I'd written about attending one of them in the winter, but didn't go. They must've been getting desperate because they wrote me a letter inviting me to yet another round of auditions in the spring. Well, I could hardly turn *that* down, so I added yet more orchestra repertoire to the pile of music I was already working on, got in my car on the day, and made the six-hour drive to Toronto. Yes, I was very young. After the audition, when the personnel manager called my name and told the rest they could go home, I was in shock. Among other things, that meant the great Karel Ančerl himself had approved my hire. I figured all those other more talented violinists before me must've had bad days and I'd had an especially good one. And that was true. To win an audition at that level you have to play very, very well, and the stakes are high. An early success with a big orchestra sets you up for the rest of your professional life. But it's also a bit of a lottery. Two candidates might play perfectly, but there was only one contract. I'd worked hard to win it, incredibly hard, but I wasn't patting myself on the back. It could so easily have gone the other way.

I knew about the Toronto Symphony—usually the TS for short, sometimes the TSO when you want to put a sport jacket on it—because a classmate of mine at the University of Michigan had won an audition for the TSO just the year before. Well, I could hardly miss it when she ran down the main hallway of the music school shouting, "I got the job! I got the job!" And I'd heard them at the Ann Arbor May Festival with Seiji Ozawa in a big program, including Richard Strauss's virtuoso orchestra showpiece, *Don Quixote*. They were impressive.

Karel Ančerl was conducting in North America, far from home and far from the great Czech Philharmonic he'd done so much to place on the international scene, when the Soviets invaded Czechoslovakia. Political reform was dead, the world was shocked, and Ančerl was out of a job. As it happened, Seiji Ozawa was leaving Toronto for San Francisco and the TSO had a shrewd and far-sighted general manager in Walter Homburger, himself a European refugee. So, thanks to the tanks and troops of the Warsaw Pact, one of Europe's greatest conductors became the next music director of the Toronto Symphony.

I'm from a part of the American Midwest now known as the Rust Belt, but it sure wasn't called that when I was a kid. Detroit then was a great manufacturing city that became home to the Motown Sound and The Supremes, as well as Chrysler, General Motors, Ford, and the Detroit Tigers. How in the world could I know what Czech music meant? Well, by playing for Ančerl, the same way I got a sense of French music from growing up with the Detroit Symphony and its exceptional French conductor, Paul Paray, and the way I got a sense of Mozart from my first years in the National Arts Centre Orchestra. You absorb the style, the sound, and the spirit. Then, as when Sherlock Holmes solves a mystery, suddenly it's obvious.

In the Toronto Symphony's years with Ančerl, when a Dvořák Slavonic dance would appear on the stands, even for a "kids' show," the orchestra would dig in with affection and a special sound, a proprietary sound.

Czech music was *our* music, the Czech sound was *our* sound, even if some Toronto Symphony members had never been farther afield than the Royal Ontario Museum on Bloor Street. I loved playing in an orchestra that had limitless admiration for its conductor and a sense of identity with the music of his homeland. It was love, appreciation, and infinite respect. And, to be honest, a certain amount of fear.

Orchestras then were not like orchestras now. With the National Arts Centre Orchestra, even in difficult music that's new to us, people are so well prepared that the first rehearsal sounds like a concert. It's the same with today's Toronto Symphony and all major orchestras. But fifty years ago . . . not so much. At its best, the TSO of those days could hold its own on any international stage and did so on many tours of Europe, the US, and Asia. But in the workshop of early rehearsals, things could get scrappy. Ančerl had no patience with that. One uncompromising way he raised the Toronto Symphony's performance standard would not be acceptable now. But it would not be necessary now.

We were rehearsing the first symphony of Shostakovich, a brilliant work that was written as a graduation exercise, believe it or not, when Shostakovich was only nineteen. Maybe the dazzling young composer was showing off for his professors, I don't know, but for whatever reason he gave the first violins an incredibly difficult passage right on the first page. It's one of those things where, if you play it well, it's impressive for a moment but, if you mess it up, it's the only thing the audience will remember. It's totally exposed, fast and high, but it also has to be perfectly controlled because the tempo isn't *that* fast. It has to be clean, clear, and rock-solid—right "in the slot." Unfortunately, in that first rehearsal it was none of those things. It was a mess. When the break was called, Ančerl asked the first violins to stay onstage and for everyone else to leave the hall. We broke out in a cold sweat. We knew what was coming.

"First stand alone."

Even then, going back stand by stand was almost never done. The unexpected shift of gears from playing in a section to playing alone can throw off even the best players. The first stand was Albert Pratz and Isadore Desser, both superb violinists. Albert was an established solo artist and had been in the NBC Symphony with Toscanini. Isadore had an effortless, sparkling technique. They played the passage perfectly. Damn. The second stand was still pretty good. But then, as the moment of truth approached for us lesser mortals farther back, things went downhill fast.

On the last stand was Cenek Vrba, a fine Czech violinist who had won the CBC Talent Competition and later became concertmaster of the Calgary Philharmonic. He played perfectly. But his stand partner, a young, energetic, but inaccurate (to be charitable) player, did not. No, it wasn't me, *grâce à Dieu*. Things fell apart, the centre could not hold. Poor Cenek began stomping his foot in a vain attempt to keep things together while the rest of us studied the floor. It was awful. When this trainwreck was over, our great conductor just looked down at his score in silence as we left the stage. Needless to say, at the next rehearsal the passage had improved significantly. We were relieved but, it turned out, not reprieved.

The following week's program included a suite from Prokofiev's spectacular ballet *Romeo and Juliet*. Most orchestra musicians prefer the stage to the obscurity of the ballet pit, but I have yet to meet one who didn't gladly accept invisibility in return for playing this glorious score. Act III has a hugely difficult, manically fast section for the violins called "Death of Tybalt." It's meant to sound like a sword fight and it succeeds brilliantly: lots of noise, lots of action, a bad end. When our much-improved dress rehearsal for the Shostakovich was over, Ančerl turned to the violins, looked straight at us and said, in a voice dry as dust, "Death of Tybalt." That meant nobody had a weekend.

Next Monday, when "Death of Tybalt" came around, we played brilliantly, virtuosically, heroically, every note clear and full of energy. We were magnificent! At the end, silence again from Ančerl, but a different kind of silence. Then he looked over at us and smiled. I could count on one hand the number of times we'd seen him smile. All was forgiven, we were back in our great maestro's good graces, and our collective blood pressure headed back down.

And that was one way, rough as it was, that Karel Ančerl raised the level of the TSO of those days to sound more like the Czech Philharmonic than it ever imagined it could. There was no resentment, such was our respect for him. We knew he was right. And, despite his declining health, Ančerl also had other ways to show what an old-school music director could be like.

The week after the Prokofiev (the performances were terrific), we had a guest conductor we didn't like. It happens, I won't say how often. All right, often. The big piece on the program was the fresh, open-hearted, beautifully written *Symphony in C* of Georges Bizet. If this vivacious piece isn't *musique dansant*, nothing is. Like Shostakovich, a youthful Bizet wrote this masterpiece as a student assignment. Then, like a student, he promptly forgot about it. A chain smoker and obsessively hard worker, Bizet died of a heart attack at the age of thirty-seven just three months after the premiere of his great masterpiece, *Carmen*. He thought it was a failure. Purcell, Pergolesi, Mozart, Schubert, Mendelssohn, Weber, Bizet—all dead before the age of forty. What a list.

The manuscript for the *Symphony in C* passed through several hands, then sat on a library shelf for decades. Sixty years after Bizet's death, the *Symphony in C* finally had its first performance. Then, of course, it was, "Wow! Where has this been all our lives?" Too late for Bizet.

Even coming from the composer of *Carmen*, one of the most hot-blooded scores in all opera, you'd think a work as early as the *Symphony in*

C must be lightweight, but you'd be wrong. The *Symphony in C* is joyous, sophisticated, exuberant, restrained, pierced with sadness (the long, poignant oboe solo in the Adagio is the most famous in the repertoire) and the "Finale," Allegro vivace, is a brilliant *moto perpetuo.* For the first violins, of course. And, like the Shostakovich, not *that* fast. Every note must be perfect.

Ottawa audiences heard the National Arts Centre Orchestra play the *Symphony in C* many times in its early years. It fit the small orchestra's crisp, clean style and exceptional technical abilities. But the Toronto Symphony's guest conductor that week all those years ago was not Karel Ančerl, and the TSO in those days was not the NAC Orchestra. As it happened, I had the week off, so I took a busman's holiday and went to the concert. Not entirely to my surprise, it wasn't very good. Actually, it was awful. Apparently I wasn't the only one on vacation. What I didn't know—what nobody knew—was that Karel Ančerl was *not* on vacation.

The following week, the first thing he did was tear a strip off the violins. He tore a strip off pretty much the whole orchestra, actually. "No matter who is conducting, you must play your best! The audience pays the same! Last week was unacceptable!" Fifty years later, I remember those words like it was last week. And so we learned that Karel Ančerl was our music director every week of the season, not just his weeks. Again, he was right.

But as the season progressed, we realized that something else *wasn't* right. The great man didn't look well. He missed some concerts.

A recording of Bedřich Smetana's mighty symphonic cycle *Má vlast* was on the schedule. *Má vlast*, in English, is usually "my country," but that doesn't come close to doing justice to the bone-deep patriotic and personal weight that title had for Smetana. Semyon Bychkov, today's chief conductor and artistic director of the Czech Philharmonic, writes:

> Má vlast, My Homeland, Mein Vaterland, Patria mia, Ma Patrie, Rodina . . . We all have one. It may be called by a different name, but the feeling is the same—the sense of identification with one's roots and of belonging. The pride we take in the best of our heritage and the pain of having to live with and come to terms with its darker pages. Smetana speaks for his country: its longing for independence at a time when it was dominated and needed to assert its national character, its language, its way of thinking. While looking at its past, he dreams of its future.

Every year for the past seventy years, *Má vlast* has been performed on the anniversary of Smetana's death as the opening concert of the Prague Spring International Music Festival. *Má vlast* was Ančerl's last recording with the Czech Philharmonic before the Soviet invasion meant he could never go home. Nothing could have been a greater privilege than to record this great work with him, but it was cancelled. We became concerned for him, and we were right. He had been the Toronto Symphony's music director for only four years, but his identification with the orchestra and the orchestra with him was complete. With *Má vlast* cancelled, we thought we might never again be so close to his heart. But on that we were wrong.

Ančerl's sixty-fifth birthday was April 11. As it happened, we had a concert with him that night so, despite his increasingly dubious health, somebody got the bright idea of surprising him. The plan was, instead of playing the swashbuckling opening of the big piece for the evening, Richard Strauss's *Don Juan*, we would play Happy Birthday instead. Then the mayor of Toronto, David Crombie, would come out and present Ančerl with a plaque. What could possibly go wrong? So Ančerl bravely starts that muscular tone poem, swinging for the fences, we play Happy Birthday instead and the poor man staggers back like he's been shot. The "surprise" wasn't funny at all, not one bit. Unperturbed, whoever was running this charade cheerfully came out with the mayor and the plaque and, oh God, a microphone, and asked Ančerl, still breathless with shock, to say a few words. Somehow he managed, but we were cringing at the obvious inappropriateness of the thing. Finally the presentation was over and Ančerl managed to conduct *Don Juan*, of all pieces, but he was clearly shaken. Equally clearly, people had not realized until then just how ill he was.

Just a month later Ančerl conducted Dvořák's *Requiem*. This transcendent work is the grief of the ages—in Latin, of course, but musically in Czech, if you can imagine such a thing. Ančerl was not himself, he was pale and bent, so unlike him, but this masterpiece from the summit of his culture held him up and us with him. The dress rehearsal had the whole Toronto Mendelssohn Choir—three hundred fine singers—as well as four soloists and the hundred musicians of the Toronto Symphony. Four hundred people onstage, but the hall was empty, it was just the dress rehearsal. But soon it became obvious it was much more than that. Nothing was said, but everyone could sense that Ančerl was looking at his last days and here we were with him, playing this immortal music that was so dear to him. Gradually, we realized that this dress rehearsal was his personal farewell to us. We played for him like we had never played before, the magnificent choir sang like they had never sung before, all to the empty hall, just for him. It became our private benediction, and his.

At the end there was no sound. Ančerl placed his hands gently on the score and looked at it for a long time. Then he slowly stood and walked off the stage, all in silence. When he had left, nobody could move. Four hundred people. It seemed to last forever. Finally a chair shifted and people quietly began leaving the stage. We were all moved beyond words by the experience we'd just had with this great, great man—our love and respect for him, his love and respect for us, expressed through the almost unbearably powerful music of his countryman.

Official records say we did another program with Ančerl the next day, music of Mendelssohn and Beethoven, but I have no memory of it. In any case, those were his last concerts with us. He died just two months later of complications from the chronic hepatitis he'd contracted in Auschwitz. His parents, his wife, and his son were murdered there. Only he survived. And we had just played the great *Requiem* of Dvořák with him, Ančerl conducting his heart out for us, us playing our hearts out for him. And for a hall full of ghosts.

The Unique, the Truly Great, the Rather Unbelievable Actually Helmuth Rilling

Art is the contemplation of the world in a state of grace.

—Hermann Hesse

I ONCE CONTRIBUTED A GRAIN of sand to the mountain of writing on J. S. Bach with an essay modestly titled "Why Bach is the Greatest Composer Ever" and nobody argued, so I guess that's settled. But where to start with Helmuth Rilling, for decades in our era one of the greatest *conductors* of Bach ever? While Herr Rilling would likely, like the rest of us, see himself as a mere servant of the great Thomaskantor, in fact his accomplishments as a musician, a scholar, and a teacher are enormous.

As a conductor, Rilling's repertoire ranged from Mozart to Verdi to Penderecki, but it was J. S. Bach upon whom he based his musicianship and his career. He founded one of the world's finest choirs, the Gächinger Kantorei, founded two of the world's great Bach festivals, the Internationale Bachakademie Stuttgart and the Oregon Bach Festival, received the Bach Medal of the City of Leipzig, whose recipients form a veritable constellation of the brightest international stars in Bach performance, recorded the complete choral works of Bach twice (170 compact discs before it was all released online) and, not least, celebrated his ninetieth birthday shortly before I wrote this.

Sadly, Helmuth Rilling left us just recently at the great, grand age of ninety-two, surrounded by his family and, no doubt, the greatest heavenly choir ever assembled.

An entire generation of musicians have come of age never having experienced Helmuth Rilling in performance. Many have never even heard of him. How fortunate for them, to be able to discover such an artist for the first time. I can't help but be personal about him because, as long as I can remember, he has been my ideal conductor: a great musician with tremendous personal presence (but not the kind that sucks all the air out of the room), a devoted, humane person, an incomparable scholar and, not least, a man of faith, lightly worn but deeply felt. I first heard him in Detroit fifty years ago when I was a student at the University of Michigan; five worshipful singers drove in with me from Ann Arbor. Supported by a grant from the German government, he was on tour with the Gächinger Kantorei and the Bach-Collegium Stuttgart, performing Bach's *Mass in B Minor* and the *St. Matthew Passion* on alternate nights all over North America. Imagine . . .

He was still in his thirties then, shaking up the staid world of Bach choral performance of those days with his brisk, unsentimental tempos and vivid illumination of the texts. Among many things we admired, it was the first time we'd heard a *St. Matthew Passion* that wasn't conceived on a geological time scale.

To really appreciate Rilling's artistry, we have to start with J. S. Bach himself. Not only did Bach write everything from monumental sacred masterworks to everyday pieces for weddings, birthdays, and even a coffee house, through the power of his unique talent (and by working harder than anybody else) Bach found ways to give musical expression to every imaginable human experience. Writes *New Yorker* music critic Alex Ross: "Bach is undoubtedly music's supreme companion of extreme distress. The human species has yet to undergo a catastrophe that Bach did not see coming long in advance." Not to forget his cantata about coffee. Bach really had everything.

So did Rilling.

Two decades after I'd first heard Rilling, and lots of water under the bridge, I was in my front chair in the NAC Orchestra and had developed ambitions to be a conductor. The great Russian conductor Kiril Kondrashin said of such ambitions, "Eees a *disease.*" But blind self-confidence will get you a long way in conducting and, in those years, I had lots of it. We were doing a short tour with Rilling and the Gächinger performing the *St. Matthew Passion* at the NAC in Ottawa, at the Notre-Dame Basilica in Montreal, at the Kennedy Center in Washington, and in Carnegie Hall. I told him I wanted to attend his summer conducting academy in Stuttgart, he told me who to write to, I was accepted. I took a crash course in German at the local Goethe-Institut and off I went.

The Internationale Bachakademie Stuttgart attracts conducting students from all over the world. That summer, many came from occupied Czechoslovakia. The course had the daunting but accurate title "Internationale Bachakademie Stuttgart, Sommerakademie Joh. Sebastian Bach 1987: Bach und die Tschechoslowakei." The theme was music related to Mary: Bach's "Mary cantatas"—*Wie schön leuchtet der Morgenstern*, BWV 1; *Meine Seel erhebt den Herren*, BWV 10; and *Herz und Mund und Tat und Leben*, BWV 147—Bach's *Magnificat*, and Antonin Dvořák's immense choral masterpiece, his *Stabat Mater*. With all that happens to poor Mary in that music, she would likely have preferred to be in accounting.

The academy was super-organized, of course, complete with three-ring binders holding all the schedules and concert programs for the course. It even had space at the end for a daily journal that came out every morning with photos and informal articles about the music of the day and the conductors involved. The last page listed conductors from ten countries, including, thank you, Canada. Rilling wore his politics lightly, like his religious beliefs, but I don't think it was just coincidence that the course focused on the music of a Soviet-occupied country and that many of the conductors came from behind the Iron Curtain. Also, several of the Bachakademie conductors were women. Forty years ago this was unusual, but it didn't seem unusual to him.

And then there were Rilling's *Gesprächskonzerte*, or "talking concerts." He would just stand there on the podium in his black leather jacket, looking impossibly laid-back, and lead the Bach-Collegium and a choir and soloists through detailed demonstrations of the works for the summer—the big themes, special examples of musical or word symbolism, details of orchestration and, when appropriate, theological background. Often, these special concerts were broadcast live on German radio. In those pre-internet days, I just took a little radio connected to a cassette recorder and taped them on the spot.

Rilling did countless talking concerts like these, including the complete *St. Matthew Passion*, the *St. John Passion* and the *Mass in B Minor*. That's a *lot* of talking. He did these in German in Stuttgart, in English in North America, and from memory everywhere, all the examples, dozens of them. No scores, no notes. The intellect that enabled him to do this would have been hopelessly intimidating except there was none of that with him. It was all about the music. And if you were all about the music, that's all he cared about.

Rilling has published whole books on just the nuts and bolts of performing Bach's big choral works. Each looks at the music three ways: the music itself (style, form, phrasing, articulation, musical-rhetorical figures, tempos), then the theology behind the music (with Bach, never far below the surface), and, last but absolutely not least, practical rehearsal issues, like preparation of the orchestra parts, who sits where, and rehearsal order, i.e., who gets to go home first. With works that last three hours, get that last one wrong and you might as well forget everything else. Which is to say, with Rilling you had profound spiritual experiences that always ended on time.

But despite the most careful organization, there's always the human side. For a big choral work with an audience, that's a lot of people in the room. The high point of the summer course was when we conducted movements of the Dvořák *Stabat Mater* with full orchestra, the Prague Philharmonic Choir, and four soloists in the big Stiftskirche (Collegiate Church) in downtown Stuttgart—essentially the Bachakademie's base of operations. These special rehearsals were open to the public and the church was always packed. During the war, the Stiftskirche was almost destroyed by Allied bombing. The few original walls that remain still bear the scars. It is impossible to describe the intensity of great sacred music heard in such a place.

The subject of the *Stabat Mater* is, of course, unbearable. It was the genius and humanity of Dvořák that turned such an overwhelming subject into great art. As it happened, just before it was my turn to conduct, there was a disturbance at the back of the church. Some poor soul had fainted and people were rushing over to help. Of course, everything stopped. Rilling stood up from his seat in the front and looked back with concern. An uneasy quiet settled over the church, except for soft voices in the back speaking to someone. After an endless minute, Rilling visibly relaxed and gently said to the audience, "She has her friends with her and is getting the help she needs." I will always remember the thoughtfulness and kindness in his voice. Then he gestured to me to conduct the next movement, "Inflammatus et accensus" (In flame and fire). Oh, God . . . now? *Me?*

The singer's text included the words "Fac me cruce custodiri, morte Christi praemuniri, confoveri gratia" (Make me to be guarded by the Cross, protected by the death of Christ, and cherished by grace). That stupendous prayer so overwhelmed me, and the circumstances in which I now had to conduct it, that I just closed my eyes and threw myself heart and soul into every phrase, every note, trying to make my intensity of expression worthy of the situation. That kind of thing is a classic formula for disaster, but the performance seemed to go well enough. Afterwards, Rilling took me aside. Perhaps, I thought in my youthful hubris, he was going to give me a compliment. He leaned down and whispered, "Don't slow down at the end. The singer will run out of air."

That's Helmuth Rilling.

Later, back home, some of my orchestra colleagues told me I should keep going with the conducting, an inexpressibly rare compliment. For reasons I still haven't quite figured out, I didn't. But that summer in Stuttgart I saw someone who certainly should have. One late afternoon in class everyone was tired, the *Stabat Mater* had been rehearsed for hours, and the young conductors were boring the orchestra to death. Intonation had gone totally off the rails, the sound was thick and unfocussed, the music directionless. Then a young woman stood up to conduct. I learned later she was a single mother from Bremen. She was slight of stature and even appeared a bit shy, most unusual for a conductor. She did not appear imposing or attention-getting in any way. But when she began to conduct, the world changed. Suddenly the orchestra and choir were in tune, the sound clear and vivid, the music full of character and vitality.

It was as if Dvořák himself had come into the room, or at least Helmuth Rilling. No, Rilling was already there, he had been for hours and was as tired as the rest of us. What the hell? She was just standing there, hardly moving. But she didn't need to. It was all in the economy and precision of her gestures, and in her eyes. She seemed to be making eye contact with everyone at the same time. Just her presence—her radiation—made the music instantly come alive. She was rehearsing the final movement, a powerful musical statement that summed up the entire work. Still hardly moving, she built it to a stupendous climax, the whole room shaking with the final, triumphant words, "*Paradisi gloria!*" At the end there was a stunned silence. Then Rilling stood up, smiled until his eyes shone and said one word: "*Ja!*"

Nobody Knew Anything Then

I don't approve of people who watch television, but I am one of them.

—Glenn Gould

IF YOU'VE NEVER HEARD A recording of Helmuth Rilling's superb choir, the Gächinger Kantorei (since Rilling's retirement renamed the Gaechinger Cantorey), you should—many can be easily found online. You won't believe what you've been missing. But Stuttgart, the Gächinger's home base, is also home to another choir that sings wonderfully well, the Kammerchor Stuttgart, conducted by Frieder Bernius. Both choirs have long been considered among the best in the world, the wonder is that the musical character of these two choirs and these two conductors could not be more different. In Bach, let's say, shouldn't one be considered more "correct" than the other?

That's like the argument from the deep dark past that Bach could not properly be played on a modern piano. All mainstream pianists play Bach on the piano now, towering above them all Canada's Angela Hewitt, who has the largest and most celebrated recorded catalogue of J. S. Bach of any pianist of any era. The "Bach on the piano debate" is laughable now, but for a long time it was a real thing. Pioneering pianists like Myra Hess, Edwin Fischer, Rosalyn Tureck, and Hewitt had to push hard at first. And, of course, there was Glenn Gould, who was a certifiable genius, but his famous *Goldberg Variations* were recorded in 1955 and nobody knew *anything* then.

As for correctness, there has never been a greater conductor of J. S. Bach than Helmuth Rilling, yet he always performed Bach on modern instruments in modern pitch. And they played with—horror!—vibrato, another dispute that, like Bach on the piano, has since evolved to everyone's benefit. Rilling argued that we can try to reproduce the instruments and the pitch of Bach's time, but we can't reproduce his listeners. We hear Bach from the perspective of three centuries of music written since Bach's time, from the "romantic classicism" of Beethoven to the wild dissonances of Ligeti. What would Bach's listeners have made of the Berlioz *Requiem*, his *Grande messe des morts,* composed less than a lifetime after Bach's death but written for a choir of eight hundred voices and an orchestra of two hundred, including ten pairs of cymbals and sixteen timpani? Plus four brass bands.

Today, fortunately, great "modern" performers and great "period" performers share the same stage. We have expanded our horizons, we now take in more of the depth and breadth of Bach than ever before, and almost certainly more than Bach's own listeners did. In fact, some Leipzig worthies found Bach's music annoying and "needlessly difficult," even scandalous, such as his spectacularly theatrical *St. John Passion*. "Opera has no place in church!" they muttered, on their way out the door.

The august Leipzig town council even pushed Bach around on occasion. Due to some intrigue unknown even to Bach himself and still unconfirmed by scholars (likely inter-church rivalry), just before one

Good Friday service Bach was told by the authorities that he "needed permission" to perform his *St. John Passion* and, not having obtained such permission, the performance was to be cancelled. Bach replied, typically, "I don't care. I didn't want to do it anyway." In fact he was deeply hurt, but he wasn't going to tell *them* that.

Listen to anything conducted by Helmuth Rilling with his athletic, full-throated Gächinger Kantorei, and then listen to Frieder Bernius with his refined, "authentic performance practice" Kammerchor Stuttgart. I dare you to say which you prefer.

I must make a short detour here to define a term I've already used: "performance practice." This isn't the answer to the tired joke "How do I get to Carnegie Hall?" Performance practice is a term of art that can mean anything from performing old music rationally and musically, based on credible historical evidence, to ideological extremes of style that must be "original" even if it sounds like a plugged-up vacuum cleaner (see "The Ghost in the Machine"). That's why performance practice used to have a dodgy reputation: "They're the ones who can't play in tune." Now, performance-practice players are some of the hottest musicians in the business, but sometimes reality changes faster than opinion.

As with Rilling years earlier, most NAC Orchestra musicians had no idea what to expect with Frieder Bernius. Actually, it was worse. Bernius had sent his own orchestra parts ahead of time and they were . . . strange. Scattered all over the music were pencil markings that looked like little parentheses over certain notes. This especially annoyed the string players because, at first glance (and when you're performing, a glance is all you get) they looked like little downbow marks. Each time you saw one, you had to remember that it *wasn't* a downbow, it was something else, but by then you'd screwed up and pretty soon you'd written the whole thing off. So we thought, "Oh no, he's one of *them.*" Meaning performance practice zealots.

We hadn't even met Bernius and already we hated him. But, as happened with Rilling, at the first rehearsal in came all these young German singers (though, being "historical," not so many black leather jackets), and from their first entrance, as with the Gächinger, their singing was simply overwhelming. *HUGE*, beautiful sound, resonant, musical, and perfectly in tune. We were stunned. If this guy could put together a choir that sings like that, this "zealot" suddenly had credibility.

And we quickly learned what the strange parenthetical markings meant. They were indications for de-emphasis, notes to be played more lightly. Bernius didn't mark where there should be more sound, he marked where there should be *less*. These "reverse dynamics" lightened the texture miraculously and moved the tone production into the performance practice world with no need for annoying admonitions like "Oh, please . . . less vibrato." Now we *loved* him.

But that was a long time ago. Now the NAC Orchestra, like all other fine orchestras, moves into "performance practice" style as a matter of course for composers like Bach and Handel, sometimes for Mozart and Beethoven, even for Brahms and Schumann, if an eyebrow is raised. This development has been so gradual and natural that it's gone unnoticed by audiences, except they remark how much they like the sound. But it's very much noticed onstage and by grateful conductors.

That's how the Kammerchor Stuttgart sang: low pressure, relaxed sound production, minimal vibrato, transparent, almost a "white" sound like a fine boys' choir, but with adult strength. They even use the same period sound in their performances of Bruckner's unearthly beautiful motets, and more "romantic" music does not exist.

You could actually see the difference. In rehearsal, the Gächinger often cupped their hands backwards in front of their ears to hear the sound reflected from behind the group, because the sound heard from *within* the group was such high voltage. The Kammerchor didn't need to do that. Two totally different concepts of sound production and two totally different approaches to "period" performance, but both persuasive, musical and, most important, beautiful. You hear either one and think, "How else could it be?"

Why? I Know It.

We did Elgar's second symphony and afterwards a board member says,
"NO MORE ELGAR!"

—Sir Andrew Davis

I WROTE THIS ESSAY BEFORE the beloved British conductor Andrew Davis passed away. Having known him, worked with him, and loved him for most of my professional life, it was indescribably difficult to revise this into the past tense. It's still hard to believe he's no longer with us. If you don't believe musicians can really have such affection for a conductor, "Why? I Know It." should convince you.

I had known Andrew since his debut with the Toronto Symphony over fifty years ago. Ever since then, whenever I ran into him, even after not seeing him for years, it was always a booming "Hello!!!" in his famous Oxbridge baritone, then a bear hug, then "Winston! How *are* you?" followed by his hearty laugh full of kindness. He was like that with everybody. Without exception, all the remembrances of him have ended with "He didn't have an enemy in the world." So far as I know that was true, amazing in our business. His death devastated the Toronto Symphony, which he'd conducted at least once every year for fifty years without fail, devastated the international music community, and devastated me.

After Karel Ančerl died in the summer of 1973—it's still such a sadness to write that, even after all these years—the Toronto Symphony engaged the devoted, under-appreciated Victor Feldbrill as resident conductor and started an international search. According to Richard Warren's book-length history of the Toronto Symphony, five names ended up on the short list but, from where I sat in the orchestra, only two names were on the *really* short list: Andrew Davis, a hugely talented young Brit with a gold-plated CV, and Klaus Tennstedt, a hugely talented German in his forties, recently defected from behind the Iron Curtain. Tennstedt had recently made his first North American appearance with us in Toronto, Andrew had also done a spectacular performance with us, which I'll get to shortly, so we had already seen and liked them both.

At the outset of his conducting career, Andrew still looked like a big choirboy, bangs and all. That was before the Toronto Symphony and, well, life, got hold of him, but the bangs held out for a long time. When Andrew first arrived in Toronto he really did look like a big kid and even sort of acted like one, until he spoke. Then his resonant, incongruously authoritative voice said he might not be quite such a kid after all.

Tennstedt barely knew ten words of English and kept losing his watch, but he was a rare talent and shrewd catch of TSO managing director Walter Homburger, just as Ančerl had been seven years earlier. With his almost non-existent English, his painfully obvious insecurities and tendency to get lost on his way to rehearsals, we felt warmly protective of him. We called him Big Bird, for reasons that are obvious to anyone who's seen him conduct. Also, charmingly, he couldn't tell time very well, whether or not he had his watch, but he was obviously a very great artist. His chaotic beat, disheveled appearance, and personal magnetism, reminding many of Furtwängler, drew a phenomenal sound from the confused but inspired musicians. We had great hopes.

But Andrew also got the rumour mill going as a last-minute replacement for Ančerl, conducting a stunning performance of the massive, highly idiomatic, and not well-known *Glagolitic Mass* by the intense Czech composer Leoš Janáček. When he got the call, young Andrew's ace up his sleeve was that his parents had given him a score to the Janáček as a Christmas present the year before and he'd learned it "just because I really liked it." So when this young conductor with the choirboy bangs upon whom serendipity had smiled so broadly launched into this monster of a work with total knowledge and confidence, we were impressed as all get out.

Imagine having two such conductors as possible music directors! But, as the story went, the difficult decision was made clearer when the chair of the board visited Tennstedt in his dressing room before his concert and found the great conductor distracted and nervous and very possibly already into the post-concert refreshments. The performance was terrific—Tennstedt's performances had an elemental power that was unforgettable—but when the same board chair visited Andrew before *his* debut conducting the *Glagolitic Mass*, he found Andrew serene and confident, the doorstop of a score lying closed on his desk. Asked why he wasn't doing some last-minute studying, Andrew calmly replied, "Why? I know it."

Klaus Tennstedt went on to a become one of the great conductors of the late twentieth century, but the TSO board was looking for brilliance in someone just a little less scary. They found their man in the gifted young Brit with the bangs.

Also, it must be admitted, while we hugely admired Tennstedt, we *loved* Andrew. At his first rehearsal as music director we launched right into the big work on the program, Stravinsky's *Petrushka*, playing the splashy, difficult piece for all we were worth. It was a thrill, until the place where everything comes to a sudden halt, the deafening silence interrupted by a short, low F-sharp on the contrabassoon, *BLAAAT!!!* Andrew gleefully called out "Flat!" and broke into almost embarrassingly foppish laughter: "Ha! First comment as music director!" Well, Mozart had a funny laugh, too. We were off to a good start.

And, shortly after Andrew arrived, a recording contract also conveniently arrived. Our first project for Columbia Records was a two-LP set of the Russian chemist and part-time (!) composer Alexander Borodin: his three symphonies, the Overture to *Prince Igor* and the famous *Polovtsian Dances* with the three-hundred-strong (in those days, very strong) Toronto Mendelssohn Choir.

The recording was made in Massey Hall, our home turf, with its friendly acoustics, if a bit dry for microphones. The producer, Andrew Kazdin, who did many of Glenn Gould's recordings (which is to say, he was very good and very patient), and engineer Bud Graham did a great job capturing the generous, woody sound of that scary old brick pile on Shuter Street. After frustrating experiences with fussy producers (one stopped a great take of Brahms's Symphony No. 4 because he thought he heard a chair creak) it was a relief to see the Columbia guys come in, set up maybe half a dozen microphones, nothing like the rainforest of mike stands you see now, and call out from the booth, "Play something loud." We played something loud, the voice from the booth said, "OK, we got a level. Let's go." So we went. Wow.

Andrew had a friendly, energetic conducting gesture that came up from the beat, not down into it. The result was a sound that was always expanding, always leading somewhere, inspiring confidence in musicians and enthusiasm from choirs. His habitual index finger and thumb in a circle—"All OK!"—just added to the "we're all in this together" feel of things with him. Andrew and the Toronto Symphony would have their inevitable ups and downs over the years, but there's a reason he became a virtual member of the TSO family, still gladly coming back to conduct year after year, and always welcomed with open arms. Didn't they just name a street after him?

Figure Out Which One You Are and Please Don't Do That

I just like this whole process of celebrating music with a whole lot of musicians.

—Trevor Pinnock

WHILE WORKING ON THIS ESSAY, I spilled a whole cup of coffee on my laptop. You know how it works. You're distracted, you put the coffee in a stupid place, you reach for something and knock it over, the whole thing goes right on the computer and you sit there, watching it slowly filter down into the keyboard. I turned the laptop upside down, drained it out and, amazingly, it still worked. It's a MacBook. This isn't product placement, just gratitude, because I was writing about Trevor Pinnock, our exceptional artistic director of thirty years ago, and I didn't want to lose my work. Then my inner Jungian connected this mishap to dear Trevor, whose extraordinary talents did not extend as far as keeping track of his car keys. Clearly, I was already in the ballpark.

Trevor is one of the most interesting musicians ever to stand on the National Arts Centre Orchestra podium. The first time I saw him was backstage in Symphony Hall in Boston while we were there on tour. Or rather, I saw a crush of NACO musicians crowding around someone rather short of stature and apparently very popular. This was several lifetimes ago, when we were touring the US with the dazzling flutist James Galway. He played the flute like nobody before or since, but he was unnervingly laid-back onstage. That night during his concerto we crashed and burned. He left out a repeat, we didn't, it fell apart. In Symphony Hall, one of the most prestigious concert halls in the world. We didn't know where to look. But he just laughed it off and calmly started over. Then, as an encore, he played "Danny Boy" and reduced the normally reserved Boston audience to tears. Not Bach, not his famous arrangement of the Paganini "Moto perpetuo"—"Danny Boy." And two thousand people were dabbing their eyes. *That* was James Galway.

Trevor had come to our concert. Backstage afterwards we were laughing and hugging him, so happy to see this long-time friend who didn't forget his repeats (but didn't play "Danny Boy," either). And five years later, after various traumas we could never have imagined back in those innocent days, Trevor was appointed our artistic director and principal conductor. I'll get to the traumas in a minute. The hope was that his brilliant musicianship and sunny personality would bring some life back to a group that hadn't seen the sun for a while. Poor guy. If he'd known what he was in for.

In those early days, Trevor brought us a desperately needed freshness of approach. He would say things like, "There are two kinds of musicians in this world, ones that rush and ones that drag. Figure out which one you are and please don't do that." Good to know he's a fan of spaghetti Westerns.

One of the first things we did with him was Mozart's manic (or manic as Trevor did it) "Paris" Symphony (Symphony No. 31 in D Major, "Paris" to be correct). Trevor's boundless energy was all over that Mannheim Rocket of a start, like a firework going off. And the virtuoso last movement saw the NAC Orchestra back to its best days, able to play faster and cleaner than anybody else. Mozart's tempo marking was simply *Allegro*, but that didn't stop Trevor from flooring it, kicking up a cloud of dust and taking the corners on two wheels. It was a thrill.

Unfortunately, between our happy meeting with Trevor in Boston and his appointment with us five years later, a newly elected Progressive Conservative government had tried to privatize the National Arts Centre, our home, so it could be used for more profitable commercial road shows. Nothing against road shows, but that's not why the people of Canada invested almost three hundred million in today's dollars to build such an exceptional place. Privatization would have meant the end to all the NAC's own presentations, an end to its support for Canadian artists, and would have put us, the only group of artists actually resident in the building, out of a home. That would have meant the end of the National Arts Centre Orchestra, historically the National Arts Centre's signature achievement.

Our fine European music director at the time, Gabriel Chmura, winner of the first Herbert von Karajan Competition, had been fired for signing a petition in support of the NAC's ushers, who were on strike. The real reason was that, with the orchestra decapitated, it would be easier to get rid of us. Yes, gone. But not our budget. It's hard to believe now that this was the goal, but it was.

As a result of all this, we ended up on strike ourselves for seven weeks. Carrying a picket sign is difficult for anyone, but for us, walking out on our loyal audience, walking out on our vocation, saying the show would not go on, it was traumatic. After that dark time, Trevor's friendly brilliance was just the ticket for us.

I *really* hate talking about the strike. It was thirty-five years ago, hardly anybody remembers it now, and those few who do would rather forget it. The action itself was very civilized, everything done by the book. The date and time were agreed upon with the NAC, the media and the public were informed ahead of time, even our faithful conductor Gabriel was in on it. The last rehearsal was pro forma and short, but he took it as seriously as everything else he did. It was just the first movement of Beethoven's Seventh Symphony, our signature piece, which seemed fitting. At the end of the movement, as the heroic horn calls we'd played so many times in so many places rang out, everyone broke down in tears. Gabriel graciously wished us good luck, we put our instruments away and, following a planned route, walked out of the building in full-dress tails, even though it was eleven in the morning. The cognitive dissonance was overpowering. We felt sick.

A large contingent of our public was outside waiting for us, and the print and television media. I was the musicians' media spokesperson and had remarks prepared for the cameras, but for a while nobody could find me. That's because I was hiding in a corner, weeping uncontrollably. It was those damn horn calls. This whole thing was wrong, terribly wrong. But I finally got it together, faced the cameras, told everyone why we were doing this and answered questions. The local paper was friendly, the national press not so much (yes, press—this is all pre-internet). Then we picked up our picket signs and out we went into a crisp, sunny fall day. Our principal flute wore a defiant Mozart wig, two other orchestra members were photographed hugging and crying, their picket signs flat on the ground. A press camera caught me at a particularly good angle while I was speaking and someone said I looked like Kevin Costner. That was the only positive thing about the whole sad event. Unfortunately, I do not look anything like Kevin Costner.

By the time the strike was over, it was dark at four in the afternoon and snow was on the ground. But we had survived. In fact, like those horn calls, we had triumphed, if one can really use such a word to describe such a survival. We had successfully pushed back against destructive policies that led all the way up to the prime minister's office. But the strike came with personal costs that only someone who has been through a protracted labour action would understand. One such cost for me—and a steep one—was an awkwardness that cast a sad and seemingly permanent shadow on my relationship with Trevor Pinnock.

Of course, we had a picket line. I get chills even seeing those words as I write them, but it was necessary and even courageous, since some of our most loyal supporters were offended by our public act of defiance. "Classical musicians do *not* carry picket signs!" Yes, they do. We dutifully picketed at pre-arranged places around the building, our lapsed Southern Baptist principal oboist called them Stations of the Cross. When I walk by those places today, almost forty years later, I still think of them that way.

By unfortunate coincidence, Trevor's brilliant period orchestra, The English Concert, was touring North America and they were booked for a performance at the NAC during our strike. It fell to me to tell Trevor why they couldn't cross our picket line.

I loved The English Concert. We all did. They'd played at the NAC a few years before and astonished all of us with their phenomenal virtuosity and no small amount of flair. Their horns swaggered their way flawlessly through such high registers in a Haydn symphony I was surprised they didn't get nosebleeds. But unlike most North American orchestras (in other words, unlike us), The English Concert paid their way through their seasons day to day, engagement to engagement, just on their concert fees.

It was an insecure existence and touring is expensive. The substantial fee from their NAC engagement was crucial to keeping their finances above water.

Needless to say, Trevor was not pleased with what I had to tell him. He understood our situation, but The English Concert really needed the money. Of course, I had to hold firm. Another NACO member threw a party for the members of The English Concert that night, so they wouldn't just be sitting in their hotel rooms watching their deficit run up. Needless to say, I didn't go. After that, every time Trevor was with us as a guest, and then later when he was our artistic director, he and I were on cordial terms—he knew how much I admired his work—but I felt there was a barrier between us. It was a constant sadness.

Trevor Pinnock's few years with us would be a book in itself. We started off with some fantastic concerts, we were thrilled to have him with us. Our tradition was to play precisely and perfectly above all else, everything rehearsed to the last detail. But Trevor approached Haydn and Mozart like jazz. We'd ask if something should be long or short, he'd say, "Just go with it." Forty-six pencils came out, dutifully marking "Go with it." It drove him crazy. But once we loosened up, working with him became a revelation. Our special identity remained, we just expanded it to include "Go with it." We all agreed it was an improvement.

And Trevor could spot talent. We had an opening for principal flute, one of the most important positions in the orchestra. Trevor persuaded the audition committee to pass over a very fine, experienced player they liked and take a chance on a brilliant, twenty-year-old undergrad from McGill who had never had a professional position, much less a principal chair in a major orchestra. But this student, with the memorable name Joanna G'froerer, proved Trevor's instinct right. From day one she was just astonishingly gifted in the position. No matter how crazy things got, Joanna always knew "where to put it." Despite her youth, she often became the de facto leader of the winds, sometimes the whole orchestra, because she was always calm, always musical, and always right. Joanna has been with us now for over thirty years and all that time she's been a peerless musician, a great colleague, and a total star every day of the week and twice on Sunday. Trevor himself is a one in a million talent. I guess it takes one to know one.

Trevor also did some serious work with new music, once again passing over a more conventional choice for composer-in-residence and hiring the more adventurous, edgier Linda Bouchard. And it wasn't just a token position. We played her work in many concerts at home, made several CDs, and included her music on a program in Carnegie Hall. Trevor, known internationally more as a Baroque specialist, was totally in on everything, old or new. It was a great adventure for all of us.

Inevitably, sometimes comically, there were some miscalculations. I'll never understand how such a hugely accomplished musician as Trevor couldn't conduct Brahms to save his life. Our grim management situation then didn't help things, either. They made life as miserable for Trevor as they did for us. So this hugely gifted artist and almost painfully sincere person ended his five-year tenure with us having had the worst time of his life. But the year after he officially left, he came back for one last performance. And it was one for the books.

It was during Lent, appropriate in so many ways, that Trevor returned as a guest to conduct Bach's *St. Matthew Passion*. And while we were preparing to perform this most revered of all sacred masterpieces, we were up to our necks yet again in that most secular of performance arts, contract negotiations. If the challenge last time had been existential (which it was), this time was even more toxic. Our excellent, hard-won contract became meaningless in the face of remorseless mendacity and bad faith. Last time, as awful as it was, at least the corner office believed its own fabrications. This time, the lies were intentional.

Things had deteriorated to the point where we had taken yet another strike vote (those were such miserable meetings) and had "run out the clock," meaning that, under Canadian labour law, enough time had passed without reaching an agreement that we could decide with no notice to simply stop playing and walk out. This wasn't the civil, carefully planned, mutually agreed-upon "work action" we had last time, difficult as it was. This was a little guerrilla war.

As it happened, our performance of the *St. Matthew Passion* was going to be broadcast on the CBC, nationwide, live-to-air. An hour before the performance, as the musicians for this big production were backstage warming up, another union asked me if we were going to strike the broadcast.

In their view, the presence of the public broadcaster's microphones created a perfect opportunity to get an instant national profile for our situation—headlines and everything. And they were right. Our strike vote, the provisions of the law, and the live microphones had put us in a powerful position. But we wouldn't, we couldn't even consider doing such a thing. Our union was our support, our lifeboat, and our negotiating power. Our union was of existential importance to us as our employer turned, like Jekyll and Hyde, into a remorseless enemy without a conscience. But this was J. S. Bach's *St. Matthew Passion.*

We could no more walk out on this performance than cut off our hands. We were in the worst possible mental and emotional place to perform this greatest of all sacred works but, ironically, in a true "last shall be first" inversion, it turned out to be the best place. To explain that, please forgive me but I must get personal.

Like all musicians, I always knew the *St. Matthew Passion* was special, but I had no idea how special until I performed it with Trevor in this insane situation. As usual, I was sitting right in front, right at the focal point of Bach's massive double orchestra and double choir. From the very first notes of that grave, E-minor opening with its heavy, relentless pulse, I was pierced through by this unearthly tragic music. The heavy, swaying pedal point on the low E of the basses, the heartbeat of the whole work, the lines in the oboes and flutes tangling themselves into a mournful call that goes straight to the heart, the violin lines entering one after another, like a funeral procession, until the first violins enter on a high B-natural, more than four octaves above the low E, as if enveloping the world in a grief too deep for words. Somehow, in the midst of unending lies, here was truth.

We are artists, not litigators. But we had just spent the better part of our fall season on a legal battlefield, trying to cope with . . . how else to say it . . . bad people. While trying to maintain the clarity of mind and integrity needed to perform this great, great work, offstage we were drowning in malevolence.

So when we started to play that grief-laden opening of the *St. Matthew Passion*, it was a revelation, a revelation of the truth of Bach's music and the truth of the Passion story as Bach portrayed it. I don't mean that necessarily in the religious sense, although it certainly was that also. With Bach, how could it not be? It was quite simply the awful truth of the price of salvation. With those opening notes, my heart was pierced through with truth.

There should be no human way to express something so transcendent, but Bach found it. And the next day, I made an appointment with an Anglican priest I knew to try to come to terms with that encounter. Yes, I said it would be personal.

Years later, Trevor came back as a guest to do Handel's ever-popular *Messiah.* We did a Messiah just a few years ago with Bernard Labadie and his phenomenal choir, La Chapelle de Québec, that was, in the opinion of many, the best Messiah we've ever done. Technically, stylistically, and musically, it was unsurpassed in my experience. Labadie's amazing choir helped. But we all reserve a special place in our hearts for the Messiahs we do with Trevor, because they always have a unique, unforced spirituality. It's odd. Trevor Pinnock and Helmuth Rilling could not be more different, but they both have a penetrating, personal sincerity in sacred music that I have never experienced with anyone else. It's not just their knowledge and their musicality and the beautiful sound they get. It's the way they look at the choir, it's the way they look at us. They are musical priests.

So I was devastated when I came down with a raging head cold just before rehearsals started for Trevor's Messiah. The last thing he needed was me coughing and sneezing right in front of him, so I didn't play. But I wrote him a letter. I told him how sorry I was not to be playing his Messiah and how special they always were to us. And I told him what his St. Matthew Passion all those years ago had meant to me, that it had begun a deep relationship with the Christian faith that, in the end, did not work out as I had hoped, but left a longing for a less ambivalent faith than mine became. Yes, I let it all hang out. Trevor had been a choirboy at Canterbury Cathedral and played services as an organist while still in his teens, so I didn't think going all churchy on him would put him off. But I never heard back from him. "Well, okay," I thought. "He's still mad at me for my part in the cancellation of that English Concert performance all those years in the deep, dark past." I couldn't blame him.

Then, just recently, Trevor came back to do another St. Matthew Passion with us. Could this performance possibly live up to that once-in-a-lifetime experience of twenty-five years ago? No, it couldn't, and it didn't. It was in January, the wrong time of year. The choir was still exhausted from all their Christmas engagements and was very short on rehearsal, the all-important Evangelist was talented but had never sung the huge role before. There were a lot of things, it's not important what they were. What *is* important is that the first time I saw Trevor backstage, not having seen him for a decade, he called out my name, rushed over to me and said, "Oh, Winston! I've been feeling so guilty all these years for not answering your beautiful letter! That was so kind of you!" And right there in front of all my colleagues, he gave me a huge hug.

That's Trevor.

A Brief Aside about Poetic Metre

I was reading the dictionary.
I thought it was a poem about everything.

—Steven Wright

SINCE I WAS JUST TALKING about the *St. Matthew Passion*, the rhythm of its solemn opening chorus—or rather the rhythm of its text, which is reflected in the music—is in trochaic tetrameter. This seems pretty far in the weeds, but it's actually important. For instance, these famous, creepy lines from "The Raven" by Edgar Allen Poe are in trochaic tetrameter:

Once upon a midnight dreary, while I pondered, weak and weary

Trochaic tetrameter is a ponderous name for a ponderous poetic rhythm of stressed and unstressed syllables, sometimes (if comically) represented like this:

"**DUM**-dah **DUM-**dah **DUM**-dah **DUM**-dah"

Somehow, that awkward rhythm seems to fit grim thoughts. (Stick with me, it gets grimmer.)

Bach's librettist, Christian Friedrich Henrici, better known by his pen name, Picander, was a poet. For the *St. Matthew Passion*, the words were written first, then Bach wrote the music to fit. Henrici-Picander would have known this poetic rhythm and its dark emotional effect when he wrote the words—the poetry—for that solemn opening chorus.

The first line, sung slowly, is,

> "**Kommt**, ihr **Töch**ter, **helft** mir **kla**gen."

An inaccurate translation (to preserve the rhythm) is,

> "**Come,** you **daugh**ters, **feel** my **sor**row."

That stressed-unstressed rhythm with which Edgar Allen Poe and Picander conjured so much darkness is the exact opposite of the friendly, better known (for good reason) iambic pentameter that merrily skips along everywhere in Shakespeare:

> "dah-**DUM** dah-**DUM** dah-**DUM** dah-**DUM** dah-**DUM**."
> "Shall **I** com**pare** thee **to** a **sum**mer's **day**?"

It's not only the subjects that make those poetic lines different as night and day. There was tragic music already embedded in the rhythm of Picander's poetry. And Bach found it.

I get into all this because the nerd in me thinks it's sort of neat. And, as academic as all this sounds, certain rhythms in words and music, like certain harmonies, do somehow have a primal connection to our emotions. I have no idea why. Oliver Sacks, the great neurologist who spent a professional lifetime trying to figure out things like this, had no idea why, either. It's magic.

Here's the grimmer. That same heavy, trochaic rhythm is used in the thirteenth-century Latin hymn "Stabat Mater," possibly the grimmest poetic text ever set to music (see the not-at-all-grim chapter on Helmuth Rilling). The first three lines are:

> **Sta**bat **Ma**ter **dol**o**ros**a,
> **Jux**ta **Cru**cem **lac**ri**mo**sa,
> **Dum** pen**de**bat **Fil**i**us**.

If you're paying attention, you'll notice a syllable missing at the end of that last line. That's called catalexis and you're welcome to look it up if, amazingly, you're really into this.

The important thing is that what the text says is unspeakable. Even if you don't know Latin (who does?) the horror of the text is obvious. Put it in Google Translate if you really want to ruin your day. And, like the *St. Matthew Passion* opening, it's in that foot-dragging trochaic tetrameter. So let's go back to our friendly, bouncy iambic pentameter:

> Shall I compare thee to a summer's day?
> Thou art more lovely and more temperate.
> Rough winds do shake the darling buds of May,
> And summer's lease hath all too short a date.
> Sometime too hot the eye of heaven shines,
> And often is his gold complexion dimmed;
> And every fair from fair sometime declines,
> By chance or nature's changing course untrimmed.

But thy eternal summer shall not fade
Nor lose possession of that fair thou ow'st,
Nor shall Death brag thou wand'rest in his shade,
When in eternal lines to time thou grow'st.
    So long as men can breathe or eyes can see,
    So long lives this, and this gives life to thee.

Isn't that just wonderful?

Kiss Me as If It Were the Last Time

Last tango in Tokyo

IN 1970, IN THE TOKYO Bunka Kaikan, a fine 2,300-seat concert hall, the Cleveland Orchestra said goodbye to their great conductor George Szell in an incandescent, lifetime of respect performance of Sibelius's Second Symphony. It would also be the last of 120 CDs' worth of recordings that Szell and Cleveland would leave behind for a grateful posterity. It's easily found online, and with a nice picture. If there's any concert that makes the case for recording all live performances so microphones are there when lightning strikes, perhaps for the last time, this is it.

For me, just seeing the words "The Cleveland Orchestra with George Szell" conjures up a whole world of the highest achievement. Because of the work the orchestra did with Szell, or perhaps it's more accurate to say the work Szell did with them, the Cleveland Orchestra became uncontestably the finest orchestra in North America and one of the greatest in the world. Yes, music lovers in Philadelphia, Chicago, New York, and Boston, the homes of the other "Big Five" American orchestras, would beg to differ, but critics agreed that Cleveland with Szell was, all things considered, the finest. I was going to say, "the best," but "the finest" is more precise because it's less about "who won" and more about refinement, culture, and discipline. And that was George Szell.

To be sure, the way Szell transformed a good regional orchestra into an international powerhouse broke some china, as they say. That's a euphemism, obviously, for people losing their jobs. A brief sidetrack:

The Cleveland Orchestra's previous music director of very brief tenure, Erich Leinsdorf, was a musician of deep background. Born into an observant Jewish family in Vienna, trained in Vienna, and assistant to Bruno Walter and Arturo Toscanini in Salzburg, at the end of 1937 he accepted a contract as assistant conductor at the Metropolitan Opera in New York. With the Anschluss occurring just months later he was fortunate to be where he was, but he had no permanent status in the United States. Fortunately, a freshman congressman named Lyndon Baines Johnson intervened on his behalf so he could remain in the US. And in 1942, Erich Leinsdorf became an American citizen.

The board of trustees of the Cleveland Orchestra had been looking for a successor to the gun-toting conductor Artur Rodziński (see "The Most Beautiful Music Ever Written by Anybody, Anytime") who had led the Cleveland Orchestra with distinction (and likely some drama) for a decade. The board's choice was the young, talented, newly naturalized US citizen Erich Leinsdorf. Leinsdorf's piercing intelligence and acerbic wit likely served him well in the interviews, and would doubtless have served him well as the Cleveland Orchestra's music director, but in 1943, the same year he began his contract, he was drafted. He told the Cleveland press, "I intend to abide by the orders of my government" and off he went to serve Uncle Sam.

It was the old story. While Leinsdorf was away in uniform, George Szell guest-conducted the orchestra and the public fell in love with him. Leinsdorf, having been there such a short time and knowing who Cleveland really wanted, gracefully submitted his resignation, opening the door for Szell to become music director. Leinsdorf's honourable behaviour in all these ways served him well. He went on to a highly successful career in the US and, no small thing, was welcomed back to Cleveland frequently as a guest after Szell died.

If you sense I have a soft spot for Erich Leinsdorf, you're right. In his excellent book *The Composer's Advocate: A Radical Orthodoxy for Musicians* (that title tells you everything), he writes, "I refuse to program either of the Chopin concertos with a fine orchestra. It's a waste of their time."

He's my man.

So now Cleveland had the masterful, Hungarian-born George Szell, a conductor with an encyclopedic knowledge of music and an iron will to impose that knowledge on anyone and everyone. Szell had been a child prodigy as both a pianist and a composer, performing in Europe and London even before his voice changed. An adoring press called him "the next Mozart." At the age of eighteen, the next Mozart was taken under the wing of Richard Strauss, no less, who, after hearing young George Szell conduct, declared that he could die happy knowing that Szell was there to take his music into the future. In fact, during a recording session for the world premiere of Strauss's cinematic tone poem *Don Juan*, young Szell was rehearsing the orchestra because Strauss had overslept. When he finally arrived at the session an hour late, he heard Szell conducting his new piece better than he could, so he told the recording producer, "Keep it." So the second half of the world premiere recording of *Don Juan* is actually conducted, not by the greatest living German composer, but by a teenaged George Szell.

Arriving in Cleveland (and no longer a teenager), Szell's explicit ambition was to transform the Cleveland Orchestra into "America's finest orchestra . . . second to none." Those were his exact words. To that end, he negotiated a personal contract that gave him total authority over programming, scheduling, recording, and, most sensitive, personnel. In a radio interview included in a seven-CD set titled *The Cleveland Orchestra, Szell—Centennial Compact Disc Edition Commemorating The 100th Anniversary Of The Birth Of George Szell* (it lives up to all those extra capital letters), Szell states evenly and mercilessly that his priority was that the orchestra reach the highest possible artistic standard, "not that every member have a secure job." Imagine that phrase delivered in a clipped Mitteleuropean accent and you get the flavour of it.

Szell did, in fact, dismiss a number of players, sometimes abruptly and with little explanation, in order to replace them with other players he believed to be superior. As in any workplace, when one employee is summarily dismissed, a dozen start looking over their shoulders. He was a total authoritarian and a micromanager—a famous story had him telling the cleaning staff how to replace the toilet paper. The worst part is, it was true. He probably knew exactly how much toilet paper they had to keep in stock. In the same spirit, Szell's office window looked out over the parking lot, so he could see how early players arrived for rehearsal and if they were carrying music. Or not. He would even comment on the car a musician was driving, asking things like, "How does an orchestra musician afford such a big car?" (Szell's car was very big.)

All this came at a steep, often not-so-hidden human cost. It affected everyone, no matter how well they played. Some of the orchestra's finest front chair soloists resigned because, as great as the music was, they felt stifled by Szell's micromanaging. But, as the orchestra's performance standard rose to become, indeed, second to none, other musicians flourished, or at least went along for the amazing ride.

Nobody questioned Szell's right to the total control he demanded, such was their respect for his musicianship. For Szell, the music was the first thing, the last thing, and the only thing. That's also what orchestra musicians believe, in their heart of hearts. The saying "the Cleveland Orchestra plays like a string quartet with a hundred members" was the result. This is the hard-core context in which the Cleveland musicians developed such limitless respect, and even a thick-skinned kind of affection, for their dedicated, all-seeing, all-knowing music director.

Orchestra musicians are in the most ambivalent of occupations. They train for years to be soloists, yet ninety-nine times out of a hundred they end up playing in orchestras where their individual personalities become subservient to a collective directed by someone else. And yet orchestra musicians *live* for the collective. That's the only way to play Beethoven and Brahms and Strauss and the rest. That's what this whole book is about, about a love for the art so deep that a total fusion of a hundred different musical personalities becomes possible.

That's how Strauss happens. That's how *Strauss* happens. And the Cleveland Orchestra with Szell played Richard Strauss like nobody else. And, in the same way, they played Sibelius like nobody else, incandescent Sibelius, and in the face of everything I've described here. So, if you search for Cleveland's Sibelius Symphony No. 2 in Tokyo (sibelius symphony 2 szell tokyo usually does it), you'll hear a one-of-a-kind live performance that will take you through every kind of human drama, both in the music and right there onstage. That's what orchestra musicians live for.

And in all his years in Cleveland, George Szell never programmed the Chopin concertos.

PART II

Soloists: Politics and snakeskin boots

If the Almighty himself played the violin,
the credits would still read "Rubinstein, God, and Piatigorsky."

—Jascha Heifetz

Ida! Don't Do That to Me!

Res severa verum gaudium

When this was a blog, I was writing a piece for Canada Day; it appears later in this book as "Shall We Ask Za Composer What He Wants?" I *love* Canada Day and I had all kinds of Canadian ideas, but then news came of the death of the much-loved, much-respected, one-of-a-kind violinist Ida Haendel. There are never that many truly great players around, but among them was this diminutive person with a megawatt personality and a once-in-a-lifetime talent.

Among many wonderful things we did with her, top of the list was an unforgettable performance of the Britten violin concerto, conducted by her long-time friend Franz-Paul Decker. If any two artists embodied the historic, oh-so-Teutonic motto of the Leipzig Gewandhaus Orchestra, *Res severa verum gaudium*—"true joy is a serious thing"—it was these two.

With Ida Haendel, nothing was ever routine. She had the smallest hands I ever saw but she got around the instrument with seemingly effortless agility and accuracy. But what was unique was her sound:

assertive, sharply focused, passionate yet full of dignity. Her instrument was a gorgeous 1696 Strad, but, as Jascha Heifetz once observed (one eyebrow raised), it doesn't play by itself. Ida was one of those performers like the great Romanian pianist Clara Haskil, whose façade of reserve concealed an iron will and a heart filled with the grief of the ages.

The Britten Concerto is not played that often, perhaps because of its lack of technical flash but more likely because of its cosmically bleak ending. I can't think of any other major work for any instrument that goes as far out in the snow, except perhaps the Fourth Symphony of Sibelius, or the bone-chilling ending of the Sixth. Perhaps that's one reason the Sibelius concerto was Ida Haendel's signature piece—Ida and Jascha Heifetz, except Heifetz's Sibelius was red-hot. Ida's was freezing cold.

For several reasons, the rise of fascism certainly first among them, the 1930s inspired a veritable encyclopedia of great twentieth-century composers to write violin concertos. Between 1931 and 1938, Stravinsky, Szymanowski, Berg, Prokofiev, Schoenberg, and Bartók, and in 1939 alone, Barber, Hindemith, Piston, Hartmann, Walton, and Britten. Of these twelve serious works, eight are now in the standard repertoire, an amazingly high proportion. And unsettling.

Young Benjamin Britten was outraged at the appeasement policy of Neville Chamberlain's Conservatives. He also had friends who had fought on the Republican side in the Spanish Civil War—Britten actually met his life partner, Peter Pears, doing a benefit recital for the Loyalists. Shortly before that war began, Britten was in Barcelona where he heard Louis Krasner give the world premiere of the Berg Violin Concerto. It was a life-changing experience for Britten, as that beautiful, grief-stricken work is for all of us. As Michael Steinberg wrote, for Britten, the Berg Concerto "provided a model for the idea of violin-concerto-as-requiem . . . a *concerto funèbre*." As it happens, *Concerto funebre* is literally the title of Hartmann's concerto and the explicit subtext of the Berg. It was a serious time.

The Britten Concerto begins with a soft five-note theme in the timpani in a Spanish rhythm—the same rhythm appears in one form or another everywhere in the concerto. And the last movement is a passacaglia, a dance form that began in Spain and became a time-honoured way of expressing grief—we meet a close cousin of the passacaglia later on in "Chaconne." That great final movement was written *in memoriam* for the British volunteers who had died in Spain, some of them Britten's friends. "Dido's Lament" from Purcell's opera *Dido and Aeneas*, Bach's Passacaglia in C Minor for organ, the monumental last movement of Brahms's Symphony No. 4, Nicholas Hooper's dignified, grief-laden music for "Dumbledore's Farewell" in *Harry Potter and the Half-Blood Prince* (yes, really), and, the crowning achievement of the form in all music, Bach's *Chaconne* from his Partita in D Minor for solo violin, are all either a passacaglia or a chaconne.

Of the Britten, Michael Steinberg writes:

> The final variation (*lento e solenne*) is the keening lament toward which the whole concerto has led. I think of Thomas Mann's phrase about "that speaking unspeakingness that is given to music alone."

Let that settle in a minute.

Left to his own devices, Franz-Paul Decker relished going head-to-head with Ida in bleakness—two wartime Europeans—so they were a perfect team when they performed the Britten with us. She played the Britten wonderfully well, as if she owned the piece, but in the dress rehearsal something more happened that was extraordinary, even for her. It was one of those once-in-a-lifetime things, mystic, wonderful, like the soul-shattering Dvořák *Requiem* with Karel Ančerl I describe in the second chapter of this book. Without anyone saying a word, Benjamin Britten, Ida Haendel, Franz-Paul Decker, and the musicians of the National Arts Centre Orchestra somehow suspended the laws of physics. We became one devastated human soul, looking into the abyss. At eleven o'clock in the morning.

I'm not exaggerating. Britten's music and Ida's epic playing totally overcame our professional detachment. They simply broke our hearts. At the end there was a long silence, some tears. We were still recovering when Decker, typically, broke the spell and barked, "Ida! Don't do that to me!"

Ida Haendel, whose old-world sense of irony surpassed even Decker's, was also affectionately infamous for her severe manner in rehearsal, the better to mask her wicked sense of humour. Ida was with us one holiday season when we did our annual Christmas charity concert. These are relaxed, cheerful affairs—lots of kids, Santa Claus—and we always have special guests come onstage with us as part of the fun. The star turn is always Leroy Anderson's quintessential holiday piece "Sleigh Ride," which is always conducted (always comically badly) by a local celebrity. But "Sleigh Ride" also has a deceptively tricky part for a whip. A percussion whip is just two long, thin wooden boards on a hinge, but when you clap them together hard, watching not to catch a finger, they make a loud *CRACK* worthy of Indiana Jones. Ida was a great friend of the orchestra, going back to our darker days when she wrote supportive letters to the editor and spiky letters to the appropriate miscreants. We loved her for that. So, since she was in town anyway, we asked her if she'd like to participate in the Christmas concert. With typical spirit, she replied, "Of course! I'd *luff* to!" We asked her if she'd like to conduct, the usual celebrity turn. "No! I vant to play the *vip*!" So she did. And she was really good at it.

And after all this, not to forget Ida's trademark knee-high leather boots, the better to support her mile-high stiletto heels. One time she came in wearing eye-popping snakeskin—huge, high, impossibly exotic snakeskin boots. An admiring orchestra member whispered, "Last surviving male and female of the species."

That was Ida.

The Virtues of Used Bookstores

On my last birthday I was ninety-three years old.
That is not young, of course. In fact, it is older than ninety.

—Pablo Casals

AUGUST 11, 2020

IN THE EARLY GIDDINESS OF Joe Biden's choice of the first woman of colour as candidate for vice president of the United States, a woman of great accomplishment and in the full flood of life, as someone said, nominated by a whiter than white presidential candidate of greater age than any in American history, this musician's thoughts turned to J. S. Bach. Really, they did. If it's earthshakingly personal, it's always Schubert. If it's just earthshaking, it's always Bach.

Actually, I was thinking of Bach's Cello Suite No. 3 in C Major played by Pierre Fournier and, from a couple of generations earlier, by the legendary Pablo Casals. Since Casals's time a century ago, many great cellists have made wonderful recordings of this music, Casals and

Fournier just happen to be my favourites. Listen to either of them playing this wonderful piece—their recordings are easy to find online—and you won't think I'm quite so strange to think of music like this on days when the universe changes.

If there were ever a Mount Rushmore for cellists, Casals would be the most prominent face on it. Bach's solo cello suites are everywhere now, even in TV shows—the prelude to the first Bach suite played on screen by Yo-Yo Ma had a starring role in an episode of *The West Wing* (he let Janel Moloney hold his Strad). But Casals did the very first recording of the Bach cello suites, back before anyone else performed them in public, back before hardly anyone even knew they existed. An amazing thought.

Before the turn of the last century, before most homes had electric lighting, thirteen-year-old Pablo Casals came across the music for the Bach suites in a used bookstore and took them home. The old edition he'd found was corrupt and full of added markings that were not by Bach, obvious even to his young eyes, so he had to figure out this great music for himself. The result, as you can hear on his recording from almost a century ago, has an energy and freshness of style that today's performance practice scholars would admire. Casals was the best from the word go.

Then, three decades later, there's Pierre Fournier. The nobility of Fournier's Bach playing always leaves me speechless. All of his playing is supremely beautiful, but if I had to single out one thing, it would be the way he sings the Sarabande from the third suite, the C major. It always brings me to tears. Obviously, underneath Bach's forbidding persona was an all-too-human heart "touched by mortal things."

Casals, on the other hand, *dances* everything. And these are, after all, dance suites, even the sarabandes. Especially the sarabandes. I like to imagine Suzanne Farrell dancing this slow, infinitely expressive music, with her infinitely expressive arms and hands. For me, with Casals everything inspires an imaginary choreography.

I don't know why, but the Bach solo cello suites feel personal for me. I'm a violinist, so I don't know the cello suites as well as I do the sonatas and partitas for solo violin and I've never had to struggle to learn to play them. Perhaps that's why my reaction to them is deeper, with the exception of the *Chaconne*, but then the *Chaconne* is the exception to everything. Perhaps because the cello is just such beautiful instrument and, unlike the crazy violin, sings in the actual range of the human voice, and perhaps because a dear friend who is no longer with us loved the cello and always had her beloved LP of Fournier playing on the turntable. She had been a professional dancer in England with what was then called the Ballet Rambert and would sometimes actually dance to the recording, especially the sarabandes, with slow, gentle, flowing gestures. So the aristocratic expressiveness of Fournier in this ultimate *musique dansant* became a poetic ideal.

And listening to Casals . . . As a student I read his book *Joys and Sorrows* over and over. There was no musician I admired more. When Casals played Bach, the rest of the world disappeared. Casals, who played recitals during Brahms's lifetime but whose career lasted into the living memory of many musicians today, including mine, basically invented modern cello playing. He was also a pioneer in the "expressive intonation" we take for granted today, intonation that takes into account the harmonic context of the notes, or "where they want to go." Which is to say, he was a pioneer in listening.

On the piano, C-sharp and D-flat are the same black key, and therefore the exact same pitch. The most common tuning system today, called equal temperament, makes that possible (it has nothing to do with the personality of the pianist). But, according to the laws of physics, C-sharp and D-flat are *not* the exact same note, and thereby hangs a complicated tale: search "equal temperament" and "just intonation" and then run screaming from the room. In practical terms, on a string instrument or any instrument that can bend a pitch—including, obviously, the voice—a C-sharp will usually be on the high side because it usually "wants" to resolve to the D just above it, but a D-flat will be on the low side because it usually wants to resolve to the C just below it. Musicians playing anything except keyboard instruments make these adjustments constantly, subconsciously, but pianists can't. They have to depend on piano tuners who are artists in their own right, the exquisite engineering of their instrument, and their own careful voicing of chords to conceal this glaring flaw.

This really is a thing. Expressive intonation locks into the fundamental physics of harmony and our brain's ineffable, primal perception of it. Expressive intonation has always been around, especially in singers, but its conscious invention was like creating a whole new system of temperament for strings, a temperament that moves like a living thing as the harmonic tension moves. Yes, cello Mount Rushmore for Casals, without a doubt. And for you, if you've hung in this far.

So, thanks to Casals, the Bach solo cello suites became the musical Bible for cellists. Cellists grow up with it. Yo-Yo Ma tells how, as a child, he learned the prelude to the first suite one measure at a time, one measure each day, until he knew the whole thing. Cellists are lucky to have this great music for the cello, which is also great cello music, if you get the distinction. This music *is* the cello. But for young violinists, the Bach solo sonatas and partitas are too difficult for the early years of study. And they are different music.

Bach threw everything he had into his six sonatas and partitas for violin alone, including three fugues with such complex counterpoint that one poor violin all by itself should hardly be expected to contain it all.

And it can't. The three Bach unaccompanied violin fugues are the highest level—Mount Everest-level—of artistic flim flam. Of course one violin can't play three or four musical lines at the same time, that's what pianos are for, so Bach's violin fugues make violinists twist themselves into pretzels giving the *illusion* they're playing all those lines. This is why performances of unaccompanied Bach on the violin always carry a hint of danger: "Will the soloist survive the many contrapuntal difficulties and manage to make music as well? We're taking up a collection for his children, just in case . . ."

And then there's the monumental last movement of the Bach Partita in D Minor for solo violin, the *Chaconne*—an immense work that lasts as long as the rest of the partita put together. Some speculate that Bach composed this one-of-a-kind piece—not only one of Bach's greatest works but one of the greatest works in all Western art—as a memorial to his first wife, Maria Barbara, who died suddenly while still only in her thirties. We'll never know, but the Bach *Chaconne* is like nothing else in music history. You can read about it in "*Chaconne*." Then sit quietly for a few minutes.

The Bach solo cello suites also have their challenges, like any great music, but with the exception of the sixth, because it was really written for a different instrument, they're not an instrumental obstacle course like the sonatas and partitas for solo violin. What you hear is just beautiful music with heart to spare. Is it just coincidence that the earliest surviving manuscript of the Bach solo cello suites was copied out by Anna Magdalena Bach, Bach's second wife, still very much in this life—and his?

As a musician, I don't think it's a coincidence at all. Johann Sebastian Bach, the greatest composer who ever lived, master of harmony, counterpoint and form, man of faith, austere Thomaskantor and composer of a cantata about coffee, could be happy like any other man and have his heart broken like any other man. Otherwise, how could he have written that sarabande?

It's Hot in Here

Interviewer to Pinchas Zukerman: "Why don't you play the Scottish Fantasy?"
Pinchas Zukerman: "Jascha played it."

"THE MOST PERFECT VIOLINIST WHO EVER LIVED." "God's fiddler." "The king of violinists." These seemingly hyperbolic descriptions of Jascha Heifetz have been around for almost a century now, and there's a reason. Heifetz made his first recordings in the Russia of Tsar Nicholas II, playing into a metal horn that engraved his sound onto a wax cylinder. By the end of his career he was recording in stereo sound on colour video.

George Bernard Shaw famously told Heifetz that he should play one wrong note every day to avoid offending the gods. The great violinist Fritz Kreisler, after accompanying a twelve-year-old Jascha Heifetz on the piano, said to a roomful of the most eminent musicians of the day, "Well, gentlemen, we might as well break our violins across our knees." And the oldest and best: pianist Leopold Godowsky sitting in a box in Carnegie Hall with violinist Mischa Elman, listening to sixteen-year-old Jascha Heifetz's New York debut recital. "It's hot in here," says Elman. Replies Godowsky, "Not for pianists."

Those stories have been told so many times. All the references to the perfection of Heifetz's playing, of his severe, imperious appearance in performance—"Old Stone Face"—of his phenomenal technique, his unique sound, all these are true. Heifetz's playing was indeed beyond superlatives. But they actually miss the point of what really put Heifetz in a class by himself and the reason he was so greatly admired by his professional colleagues. The most accurate quote of all, I think, is "Kreisler is the king, Heifetz the prophet." This is variously attributed to Nathan Milstein, David Oistrakh, Arturo Toscanini, Eugene Ormandy, and Mischa Elman. And maybe Sir Thomas Beecham and Eugene Goossens. I heard somebody say it just yesterday. Everyone seems to claim it. Because Heifetz *was* a prophet. He changed violin playing forever.

Truth be told, he even changed himself forever. As a child he was just one amazing prodigy in Leopold Auer's Saint Petersburg class full of amazing prodigies. His earliest acoustic recordings at age ten reveal his trademark technical facility, obvious even through the primitive technology, but not yet the sizzling sound and heroic style that would make *every* violinist think, "It's hot in here." All the admiration for his spectacular technique misses the point: he also developed a way of singing on the violin that had never been heard before and has not really been heard since.

Yes. Where Heifetz was really unique, where he was truly a prophet, was in long, singing lines. Even his earliest acoustic recording of the Schubert "Ave Maria"—nothing fast and flashy there—shows that he was, at heart, a great singer who just happened to play the violin phenomenally well.

There's a recording of Heifetz, made ninety years ago, playing the third sonata of Edvard Grieg. It's easy to find online. As with all of Heifetz's recordings, the microphone was placed very close to the instrument, seemingly right under the strings. All you hear is the violin, right in front of you, with no forgiving acoustic to put a flattering sheen over imperfections. In fact, this particular recording has many imperfections; it was rejected by Heifetz and never publicly released during his lifetime. The piano is out of tune, here and there Heifetz plays sharp, perhaps disturbed by the mistuning of the piano, and the pianist plays as if he wishes he was anywhere else. Nobody was having a good day. But the sizzling heat of Heifetz's sound is still there and, most important, his unique way of singing on the instrument. With a "voice" like that, imperfections don't matter. George Bernard Shaw would've been happy.

Chopin biographer Alan Walker writes, "Inside every successful Chopin interpreter is a singer trying to get out." There's an exquisite recording of Chopin's nocturnes by Arthur Rubinstein, recorded in Italy in the 1960s, that has a singing sound like that. Again, the microphones are very close to the strings, so all you hear is peerless playing and his signature sound. It's as if you're sitting on the piano bench right next to him. To be fair, unlike the rejected Heifetz recording, Rubinstein makes no errors and the piano is tuned and voiced to within an inch of its life. But, as with the Heifetz recording, you hear everything. The point is, recordings like this are, above all, *honest.*

So I think it's more useful to admire Heifetz for what he was uniquely good at. He was not, in fact, a flawless player. He preferred to do his recordings in one take, with as little splicing as possible, so of course there are imperfections. The Grieg had to be that way, since back then recordings were made directly onto the master disc. During one recording session Heifetz's bow made an obvious squeak. The producer prepared to fix it, but Heifetz said, "No. Leave it in. It'll make a lot of people happy."

In his second recording of the Sibelius Concerto, the one with Chicago, a year after he'd had a serious fall, the clear, modern stereo sound puts you right on top of his violin as he sears his way through this great concerto that he essentially owned. Listening to it on headphones is a violin experience like no other. But he misses a slide, he fudges one of the runs of thirds in the last movement, a few notes don't speak clearly, and it's all a bit scratchy. But with leave-it-all-on-the-field playing like that, who cares? In his student days, Walter Prystawski, later the founding concertmaster of the National Arts Centre Orchestra, attended a rehearsal of Heifetz with the Toronto Symphony. I recently asked Walter what it was like. "Was he amazing?"

"No." Walter replied. "He played badly. Bless him!"

Music's Brightest Light

What's even worse than a flute? Two flutes!

—Wolfgang Amadeus Mozart

SEPTEMBER 3, 2020

A WEEK BEFORE I WROTE this, for the first time since the beginning of the pandemic, a more or less full-size Berlin Philharmonic played in the presence of a distanced, live audience. As with their earlier pandemic concerts with smaller ensembles, sitting far apart and playing to an empty hall, it was streamed live. The great orchestra was still spread out as much as possible and visibly uncomfortable—string players on separate stands, winds widely separated, brass and timpani way out by the airport. They even struggled a bit with the music, their excellent conductor Kirill Petrenko's ideas about Brahms being quite different from the way the Berliners have been lovingly playing that great music since Brahms was alive. But this live stream was a century later, music in the time of COVID, so they were facing challenges Brahms never imagined.

The Berlin Philharmonic feels proprietary about Brahms—Brahms is their music. And yet here, in their first public concert in six months, they were still adventurous and artistically generous enough to try something new. Taking that risk, how Berlin-like, honoured the composer, the orchestra, their principal conductor, and their courageous, music-loving audience. If that concert wasn't quite like a Myra Hess recital at the National Gallery during the Blitz (perhaps not the most diplomatic comparison), it had something of that defiance against the unseen. It's on their Digital Concert Hall, August 28, 2020. If you subscribe, which I highly recommend, you can see it.

In this early, distanced concert, they knew they were, in Petrenko's words, "on very thin ice." But despite the pandemic, Petrenko said he hoped with his whole heart that they would be able to put a large enough orchestra onstage to play Brahms for their first concert back. Apparently it was touch and go for a while, but they managed it. All they wanted was to be with Brahms, their best musical friend, and their audience.

Just today the members of the NAC Orchestra received an outline of a rehearsal schedule for this fall. Since this is already September, that means right now. Usually a detailed schedule for the fall is released to the public in March, but obviously March this year had other ideas. But now, a schedule! We might be back onstage after all. But there was still no actual programming, just a "save this space." And we're hoping against hope that, when it happens, we can come back with the NAC Orchestra's best musical friend, Mozart.

The National Arts Centre Orchestra used to live with Mozart the way the Berlin Philharmonic lives with Brahms. It was *our* music. Our repertoire has expanded exponentially since our first season fifty years ago, but the orchestra still has a special affinity for music's brightest light. Like Brahms for the Berliners, Mozart has been our music from day one.

"Historical performance practice" has come a long way since the opening of the house that Lester B. Pearson built, but even back then we knew that, when Mozart was on the program, nobody else in the world played it with such precision, vitality, and grace.

How many orchestras really have "their" music? The NAC Orchestra, like Cleveland with Szell, has Mozart and Haydn. Berlin has Brahms, Vienna has Johann Strauss, the Dresden Staatskapelle has Richard Strauss, the Czech Philharmonic has Dvořák, the Concertgebouw has Mahler. How many others? Be honest, now. All right, the Bayreuth Festival Orchestra has Wagner, but I don't like to talk about Wagner.

In fact, the last piece the NAC Orchestra played before the world fell apart was a barnburner performance of Mozart's Symphony No. 41 ("Jupiter"), with one of our favourite conductors, Xian Zhang. What a way to go. Now, like the great Berliners with their Brahms, it would be fitting, and just plain wonderful, for the NAC Orchestra to re-enter the world with Mozart. Like Petrenko in Berlin, I hope with all my heart that it happens.

And speaking of Mozart, for almost five decades the world's stages were graced by one of the greatest violinists Canada has ever produced, Steven Staryk, now retired to Sun City, Arizona to count his Strads. An outstanding solo artist, Staryk, at one time or other, was also concertmaster of the Royal Philharmonic, the Royal Concertgebouw Orchestra, the Chicago Symphony, and the Toronto Symphony. Somewhere in there he was invited to be concertmaster of the Berlin Philharmonic, but he turned them down.

Fifty years ago, Staryk recorded two of the most popular Mozart violin concertos—the D major and the A major—with the NAC Orchestra. Staryk was known for saying, "For an audition all I need to hear is the first page of the Mozart A major. That tells you everything." Fortunately, there is a brilliant recording online of Staryk playing the Mozart A major with the NAC Orchestra. But it's been viewed only a few times, probably because it's next to impossible to find. I did find it once, but never since. Maybe you'll have better luck, it's worth it.

Staryk's story is unusual. Violinist, luthier, and violin expert Jaak Liivoja-Lorius wrote this for *The Strad* in 1983:

> Although Steven Staryk is the epitome of the well-schooled violinist, no one teacher stands out as more important than another in his development during his student years. Indeed, Staryk has often said that it would be unfair to single out names since he studied with or observed virtually anyone he felt had something to offer. Obviously a much safer, albeit more conservative approach would have been to have persisted with a smaller number of teachers and to have remained with one for a longer period of time. At least this is the traditional process which eventually allows the player to be categorized as, say, an Auer, Rostal, or Galamian student.
>
> In Staryk's case such categorization is impossible. Within the most organized sense of the term, Staryk really should be considered a self-made violinist. This is not to say that he has done it completely unaided—far from it—but it is no small credit to him that he succeeded in assembling a complete technical mastery of the violin and bow by combining many different influences into one superbly functioning entity. And, since Staryk was the architect of his own technical apparatus, he has gained immense insight in the practical relationship between technique and music-making.

I was fortunate to be able to study with Steven Staryk for a few years when he was living in Toronto. Jaak is spot on. Staryk's flawless playing was assembled by himself, one technical brick at a time, into a bullet-proof virtuoso technique. And because he knew how he'd put it together, he could teach it. For him, learning to play the violin was like going to the gym every day, each exercise carefully measured and coordinated until you had gone as far as your talent and musculature would take you. Behind such ambition was, of course, a deep love of music, but also a cold, clear eye on the gritty side of the music business. He had good reason.

In 1951, nineteen-year-old Steven Staryk was a section player in the Toronto Symphony. He was already a soloist, but he needed the income. Lucky TSO. But in November of that year, when the orchestra went on tour, he was denied entry into the McCarthy-era US. Five other members of the TSO were also denied entry, with "possible Communist associations" given as the reason. Some wryly said it was because they could read. Anyway, at the end of that season, citing "inability to fulfill their contracts," the Toronto Symphony management fired them. Yes, all of them. They became a *cause célèbre* known as the "Symphony Six." Look it up.

At the height of America's anti-Communist fervour, having a Ukrainian last name and performing at Ukrainian events was apparently enough to flag a passport. But it wasn't just the Americans. The Toronto Symphony's highly esteemed conductor, Sir Ernest MacMillan, and even the musicians' union, unbelievably, wouldn't lift a finger to help them. Even their own colleagues were caught up in the paranoia of the time and refused to support them, some even avoiding them on the street for fear of guilt by association. One of the players who was fired said she'd hear colleagues commenting about her, "She reads so many books she *must* be a Communist." (That player was bassist Ruth Budd. She was later rehired by the Toronto Symphony and became a force of nature in Canadian music for over half a century, passing away not long ago at the age of 97.) Even Lester B. Pearson, then foreign minister, dodged the issue, saying a review of the situation "would not be productive." Yes, the same Lester B. Pearson who, two decades later as prime minister, financed the construction of the National Arts Centre. There's nothing new under the sun.

A few years after all this, the talented, entertaining, and wealthy conductor of the Royal Philharmonic, Sir Thomas Beecham, hired young Steven Staryk as concertmaster. After hearing Staryk play, a euphoric Sir Thomas said, "Finally, I can record *Scheherazade*!" And he did. And over sixty years later, that recording, with Staryk's masterful solos, is still in the catalogue in the EMI series Great Recordings of the Century. Talk about landing on your feet.

Later, when Staryk was concertmaster of the Royal Concertgebouw Orchestra, that orchestra was also planning a tour to the US. Several members, as happened with the Toronto musicians, were denied entry. But, unlike the Toronto Symphony, the Concertgebouw Orchestra just cancelled the tour. A few years later, for a second tour to the US, it was felt that the orchestra could not turn down another invitation, so they performed with substitute players. But the regular players weren't fired. When the Concertgebouw Orchestra left the US and came to Canada, the regular players rejoined the orchestra onstage as a group, to a standing ovation by their colleagues.

As it happened, Steven Staryk had never been formally cleared by the US authorities, but as concertmaster, he was allowed in anyway. Mozart would've loved it.

She Sings as If She Doesn't Care If It Kills Her

Scary singing

MAY 22, 2020

FOR SOME REASON, OUT OF nowhere, the long-running CBC show *Saturday Afternoon at the Opera* came to mind. Why Saturday? Perhaps because the Metropolitan Opera, which dominates the programming during the season, thought Saturday would be the most convenient day for people to "tune in" while they do housework or wash the car or drive to the store for groceries, while listening, sort of, to the most complex, most difficult, most intensely human, and most expensive art form, well, ever. Opera is the bumblebee of art forms. It shouldn't be able to fly, but it does.

If you go online for the music I'm going to talk about here, you won't go shopping or wash the car, will you? Please, not to this music, or for that matter not to *Der Rosenkavalier*, either, which I talk about in the first chapter. I'm being a bit offhand here because, truth be told, I'm in big trouble with this music.

This morning I got an email from one of my closest friends. We'd been talking about The Most Tiresome Topic in our musical world, the future of symphony orchestras. The question has been around forever, the "immortal art" vs. "dinosaur" debate seems to peak every ten years or so, like sunspots. But it's a whole different issue when we have overflowing emergency rooms and empty concert halls. In unguarded moments, the words "existential threat" come to mind—an unwelcome guest who enters without knocking.

Mixed in with pandemic anxieties like "Will audiences ever come back?" and "How can we even rehearse without risking our lives?" I replied that the key to our musical survival is, well, love. The kind of deep-rooted devotion that makes something essential, love for an art that is larger than life in every sense, love for the kind of music one wants most to hear before departing for the undiscovered country. These days those are tall words, but that's really where the meaning in our work comes from.

And, of course, the pandemic added the existential question "Will we survive at all?" It wasn't just asking ourselves why we're here and will people get used to not having live music and will musicians ever be able to make a living at it again. We ask ourselves, *Is it worth it?*

Wouldn't we be more useful as, say, civil rights lawyers, correcting centuries of injustice? Or teachers, awakening young minds to the lifelong joys of reading and the difficult art of understanding what they read? Or physicians "saving lives while the city sleeps?" At one point I actually started down that road but, just in time, saw the light (see "The Life It Brings"). So, here I am, in my seventies, still playing the violin in an orchestra. A very fine orchestra, to be sure. That helps.

Anyway, the email from my wise friend said, "When you have doubts, listen to 'Dido's Lament' and the last twenty minutes of *Rosenkavalier*."

Gifted as we are with musical riches simply by entering a few words in a search box, search "janet baker dido's lament." You will hear a live performance from half a century ago where the inexpressibly beautiful music and life-and-death commitment of the performer touch the sublime. I use the priceless word "sublime" carefully. Here, I take it to mean the invisible miraculous.

"Dido's Lament" is the final aria from the opera *Dido and Aeneas* by the great English composer Henry Purcell. Written around the time J. S. Bach was born, there was one English opera written a couple of years earlier but *Dido and Aeneas* was the first to be recognized as a masterpiece. Purcell died at only thirty-six for reasons that remain unclear, though Purcell, unlike J. S. Bach, did realize where things were going in time to write a hasty will. Despite his brief career, the powers that be held him in such high regard that they agreed unanimously to give him a no-expense-spared funeral at Westminster Abbey and buried him next to the organ. *Dido and Aeneas* was one of the reasons he received such a high honour.

Officially, *Dido and Aeneas* is an adaptation of the dramatic story about Dido in Book IV of Virgil's *Aeneid*, but essentially it's about a woman who falls in love with a man who then leaves her. This depressingly common story is bad enough, but in Virgil it goes nuclear: Dido sings heart-rendingly of her grief, climbs to the top of a flaming funeral pyre and stabs herself to death. Purcell's simple, exquisitely beautiful music transforms this melodramatic scene into great art.

Here, we're talking about a grainy, black-and-white video of the British mezzo-soprano Janet Baker, arguably the greatest British classical singer of the twentieth century. The early video is from a live performance at Glyndebourne sixty years ago, conducted by Charles Mackerras; it would be another decade before he became Sir Charles Mackerras. The recorded balance between the voice and the orchestra is not ideal and the orchestra is, well, also not ideal, but young Janet Baker gives it everything she's got, and then some. She sings as if she doesn't care if it kills her. At that moment, I'm absolutely sure that was true.

What makes this piece of music so powerful? The real answer is that it just is. It just is. It's the unexplained miracle of human perception that makes certain musical pitches, or rather the mathematical relationships between the frequencies of those pitches (here we go) that make us feel certain ways, in this case dissolved in tears. It's all about feeling. Not touchy-feely sentimental feeling, but feelings that can raise your blood pressure or lower it, make you laugh or make you cry, a feeling that makes you want to dance, or a feeling that a certain piece of music is the last thing you want to hear on this earth. As Brahms said, "A symphony is serious business." *Res severa verum gaudium.*

If you'll indulge me, following are a few paragraphs about the physics of music and its dramatic structures, but you're more than welcome to skip to the end if you'd like. I get technical in a few other places in this book and you're welcome to skip them, too. Some people like to know what's going on under the hood, others couldn't care less, so long as it runs. I think that what goes on inside an internal combustion engine is fascinating, but that's just me. Don't worry. Other than here, this book contains only the briefest mention about internal combustion engines.

A cold-hearted theorist might say that the reason "Dido's Lament" moves us so much is because of the power of the dominant function. That's a lofty, technical term for the ineffable fact that our mind perceives one particular chord in music as an "away" chord, called the dominant, that wants to "resolve" to a home chord, called the tonic. "Going home, going home . . ." These chords can be analyzed mathematically, that's part of the wonder, but the math says nothing about why those chords make us feel the way they do. It's literally all in our heads. Yet that simple principle has powered everything from Gregorian chant to rock music, from pop songs to five-hour Wagner operas. And "Dido's Lament." It's amazing.

The greatest minds in neurology have never figured out why the mind perceives tones this way, much less understand what possible evolutionary advantage our ancestors had who could perceive a dominant function over other ancestors who just had bigger, hairier arms. It's in our brains, hard-wired it seems, and it's where music's primal power comes from. It's the engine that powers music. In some music—say, Wagner—it's an industrial diesel.

A less mystical-physiological-mathematical way of looking at it is to go back two millennia to Aristotle's *Poetics*, the earliest writing we have on dramatic theory (if you've stuck with me up to now, you'll be fine with this). *Poetics* describes the elements of effective story-telling—what creates drama, what holds an audience—basically, what makes us give a damn. Screenwriter Aaron Sorkin, creator of *The West Wing*, *A Few Good Men*, *Sports Night*, and *The Social Network*, will cite *Poetics* at the drop of a hat. Says Sorkin: "I worship at the altar of intention and obstacle." Someone has to want something, or, better, need something. Then something gets in the way. Someone else gets the job you desperately need, the person you love more than life goes off with the jerk in human resources or, as in the *Epic of Gilgamesh* four thousand years ago and innumerable stories since, you don't want to die. Character is then revealed by the way the person tries to overcome those obstacles. Or, in the *Epic of Gilgamesh*, the Bible and the Harry Potter novels, how they accept death. Success isn't necessary, only intention. In the best stories, passionate, even desperate intention. See the poem "Di rayze aheym" in "Frantic, Fierce . . . and Hopeless."

Somehow, great music creates such characters in its themes. The theme is driven away from home, harmonically, and our perceived need for the theme to return home drives the musical drama. Harmonic and thematic obstacles get in the way and we, as listeners, get caught up in it. If the music is beautiful, or at least well-written, we want to get back home, too. This harmonic drama can be as short as a two-minute song or as long as that five-hour Wagner opera. The basic principle is the same.

To paraphrase the great British writer Julian Barnes, music, like love, is the meeting point of truth and magic. The truth is that, when a theme moves away, we want it to get back home. The magic is that this desire exists in the first place.

And what transforms this desire for "the return" into great art is the composer of genius, otherwise music wouldn't have progressed past Happy Birthday. Take our indescribably beautiful aria from Purcell's opera, "Dido's Lament." It begins, "When I am laid in earth . . ." Those grim words begin "Dido's Lament," and a lament it most certainly is. But in musical neurophysics, it's just one long frustration of the harmonic desire to get home. Combined with a passacaglia-like bass—the repeated descending pattern in the bass line of "Dido's Lament"—somehow we perceive that harmonic frustration as profound grief. This music reaches inside us to places we almost wish it hadn't. Music theory accounts for this very untheoretical power, but doesn't explain it.

But, as in everything, theory follows practice. Just listen to Janet Baker. Her sublime singing will take all this intellectualizing and brush it aside like dryer dust, on its way to breaking your heart.

Shall We Ask Za Composer What He Wants?

The end of time

DURING HIS LIFETIME, R. Murray Schafer was considered by many to be Canada's greatest living composer. During his long, productive, and widely celebrated career, he was especially well known for unconventional works intended to be performed in unusual formations, in addition to more traditional works such as his thirteen string quartets. He was also admired as a writer, a music educator, and an environmentalist. His well-deserved recognitions include the Governor General's Performing Arts Award, the Jules Léger Prize for New Chamber Music, the Glenn Gould prize, the Walter Carsen Prize from the Canada Council, two Juno awards and the Order of Canada. He passed away at the age of eighty-eight after facing Alzheimer's with courage and grace. I admire him too, with the caveat that performing some of his more experimental works or encountering him personally could result in more nuanced views of him.

Canada Day is surely one of the most joyful, most affectionate, and least jingoistic of national holidays. We all wear red (the colour of maple leaves in the fall, not a partisan statement) and wave Canadian maple leaf flags (also not a partisan statement) and generally have a good time. So on Canada

Day this year I decided to write about the cycle of six beautiful, gently exotic songs by Canadian composer R. Murray Schafer titled *Gitanjali* and written for the joyful, expressive, virtuosic, crystal-clear voice of the utterly beloved Canadian soprano Donna Brown. Yes, I'm a fan. And there exists a real, all-Canadian cast recording of *Gitanjali*: the indelible R. Murray Schafer (born in Sarnia), the above-said totally wonderful Donna Brown (born in Renfrew), conductor Mario Bernardi (born in Kirkland Lake) and the National Arts Centre Orchestra (born in Ottawa). Too bad it's not cold enough for BeaverTails. If you don't know what a BeaverTail is, you'll have to visit Ottawa in the depths of winter to find out, which means likely you'll never find out. Your loss. Did you know that Ottawa is the coldest capital city in the world, aside from Ulaanbaatar, Mongolia?

I thought several times (yes, no, yes, who will be offended?) about including here, unexpurgated, the program notes for *Gitanjali* written by the composer himself. Then I thought, hey, it's Canada Day. Why deny the fact that, contrary to world-wide opinion, not all Canadians are unfailingly polite? Let's celebrate *everything*! So, here goes:

> This joyful work for lyric soprano and orchestra is a setting of five of the poems from Rabindranath Tagore's ecstatic collection entitled *Gitanjali*. I had set one of these poems, "Light, my light," in the original Bengali in the third movement of *Lustro*, 1972. In fact, I once had a recording of Tagore singing this and other songs from *Gitanjali*, but my settings are very different. Tagore translated *Gitanjali* into English, with help from W. B. Yeats and advice from Ezra Pound. The success of the English version won him the Nobel Prize for Literature in 1913; he was the first non-European to win this prize, and when he heard the news he said, "So, they give it to a Hindu?"

What I said.

> Of all my works for solo voice, *Gitanjali* is undoubtedly the most ecstatic. The influence of Richard Strauss is perhaps more felt than actually present in the tonalities of the songs. I wrote the work for Donna Brown, a soprano with a serene and flexible voice.

Her voice is indeed that, but much, much more.

> The première was conducted by none other than my old friend Franz-Paul Decker, who wasted no time in insulting both Donna and me. First, he recalled (my piece) *Son of Heldenleben*: "Let me see . . . ven vas dat? I did it in Montreal and in Rotterdam. It had a disgraceful reception. Zay didn't like it at all!" He then picked out some passages in the new score that he thought should have been notated differently. He tore into Donna when she hummed a wrong note. "Do you have perfect pitch? No? Shall we ask za composer what he wants? He ought to know."

Unfortunately, all this is true. I was there. Franz-Paul Decker was a gifted conductor and we loved him, but he could do this kind of thing (see viola section in "Ida! Don't Do That to Me!").

> Donna sang the work three times: at the premiere in Ottawa, for a CBC recording, and with Esprit Orchestra in Toronto, but my hopes for a wide acceptance of the piece were premature.
>
> —R. Murray Schafer

I must add immediately that the lack of "wide acceptance" was not through any fault with Donna Brown's absolutely glorious singing. It may have had more to do with the fact that among R. Murray Schafer's many talents was a particular flair for annoying people, or at least thoroughly confusing them.

A friend and musical colleague once participated in one of R. Murray Schafer's more rural compositions, *Music for Wilderness Lake.* The instrumentation specified was "twelve trombones and wilderness lake." A CBC recording was commissioned, which involved placing a broadcast-quality tape recorder on a raft in the middle of the lake. According to my colleague, the recording and the costly recorder were lost when the raft sank.

And then there was *RA*, a work intended to last all night and first produced in Toronto in 1983 at the Ontario Science Centre.

An aside: the Ontario Science Centre was a superlative educational complex designed by celebrated architect Raymond Moriyama. Nestled in the Don valley just outside downtown Toronto, it opened many years ago to great acclaim. It was especially well-known for its many science and environmental programs for young people. The green, rolling Don valley was also the setting for Ernest Thompson Seton's famous book *Wild Animals I Have Known* that has given generations of young people (like me, I read it when I was ten) a lifelong affection and respect for wild animals. Unfortunately, the Ontario Science Centre was later allowed to fall into disrepair, although exactly how much disrepair is disputed. The Centre was recently closed permanently without notice by the Ontario government, followed by proposals to move it to a smaller location downtown. It may or may not be relevant that a housing development is being proposed for the address of the now-closed Ontario Science Centre.

Back to *RA*. *The Canadian Encyclopedia* describes *RA* as: "A dusk-to-dawn musical/theatrical ritual . . . scored for 7 singers, 4 actor-singers,

8 dancers, belly dancer, dwarf actor, various extras (actors and singers), 8-voice male chorus, violin, harp, percussion, ud, qanun, darabukkah, and other Middle Eastern percussion, tape and electronic sounds, and a participatory audience of 75 members."

Despite the unusual (to say the least) performance requirements, it was a serious work. Among the eminent soloists were Donald Bell, Eleanor James, and Maureen Forrester. But a musical colleague who participated in the premiere also told entertaining tales of certain members of the participatory audience in the darkened science centre at 4 a.m. Apparently the parameters for their participation were not clearly defined.

And then there was *Cortège*, written for conventional orchestra, which the NAC Orchestra once infamously took on tour to Europe. Infamously, because a complete performance originally involved the musicians wearing masks like the Phantom of the Opera and goose-stepping around the stage. Needless to say, this bit of theatre was excruciating to perform in Germany. We played *Cortège* again some years later, but by that time the goose stepping had been shelved, along with the masks. Literally. For many years, on a top shelf in the music library gathering dust was a cardboard box with lettering in magic marker saying, "These are the masks."

Which, patient reader, brings us to *Lustro.*

I came to Canada straight from the University of Michigan, a "public ivy" university in a livable part of the US, and grew up in 1950s Detroit, just across the Detroit River from Windsor, Ontario. My Victorian British father (totally unreformed) would take his British parents to Windsor, betimes, to buy Bird's Custard, Lyle's Golden Syrup, and to marvel at the road signs which, in those days, were in the shape of the British crown. They felt right at home.

We greatly admired the CBC—for any readers outside Canada, the Canadian version of the BBC—which we could easily receive from across the river. In addition to civilized news programs and intelligent conversation, the CBC broadcast a lot of classical music, all this distinguishing it from anything we could get on commercial American radio. The CBC was "the good radio." So my admiration for both Canada and the CBC was limitless when I won an audition to become a member of the Toronto Symphony. From day one, in a tiny, rented apartment on Yonge Street, I loved everything about Canada, even though it took me a while to believe that its colourful currency would really be accepted in return for a Big Mac. And, in my very first year, the Toronto Symphony was hired by the CBC to make the world premiere recording of a new piece by R. Murray Schafer. It was scored for mezzo-soprano, voices, multipart orchestra and tape recorder and titled *Lustro*.

The writer Stephen Adams describes *Lustro* affectionately:

> *Lustro* . . . this monumental work, is at least as imposing as (Schafer's) stage works—perhaps more so. *Lustro* is a triptych of three large compositions: "Divan i Shams i Tabriz," "Music for the Morning of the World," and "Beyond the Great Gate of Light." The outer two are primarily orchestral but include seven or eight voices in their complex texture; the middle part is for mezzo-soprano accompanied only by tape. With its large orchestra dispersed through the concert hall and its masterful manipulation of four-track tape, the work compels in its hearers a "sensation of wandering in sonic space." The whole is an evocation of mystical experience, certainly one of the most powerful attempts of its kind by any composer. "If the Patria sequence at all resembles Wagner's *Ring*," then, says Schafer, "Lustro could be called my *Parsifal*."

Yes, I'm setting you up.

The recording sessions were held in Eaton Auditorium, a medium-size concert hall with excellent acoustics that was attached to Eaton's department store at Yonge and College Streets. Unfortunately, both the fine auditorium and the fine department store are long gone, such is progress. The hall, built in the classic shoebox design, hence the good acoustics, was a popular venue for ensembles of all sizes, including the Toronto Symphony. It was also a preferred recording location for Glenn Gould who, perhaps not entirely coincidentally, lived just a couple of stops north on the subway.

We Toronto Symphony musicians arrived to find ourselves divided into sections and placed, as described above, in five different locations around the hall: two small groups in the back corners of the ground floor, two small groups in the back corners of the balcony and a lucky larger group onstage. I say lucky because the musicians onstage were the only ones who had any idea what was going on, because they had the conductor. The rest of us were supposed to be "conducted" by large clocks set on stands in front of each group, the hands set precisely at noon. Or midnight, depending on your frame of mind.

The fine singer Roxolana Roslak, who three years earlier had won a Juno Award for best classical album of the year with Glenn Gould, was placed in a far corner totally in the dark, to be illuminated, eventually, by a single candle on a tall, black pavement stand, as used in Catholic and High Anglican churches to emphasize the gloom on Good Friday. I don't recall whether she ever sang while we were playing, the description above would imply that she didn't. I only recall seeing her and the candle barely visible in the darkened hall. In the confusion it was hard to tell.

What I do remember was the manifest inability of those in charge to realize that those of us in the groups scattered around the hall had no idea when we were supposed to play. This was because the clocks weren't connected to anything. So, as things progressed, or not, most of us sat in the dark being yelled at by the conductor sixty feet away that we weren't playing in the right place. So we yelled back, "The clocks aren't running!" Perhaps that adversarial atmosphere was the composer's intention, but even with R. Murray Schafer, I doubt it.

I'm sure *Lustro* is the magnificent achievement described above by Stephen Adams, but those of us who were actually there for the recording mainly remember the unplugged clocks and, during the long periods of darkness and confusion, wondering how much all this must be costing.

Thus, my somewhat compromised introduction to Canadian music and working for the CBC. Much better experiences followed, I'm glad to say, but that first impression left its mark.

Donna Brown, however, was, is, and always shall be, totally wonderful.

The Ghost in the Machine

This book told me more about penguins than I wanted to know.

—Small boy to teacher

"WITH THE PERFECT PLACEMENT AND live acoustics, volume is not important. Articulation and texture and beauty of sound are everything." Surprising words from a concert organist who contrived his public name through such permutations as E. G. Biggs, Edward G. P. Biggs, E. G. Power-Biggs, Edward Power Biggs, and Power Biggs, before settling on E. Power Biggs, the name he would make synonymous with the mighty pipe organ. No way to miss the word that most characterizes the organ in the public mind. But now, "volume is not important"?

Before we go on, fair warning. This rather lengthy essay wanders a bit. My editor wanted it divided into at least two, perhaps even three separate parts with more individual focus. As you will see, he had a point. But this is an attempt to describe a great love. If you're being honest, that's usually messy.

My British father was a fine organist, trained at Coventry Cathedral before the war. His noble playing was my first impression of great music grandly played. Seeing my father at the console on Sunday mornings, in those days wearing full morning dress, made the kind of indelible impression that can be made on a small boy by a father who can do something extraordinary. So please bear with me. While the organ is not everyone's cup of tea, as it were, for me the instrument has been a lifelong musical inspiration, a visceral thrill, and a solace. And, from my youngest years until today, three-quarters of a century later, a vivid reminder of a father who, in my mind, still stands miles above all others. Yes, I was blessed. Twice. Three times.

In my experience as an orchestra musician, the organ is the most admired (look at all those keys) but also the most disliked of all the great musical instruments. And it's not just the church thing, though for sure that doesn't help.

A fine violin has a soul. It's unmistakable. To play the violin well is a complex act of respect, technical mastery, and, in the best sense (and in both directions), a kind of seduction. Play a violin with ability and love and it will come alive in your hands. It's magical, really. But a pipe organ is a machine built in a factory, a mammoth machine weighing several tons with thousands of moving parts. In a large organ, the highest-pitched pipe could get lost in a shirt pocket, the lowest-pitched pipe can be higher than a house—not exactly something you would polish lovingly and place under your chin. Individual organ pipes, if made by a master builder, can make beautiful, compelling sounds. But they will make exactly the same sound if the key is pressed by the gentle finger of a great artist or, using an analogy from the piano world, by the point of an umbrella.

That said, the very best organ builders somehow manage to instill a soul into their instruments anyway, "the ghost in the machine"—a phrase by an Oxford philosopher that goes back to the Cartesian idea that the mind and the body are separate. Never mind that, just enjoy the metaphor.

Online you can hear an absolutely breathtaking example of a machine with a soul by searching "fox komm" (no, that has nothing to do with an Asian factory that makes iPhones). That should bring up the inimitable Virgil Fox playing his completely over the top arrangement of the Bach chorale "Komm, süsser Tod" (Come, Sweet Death). Yes, it's easier to take in the original German. Fox and his friends just called it "CSD."

A department store would be the last place you'd expect to find one of the largest pipe organs in the world, but that's where the Wanamaker Grand Court Organ can be found, in the ten-storey-high grand court of Macy's Center City Philadelphia. Ask any Philadelphia native to "meet me at the eagle"—the magnificent ten-foot-high, nine-foot-long, 2,500-pound bronze eagle that has dominated the exact centre of the store's vast ground-floor retail space for the past century—and then look up. There it'll be, the Wanamaker Grand Court Organ, going all the way up to the top.

It's called the Wanamaker Organ because the Macy's building was originally the Wanamaker Department Store. The huge instrument was constructed for the 1904 St. Louis World's Fair, an international event grandly titled the Louisiana Purchase Exposition. Like the Louisiana Purchase, which contained roughly a third of the land mass of today's continental United States, the exposition was really big. That's where the big eagle came from. The fact that Native Americans had lived on that land since the last Ice Age was not much of a consideration in the negotiation.

Five years after the fair, the huge organ and the big eagle were purchased by John Wanamaker and shipped to Philadelphia in thirteen freight cars. The byzantine, occasionally heroic background of this mammoth instrument would be a book in itself (in fact there are several) but for our purposes it's enough to say that it's just mind-boggling. Its 28,750 pipes and all their associated blowers and wind chests and other machinery were built to the highest standards of craftsmanship. Its towering golden façade is perhaps a bit cheesy, but its sound is beyond belief.

Of no relevance at all to the organ is that the original Wanamaker store (this is the late 1800s) provided its employees with free medical care, a profit-sharing plan, and a pension. It was also the first department store to have electric lighting and a telephone, its ads were honest, and they invented the price tag.

Back to the music, the original four-part chorale "Komm, süsser Tod" is supremely beautiful just by itself, but it can be played in a minute. But that was before twenty-seven-year-old Virgil Fox was asked, almost a century ago now, to play a recital for the American Guild of Organists on the Wanamaker organ. He decided to do something beyond spectacular to impress them. Of course he did. He was Virgil Fox.

Fox was a big fan of the fabulous Philadelphia Orchestra, its flamboyant organist-conductor of that time Leopold Stokowski, and especially Stokowski's lush orchestral arrangements of J. S. Bach. Fox loved Stokowski's "Fabulous Philadelphians" take on "Komm, süsser Tod." Thus inspired, Fox spent several nights alone in the dark with the huge instrument (imagine how creepy an empty ten-storey-high department store would be at four in the morning) and came up with his own arrangement of such mastery and heart-rending beauty that it made him instantly famous, at least in the organ world. And now it can be heard from anywhere, anytime just by searching "fox komm." In my view that's a somewhat ambivalent kind of progress, but I'm emphasizing the positive here. If you do actually listen to it don't be shy, turn it up. You'll need good speakers and understanding neighbours. And, just so you know, when you think it's over, it's just getting started.

Virgil Fox used to tell his students that, to play the organ well, you have to do three things at the same time. First, play the notes. No small thing, considering that you have, in effect, fourteen fingers to coordinate (both hands plus the toes and heels of both feet). Second, work the machine—selecting the combinations of stops, sometimes from more than a hundred (the Wanamaker organ has 464), moving the swell shades with pedals to make the sound louder or softer (the Wanamaker organ has eleven of them), deciding which of two or three or four or more keyboards to play on, often two at the same time, sometimes three by using a stray thumb (the Wanamaker organ has six keyboards)—and third, whew, while doing all that, somehow make music. With tons of machine parts under your chin, so to speak, that's the tough one.

I've often wondered what possible evolutionary pressure could have evolved the astonishingly fine muscle control needed to draw a slow, steady downbow on a violin. The smallest trace of unsteadiness, any stray impulse of even a single muscle fiber will cause the bow to start jittering on the string, betraying your anxiety to all the world. What hunter-gatherer came in with a wildebeest over his shoulder and increased his reproductive chances with his ability to set down the wildebeest ever so slowly and gently, instead of the big hairy guy who just bashed in and threw two wildebeest on the fire. Wildebeests?

The same could be said of organ playing, which redefines the word "multi-tasking" exponentially. Did our pre-organist hunter-gatherer come in dragging fourteen wildebeest over his shoulder, having killed them all at the same time?

Be all that as it may, roughly a decade after the Second World War, the hermetic organ world began to drift into two camps: "bigger and louder" and "historical fanatic, must be original even if it sounds like a plugged up vacuum cleaner." OK, that's an exaggeration, but something similar happened in all of music. It was big. Of course, the best artists were in neither camp, they never are. They looked for the best sounds and the best music and the best way to play it, however they could figure it out. And E. Power Biggs (he really did get the name right) was the first major post-war organist to look seriously at historic organs in Europe—Bach era and even older—with a mind to preserving their original sounds.

This is important because old organs are not just musical machines. They are time machines. The countless little leather valves in an organ, the delicate linkages between the keys and other finicky moving parts can break down over time. But most of the pipes are made of metal. They don't dry out or crack or rot and they never move, so they are virtually ageless. Alone of all musical instruments, a three-hundred-year-old organ will sound exactly the same as the day it was made. And, no small thing, if left unaltered it will be in the same *pitch* as the day it was made. Which is how, looking back from our standardized age of A-440 (442 in New York or 444 if you're a high-strung European) we know that pitch in Bach's time was all over the place. "Period" instruments are now tuned roughly a half-step lower than modern instruments—the lower pitch is fundamental to the more relaxed period sound on string instruments and it's a godsend to voices. But it makes no difference to an organ pipe.

So, roughly seventy years ago now, our hero Mr. Biggs began travelling all over Europe, playing and, hugely important, *recording* old organs before they were . . . improved. As Helmuth Rilling said, we can try to recreate the instruments and performing styles of centuries ago but we can't recreate the listeners of that time, because they'd spent their lives in a world quieter than ours by several magnitudes. Old organs, with pipes in their original state, can tell us exactly what sounds those lucky, non-hearing-impaired people heard. And organ builders today are re-creating those historic sounds.

Enter Dirk Andries Flentrop of Flentrop Orgelbouw in Vandaam, Holland, makers of exquisitely crafted instruments using the organ technology of Bach's time. And enter our Mr. Biggs, who appreciated those sounds of a vanished world and ordered an organ from Mr. Flentrop for the Busch-Reisinger Museum at Harvard, with the impressive stipulation that "volume is not important, beauty of sound is everything."

After all this, time to come clean. I have worshipped the sound of the Harvard Flentrop since I was a student. I bought E. Power Biggs recordings made on the Harvard Flentrop as fast as they came out. I find the Flentrop's clarity, articulation, and transparency—its beauty of sound—just miraculous. As organs go it's not loud, because the wind pressure blowing the pipes is very low, human scale, barely more than you would use playing a flute or a recorder. The Flentrop organ uses quality of sound and natural resonance to create power, not force. Try listening to Biggs's Harvard Flentrop recording of Bach's *Passacaglia and Fugue in C Minor* and, at the opposite end of the severity spectrum, the "Siciliana" from Bach's *Pastorale in F Major*. They're both easy to find online. There are a lot of recordings of this famous music, but not like these.

The imposing "Passacaglia" begins quietly, almost mysteriously, with only a few stops drawn, only a few pipes speaking, but immediately you can hear the tonal refinement of this wonderful instrument. As the music builds and more and more pipes are brought into action, the sound grows with natural authority. By the end, at its biggest, the sound has gained great range and power but lost none of its miraculous transparency. I have no idea how that acoustical magic trick is achieved.

In the gentle "Siciliana" you hear a flute stop with its natural "chiff"—on the Harvard Flentrop so pronounced it sounds almost like woodblocks. A chiff is the knocking sound that happens when air is first released into an organ pipe, before the pipe has had time to resonate on its intended note. On later, more "romantic" organs, this chiff sound is intentionally eliminated by cutting grooves in the mouth of the pipe (yes, sounds like something they do to a tomcat). This alteration makes the sound smoother, more "romantic," but at the cost of character. But that's not a criticism, not really. Like string instruments set up for the lower pitch and lower tension of the Baroque and Classical periods, or instruments set up to play in our higher-pitched, more aggressive sound-world, all have something musical to say. And that's not just musicological political correctness.

The National Arts Centre owns two beautiful Flentrop organs, presented to the newly built NAC by the Ottawa Dutch community "in appreciation of the role played by Canadian troops in liberating the Netherlands in 1945." Lest we forget. And also, lest we forget, on display in a glass case in the NAC lobby there used to be a handsome, leather-bound volume listing the names of every individual who contributed to these priceless cultural, political, and musical gifts. Then, several years ago, the volume mysteriously disappeared from its case. Whoever took it, it couldn't have been easy. It was BIG. One hopes that this inexplicable theft is like other thefts of artworks that remain unsolved for many years until they're discovered in an attic somewhere. I certainly hope so. The book was full of heart and history. And it was beautiful.

One of the NAC Flentrops is a small, single manual, six-stop *positif* organ, used to accompany choirs and small orchestras in Baroque repertoire. You could lovingly lean against it, but not too hard. The other Flentrop is a stunningly beautiful, thirty-foot-high, two-manual, twenty-one-stop concert organ. On the Southam Hall stage it towers majestically over everything, lean all you want. The Harvard Flentrop on Biggs's recordings is somewhat larger, with twenty-seven stops and three manuals, but its sound and appearance are very similar. The big NAC Flentrop is basically the Harvard Flentrop "without the backpack," that is, without the *Rückpositiv* or "behind organ" (loosely translated) played from the third manual—really a separate, smaller organ mounted behind the performer.

With the big pipes in front of the organist and the smaller ones behind, a common Baroque design, the Harvard Flentrop looks just impossibly grand. The NAC Flentrop is no less grand and, unlike the Harvard instrument, you can see the player. Its imposing presence and exquisite design are like a benediction for the hall.

To be honest, I've always felt a little sorry for the big NAC Flentrop, because it's not in the kind of resonant acoustic that would allow its beautiful sound to bloom. Organ pipes are designed to have overtones that will "fill out" in the reverberation of a generous acoustic. If you could blow into an organ pipe in your living room, it would sound surprisingly small, hollow, and edgy. Organs need space. The great nineteenth-century French organ builder Aristide Cavaillé-Coll, who built magnificent organs for many of the great churches and cathedrals of France, including Notre-Dame in Paris, was famous for saying, "The most important stop on my organs is the acoustic." Biggs referred to the "live acoustic" of the Busch-Reisinger Museum in his original proposal to Dirk Flentrop. In addition to Biggs himself, that is doubtless what attracted Flentrop to the project.

Organ sound is fundamentally different from the sound of any other instrument. The sound of a piano, no matter how beautifully played, begins to decay the instant the note is played. Piano sound is always dying. Concealing that sad fact is part of being a fine pianist. Wind and brass instruments can play a phrase only as long as the player's breath holds out. Making the necessary breaths inconspicuous or part of the musical line is part of being a fine wind player. Strings can play a seemingly endless line, but actually the longest a string player can sustain a note without a bow change is ten seconds, plus or minus, in performance usually much less. Concealing those frequent bow changes is part of being a fine string player. Now the organ is a wind instrument—its pipes are just glorified versions of the little recorder that is often a child's first musical instrument—but it doesn't breathe. The electric blower that supplies the wind pressure takes in air continuously. It is the only musical instrument that can sustain a note indefinitely. Forever.

Organ2/ASLSP (As Slow as Possible) is an unusual organ piece by the celebrated composer John Cage that exploits this unique characteristic of the organ to its logical, if absurd, conclusion. The piece is currently being "performed" on a specially constructed organ in a church in Halberstadt, Germany. The organ has only three pipes, it's actually quite beautiful to look at, if strange. The keys are held down by sandbags. The "performance" of *Organ2/ASLSP* began in 2001 and is due to end in 2640. That's not a typo. The intended length of the composition, 639 years, marks the time between the first permanent organ installation in Halberstadt Cathedral in 1361 and the composition's originally planned start date in 2000. It started a year late due to lack of funds. Don't smile.

This "immortal" quality of organ sound is one subconscious reason, perhaps, that the organ has always been identified with the worship of God. As if "endless breath" wasn't enough, the other magical part of organ sound that Cavaillé-Coll found so important is that the sound actually *increases* the longer a note is held. Or rather, in an acoustic with a long reverberation time it does. If a space has a reverberation time of, say, five seconds, calculations show it takes roughly three seconds for the acoustic to "fill" with sound. So, during those three seconds, a note or chord held on the organ will actually produce a crescendo of sound. Shorter notes, less crescendo, longer notes, more crescendo. This is the secret sauce that enables a fine organist to conceal the fact that the organ is a machine and turn it into an expressive musical instrument.

In its rich acoustic, the sound of E. Power Biggs's Harvard Flentrop has beauty and authority but does not try to overpower you. It invites you in with its nobility of spirit. It's a sound our own beautiful Flentrop has been trying to produce for fifty years but can't, not where it is. But it's still there, trying to express, against all odds, like the rest of us, what's in its heart. The ghost in the machine.

* * *

Sadly, since this was written, Macy's City Center Philadelphia has closed. A developer has plans to convert the huge building into "mixed-use space" including retail, residential, and office space. There are assurances that the organ will be protected—a concert series on the organ was presented with the first performance titled Meet Me at the Eagle. It was sold out. But many have expressed concern for the longer term. Developing the immense space will be a very large project, and very large projects don't usually mix with very large pipe organs. Watch this space, or rather, watch that space. With fingers crossed.

Thank You, Thank You, Thank You

DUKE: And what's her history?

VIOLA: A blank, my lord. She never told her love.

—Shakespeare, *Twelfth Night*

THE SIX SHORT SONGS BY Hector Berlioz that go under the unimpressive title *Les nuits d'été* also look unimpressive in the score, like a lot of Mozart. As Salieri says in the play *Amadeus*, looking in astonishment at a Mozart manuscript that he has manipulated Constanza into showing him, "There's nothing there." But get past all the empty space and you'll find what is possibly the most intimate, otherworldly beautiful, *sublime* music ever written.

"Sublime" is such an easy go-to word. It can mean whatever people want it to mean, because it sounds so . . . meaningful. Kenneth Clark thought Turner's dramatic paintings of storms at sea "touched the sublime," which they certainly do. They're scary paintings. Kenneth Clark's use of the word is related to great forces of nature depicted in heroic style. Looking up the word, "sublime" can also mean "elevated, taken to a high degree of spiritual refinement," but that definition is, for me anyway, a bit too much like raising your little finger whilst drinking tea. I prefer to think of the word as it's used in chemistry, where a heated solid is said to "sublimate" when it turns into vapour without passing through the liquid phase. It can go the other way, too, it seems counterintuitive. Don't things usually melt first? The solid into vapour transition with nothing in between is mystical. It's magical. It's sublime.

In that sense, I find these Berlioz songs sublime. The music and the carefully intimate poetry by Théophile Gautier, like the apparently simple score, are not imposing. With the exception of one or two places, the songs are not heroic, they're not virtuosic. What they are is beyond belief sensitive to what really goes on as love comes into a soul and when it is taken away, those supremely human transitions, which are sublime because there is no in-between state. The whole human drama exists precisely in the invisible in-between state, the transition that does not exist.

For a song cycle, *Les nuits d'été* is also pretty unusual. The songs were originally written for voice and piano but are now only rarely performed that way, since Berlioz himself, one of the greatest masters of orchestration, ended up arranging them for orchestra himself. And no one voice can sing all of them in their original keys. Many years ago I learned this the hard way, when I had the kind of hubris young conductors have who don't have a clue what they don't know.

My first act of hubris was to ask Lois Marshall, only one of Canada's greatest singers, to appear with me and my amateur orchestra in Peterborough. To be fair, many members of the Peterborough Symphony were attached to Trent University and they played in a boxy old high school auditorium with warm, forgiving acoustics, which inspired confidence and made them sound bigger than they were. And they were a wonderful group of people—musical, sensitive, and generous. We made a lot of music together.

My second act of hubris (I still can't believe I did this) was to ask Lois to sing *Les nuits d'été* with us. She gladly accepted because she loved the songs and rarely got a chance to sing them. And also because Lois and I had already done some other programs with a professional group in Toronto, so she knew I was a decent musician, just inexperienced as a conductor. Which I found out when she remarked, oh so casually, "Of course, you have the usual transpositions." Of course I did.

Of course I didn't. In a panic, I appealed to my colleagues in the Toronto Symphony music library, but their strict policy was that their music could not be lent out to other orchestras. Sensible, actually. I thought all was lost, but then I remembered the library of the former CBC Symphony Orchestra, a marvellously well-organized collection with friendly librarians who were more than happy to help out a young stick-waver who'd got himself in over his head. They lent me their transpositions, all carefully bound and in perfect condition, as were all the parts in that impressive collection. Even more impressive, their transpositions were original manuscript parts, beautiful pen and ink. "You're lucky we're here," they said. "Not many libraries have these." I was saved. I photocopied the rare originals and returned them right away, so I wouldn't have to worry about losing them. Close call.

The day of the concert I drove Lois from Toronto to Peterborough, a good two-hour drive. We had a great long talk in the car about everything and everyone. I was, as they say, in the tall cotton. But when we got to the old Peterborough high school, I suddenly remembered that the only way in was up a long flight of concrete steps (this was decades before equal accessibility codes). My heart sank. I'd conducted there many times, how could I have forgotten about the steps? With her lifelong disability from polio, dear Lois could hardly walk, much less climb steps. It's why her glorious voice was seldom heard on the opera stage. How in the world would she get in? Well, to let me off the hook, she got in like the good-hearted, courageous person she was: one step at a time, crutches in both arms. It took her forever, step by careful step, this great artist who had sung for Toscanini, but she made it to the top without a word of complaint. I died a thousand deaths slowly climbing the steps by her side, trying not to hover, trying not to imagine the worst, but she made it. If you're getting the impression that I thought the world of Lois Marshall, that doesn't begin to describe it.

There are many recordings of *Les nuits d'été*, but, in my view anyway, the subtle character of these songs eludes almost every voice, such is their delicacy and sophistication. But their character does not elude Janet Baker (her matchless recording of *Les nuits d'été* with Sir John Barbirolli is online). Among other reasons, this is because Janet Baker's infinitely expressive voice always carried an undertone of secret sadness. And their character did not elude Lois, for the same reason.

Les nuits d'été finished the first half of the program. During intermission, I noticed members of the orchestra going off by themselves down hallways, disappearing around corners. This was odd, the friendly group would usually spend intermission backstage talking and having coffee. Then I came across our principal oboe, a good friend, hiding in a classroom doorway dissolved in tears, overcome by the music and by Lois Marshall. When she saw me, all she could say was, "Thank you, thank you, thank you." And it wasn't for me.

But that's not the end of the story. A few weeks later I got a call from my colleagues at the Toronto Symphony. As it happened, they had a famous singer coming to sing *Les nuits d'été* and, at the last minute, they discovered that they did not, in fact, have the usual transpositions. They asked . . . um . . . could they borrow mine? Of course I was glad to help them, but I hesitated just long enough to make it art.

The Answer to All Questions

First comes the sweat. Then comes the beauty,
if you're very lucky and have said your prayers.

—George Balanchine

FOR NO PARTICULAR REASON, I was thinking that someone should do one of those long-form *New Yorker* pieces on everything that has to happen to get a head of lettuce to your local grocery store, maybe someone like the great John McPhee. Over the last sixty years, McPhee has contributed over one hundred articles to the *New Yorker* and written thirty books. One of his first books was about oranges.

Start with who owns the land the lettuce will grow on. How was it financed? Was it perhaps passed down in a family, generation to generation, or, more likely now, owned by a big corporation? If so, what happened to the family that originally owned it? Then, how does the lettuce get planted, how are the seeds and varieties developed? Are they GMO? Who actually does the planting, how are they hired, how much are they paid, are they unionized? (Well . . .) And then harvesting the lettuce and shipping it—not a trivial matter, they're not ball bearings. Each step in the process could be a book in itself. John? As of this writing, you're still around, thank heavens. You've already done a fine book on oranges. How about lettuce?

It's like thinking about everything that has to happen to produce a great work of art, a beautiful piece of music, say, that someone composes and someone else publishes or, in some places, bans (time to watch *The Death of Stalin* again). Then someone else performs it and eventually it gets recorded and you buy a CD of it or download it or stream it or, best of all, you hear it performed live right in front of you by actual, living, breathing musicians. And not to start in on the astonishing neurology of hearing and the unexplainable emotional perception that makes certain frequencies of air vibrations sound like music. Each is a step in a long, risky process, the coming together of talent, culture, personality, politics, finance (composers have mortgages, too), physiology, neurology, and, behind everything, luck. Always luck.

After all this, the four suites for orchestra by Tchaikovsky come to mind. Yes, I'm a musical nerd, but really, they do. Lyrical, energetic, mostly dance music, wonderfully orchestrated and beautiful, yet somehow not played that often. Almost never, actually. Why?

Take the imaginative, unbelievably colourful first movement of Tchaikovsky's Orchestral Suite No. 2, "*Jeu de sons*." On the first-class LP recording with Michael Tilson Thomas and the Philharmonia Orchestra, it's the kind of thing where you wonder where it's been all your life. But then, well, the whole suite is pretty long and not all of it quite lives up to its billing, except for the dynamite third movement, "Scherzo burlesque," with its four accordions. Four accordions! That's *crazy*. OK, what's on the other side of the record? Ah, Orchestral Suite No. 4, *Mozartiana*.

Wonderful! Perfect! Gorgeous music. And in a fifty-year professional career, it's the only one of the four Tchaikovsky orchestral suites I've actually played. Not for want of trying.

There's so much great music out there that's not played, like Dohnányi's *Symphonic Minutes,* an absolutely brilliant piece. When was the last time you saw it programmed anywhere? Yes, it's done, probably more often than Tchaikovsky's second suite, but really, when? Ok, yes, other than the Berlin Philharmonic (of course) and a recording by the fine Swiss conductor Matthias Bamert with the BBC Philharmonic and a few courageous entries on YouTube. Which is to say, almost never.

Let's talk about the beautiful, more-there-than-you-think-at-first Suite No. 4, *Mozartiana.*

There are good reasons it's the most popular of the four Tchaikovsky suites by a long shot. First, it's not too long. Second, it's inspired by Tchaikovsky's favourite composer, who's everybody's favourite composer. And last, but very much not least, it has a movement based on Mozart's brief, unearthly beautiful motet "Ave verum corpus," a setting of an ancient Catholic Eucharistic text that's either unbearable or transcendent, depending on your point of view. The text, I mean, not the music. *Everybody* loves the music. And it was the music for one of George Balanchine's greatest ballets. And now we're in another world.

The National Arts Centre Orchestra has played *Mozartiana* many times because it fits the orchestra perfectly and it's Mozart. Well, Mozart once removed. We played *Mozartiana* for the Balanchine ballet of the same name when the Pittsburgh Ballet paid us a visit. But *Mozartiana* is even more than a great Balanchine ballet. It's Balanchine's *last* ballet. Yes, this is huge. I looked up the chapter in Suzanne Farrell's riveting autobiography *Holding On to the Air*, and now I remember. We've just stepped off the edge of a cliff. And not just because Balanchine was the greatest choreographer of the twentieth century and Suzanne Farrell one of the greatest dancers of the twentieth century, Balanchine's last and perhaps greatest love, and the only one of his muses who wouldn't marry him.

The music is just gorgeous all by itself, you don't need to know anything about the ballet to love hearing it, but I have to talk about the ballet anyway. The music in the ballet version starts with "Preghiera" (the "Ave verum"), which is actually the second movement of the suite, but Balanchine changed the order to make it the first. Tchaikovsky should have, too.

As I write this, in late August, everybody's at their cottage, or wanting to be, holding on to the summer like Farrell holding on to the air. If you're of a mind, listen to the "Ave verum"; it's easy to find online. There it is, the deep difficulty of excellence. And of life, and of big love. And, in this ballet, whatever is beyond all that.

In her autobiography, which, if the subject of this essay moves you at all, you *must* get, Suzanne Farrell describes it this way:

> By the spring of 1981 Balanchine was working on not one new ballet but four. He had announced a festival to honour Tchaikovsky, the composer who, along with Stravinsky, was the most influential in his life . . . . Of the new ballets there was one that took on a permanent life in the repertoire after the festival was over. It is one of Balanchine's greatest works and a ballet that has been surrounded by a mystique rare even for Balanchine.
>
> I acquired a tape to listen to the music. I knew by now that this might be his last ballet . . . . To my astonishment, I suddenly heard music I had known all my life. I had sung Mozart's "Ave verum" in church as a child, and I thought how wonderful it was to have this music enter my life again at this moment.

That night I had a dream so vivid I could not distinguish between sleeping and waking. Although we had not begun the ballet and I had no idea of its format or implications, I dreamed about *Mozartiana*. I was in a place composed of tall spires. There was sound, not *Mozartiana*, but a kind of shattering, prophetic, organ-like sound, and I was walking on the vibrating spires upward from one pinnacle to another. It wasn't precarious. My footing was very stable; I was holding on to the air.

As I climbed, the light got brighter and brighter, whiter and whiter, until finally I could see, really see. Suddenly the scene changed, and I was walking on the sand by the ocean with Mr. B. It was still very bright, and people came up and looked at me. I responded to their silent, puzzled looks by saying, "Oh, yes . . . that's *Mozartiana*." It was the answer to all questions.

The curtain rises on *Mozartiana* in silence . . . . With the lifting of the curtain, a ghostly breeze fills the stage. The air of the auditorium meets the space of the dance. The quiet music of Mozart's "Ave Verum" begins, and I feel the draft touch me. Slowly, my head rises, propelling me up onto pointe. I bourrée forward, opening my arms, palms slightly upward. It is a pose from a statue of the Virgin at the Church of the Blessed Sacrament on 71st St. and Broadway that Mr. B knew I attended. Although it is not technically a ballet position, he wanted my arms to open very, very low. It is a humble offering and divine supplication that heralds the beginning of the "Preghiera" . . .

Technically, this dance was short and simple, but it required a state of mind beyond anything I had ever attempted before. It was a hymn shared by George and me, an offering that could happen only in movement and music, not in words . . . . He had not just

> made a ballet with *Mozartiana*, he had altered and extended the spectrum of my life . . . the pervasive calm and corresponding strength I felt while performing it were truly transcendent.
>
> Balanchine at the age of seventy-seven had given us a vision of heaven . . . . My dream of climbing spires was answered—*Mozartiana* was the light. It was because this ballet existed that I could survive the death of the man who made it.

I hope you see now why you have to get her book.

After all that—and that's a lot—the thing I admire most about Balanchine is that he always put the music first. In school he studied piano, composition, harmony, theory, and counterpoint. He *loved* music. I also admire his practical, craftsman-like approach to his work. He said, "I am like a cook. And if I didn't cook, we wouldn't have a company." And all that cooking was a lot of work. Farrell, not having a great day, recalls saying to him, "I'm sorry you have to work so hard to make me look good." He replied, "I have to work hard to make all of you look good."

It's the answer to all questions.

Shall We Dance?

Quantum of solace

THIRTY YEARS BEFORE THE TURN of the last century (I mean 150 years ago), an ambitious student in Munich named Max Planck wanted to study physics. But a stiff-collared professor of great repute advised him to study something else, anything else, because, "in physics, almost everything has already been discovered." Incredibly, this is actually what physicists believed then, back before electric light, automobiles and, almost, indoor plumbing. Albert Einstein's *parents* hadn't even met yet.

Fortunately for physics, Max Planck did not follow that spectacularly flawed advice. Instead, he went on to become a physicist, discover energy quanta, which led to quantum theory, which led to a Nobel Prize. Then, just before Ford's Model T appeared on the streets, Einstein's paper on the photoelectric effect would turn physics upside down by radically extending Planck's quantum theory to account for observed effects of light which classical physics couldn't explain. It was a revolution into the counterintuitive from which physics still hasn't recovered. Nor have we.

That stiff-collared professor reminds me of the proudly confident *Encyclopaedia Britannica*, Eleventh Edition, published only a decade after Planck's discovery and four years before the war to end all wars—the war from which the world still hasn't recovered. The Eleventh Edition is full of absolute cultural and scientific certainty, tables of numbers precise to the last decimal place, written by the best minds of its time and impeccably produced—forty thousand articles without a single typo, at least not that anyone has found yet. The 32,640 India paper pages of my copy are as crisp and bright as they were a century ago, like a Bible. Well, it *is* a Bible of sorts. The Eleventh Edition is the high point of nineteenth-century industry and scholarship all on one shelf. Fifteen hundred scientists and scholars contributed to it. Yet Einstein's revolutionary paper on the photoelectric effect, "Über einen die Erzeugung und Verwandlung des Lichtes betreffenden heuristischen Gesichttspunkt" (On a heuristic viewpoint concerning the production and transformation of light), published in the most prestigious European journal of physics six years before the Eleventh Edition was published, is not in it. Six years. Einstein's name does not even appear in the index. So the best minds of the time were either so conservative they were waiting for wider recognition of Einstein's admittedly incredible theory, or they were afraid of him. Probably both. In any case, they couldn't accept that their comfortable certainties would become uncertainties, even to the point of having an actual Uncertainty Principle that describes, mathematically, how it is actually against the laws of the universe to know everything.

They didn't see the war coming, either.

For fifty years I've been playing "classical" music professionally (stick with me, there's a connection). I love jazz, growing up in the 1960s we had the *best* pop music (of course), and after midnight, through the haze, we zoned out to ragas played by Ravi Shankar. At least I think we did. But my whole life I've lived for Bach and Mozart and Beethoven and the rest, and I don't want to hear *one word* about elitism. I grew up in Detroit, where I got beat up in gym class for lunch money.

I start from the old-fashioned premise that the high art music of our Western tradition is one of the highest achievements of humanity. Not the only high achievement, to be sure, and not only Western, but it's the one I know best and have loved since before I can remember. Yes, its origins can be traced to people of a certain culture, race, and gender, but it is not *about* any of those things. And besides, look back far enough and *Wir haben alle Scheiße an unseren Schuhen*.

And, ironically, "Western high art music" is actually a primal art, as much as the mind-bending rhythms of a drumming group from Sierra Leone I once heard that made our Western percussion sections sound like an Orff class. And the best thing is, after performing Bach and Mozart and the rest professionally for all these years, I realize they're even more amazing than I thought when I was starting out. I think only musicians and physicists get to say that.

My otherwise excellent professional training, as for most of my generation, was unconsciously narrow and, like the authors of the *Encyclopaedia Britannica,* Eleventh Edition, and Max Planck's stiff-collared physics professor, presumptuous.

The great period keyboard artist Malcolm Bilson recalls fourteen-year-old Richard Taruskin, who would later become a controversial music historian (the best kind), taking a piano lesson on a short piece by Prokofiev titled "Gavotte." Young Taruskin, a thorough researcher even then, had found a recording of Prokofiev himself playing it. The great composer's playing was elastic, free and dance-like, so young Taruskin played it that way. His stiff-collared professor was horrified. "Do not play like the composer! You must play what is on the page!"

Well, Prof. Eleventh Edition, what *is* on the page?

Not mathematics, for sure. As someone said, "Mathematics will get you in the ballpark, but it won't tell you how to hit the ball." Yes, I just made that up, but it's valid. What's on a page of printed music looks neat and precise, but it's really just a form of shorthand. And the essence of shorthand is leaving things out. Rhythm that's alive, a compelling style, and, as C. P. E. Bach wrote, "above all, beauty," have to be reconstituted from the printed page like freeze-dried food. How? As the great keyboard artist Greta Kraus (a Viennese who'd had a *good* education) liked to say, "Ha, children! Look at the music. Then use your *intelligence* and *taste*."

Now that's a tall order. But she'd studied privately, not at the famous school, and her musical idols were, with the exception of the pioneering music theorist Heinrich Schenker, not intellectuals but the great turn-of-the-century singers of the Vienna State Opera. Singers. There you go.

Greta often invited me to her house to listen to music and singers and talk about music and singers and, not entirely coincidentally, bring dinner. I usually went with a dear friend, a painter and former dancer, whom Greta loved. We respected Greta's Viennese tradition of punctuality to the letter, always arriving early and standing on her front porch listening to her practice until the exact time, to the second, when I would ring her doorbell. That was fun. Greta would answer the door, an eighty-eight-year-old in blue jeans, sweater, and colourful scarf that somehow, on her, looked like haute couture, and she would say, "Come in, children!" *So* Viennese. We would hang up our coats and follow her into her lofty, wood-panelled living room filled with books and sculpture and art, a fireplace you could almost stand up in, and a Bösendorfer Concert Grand 290 Imperial piano. We would always think of the *New Yorker* cartoon she had in her kitchen showing two cows standing placidly in a pasture. One cow says to the other, "No, we're Holsteins. Bösendorfer is a piano." Well, you had to see it. Then she would laugh and say, "You are the perfect guests! Not only are you never late. You are never early."

When Trevor Pinnock came to the National Arts Centre Orchestra, he loved us and we loved him. But the way we worked drove him nuts (see "Figure Out Which One You Are and Please Don't Do That"). The NAC Orchestra of thirty years ago was still trained to within an inch of its life to do everything as planned in rehearsal, precisely, predictably, the same every time down to the smallest detail. Our more recent years with our Italian *personaggio vivo e straordinario* Franco Mannino had been a passionate affair, but we still woke up in Ottawa where, as it went, "the winters are long and the notes are short." Spontaneity was not in our repertoire. Trevor would say, "Let's try this a little shorter," and forty-six pencils came out to mark "shorter." "No, no! Just *go* with it!" he would say. And forty-six pencils came out to mark, "Go with it." The poor guy. He wanted us to play Haydn like jazz but we just couldn't loosen up. Our many years of working for precision seldom included "Go with it."

Then, in something Baroque, would come the acid test. "Trevor, do you want this double dotted?" Poor Trevor. The question doubly annoyed him because it showed just enough knowledge to say something stupid. Of course, in Baroque music, dotted rhythms are always given an extra flip, a swing, a sort of bounce. Like jazz. But "double dotted" is to say, instead of a dotted eighth note followed by a sixteenth note, you would play an eighth note lengthened by exactly 50 percent to become an eighth plus a sixteenth, and shorten the following sixteenth by exactly 50 percent to become a thirty-second. And if you do it precisely, it sounds as tedious as that description.

And so Trevor would reply, trying to keep it light, "Well . . . play . . . um . . . an eleventh note." Of course, there's no such thing as an eleventh note. He was saying, politely, "It don't mean a thing if it ain't got that swing." Everything Trevor did with us was swung. Feel it in the moment, look at the other guys and go with it. Now, we do that without even thinking. Back then, not so much.

The highly esteemed pianist and musicologist Malcolm Bilson liked to ask his graduate class at Cornell, "What's the difference between a half note and a quarter note?" Sensing a trap but not wanting to look asleep, someone replied with the obvious, "A quarter note is half the length of a half note."

"*Ja*!" the stiff-collared professor from The Old Country would say. "*Nein*!" Malcolm Bilson from Cornell would say. "The quarter note is *lighter* than the half note." What, no math?

Bilson would ask, "Here are four notes under a slur. What does the slur mean?" Knowing this had to be another trap, but game, a student shyly answers, "Um, it means the notes are connected?"

Bilson: "Fasten your seatbelts. Leopold Mozart tells us that a slur means *diminuendo*. And that the last note is short." Gawd, you can't win with this guy.

Bilson digs in: "These four quarter notes have dots under them. What does *that* mean?" Of course, dots usually mean short. But, twice bitten, nobody's going to dare say something so obvious. So Bilson continues, with a twinkle in his eye, "It means the notes are as *long* as possible, and emphasized."

Seeing his prize students eyeing the door, Bilson says, "What is the single most important thing? That *nothing* is played evenly. Four notes are not four nice even notes, the way they look so neatly printed on the page. They get faster or slower, some get longer, some get shorter."

Like jazz.

Is this distinguished professor saying everything we were taught in school was wrong? Well, yes. And no. But yes. Of course rhythms are mathematically related and a slur connects notes together and dots usually mean short. What he's saying is that we don't know *everything*, not even close. This is musical quantum mechanics. We're young Max Planck.

The "old school" way of playing was sort of like those intimidating yellow signs you still see sometimes in Germany, printed in forbidding black Fraktur:

Unbefugten ist der Zutritt verboten!

Unauthorized are forbidden access!

But old-school performance style was actually, at one time, a dynamic, flexible style handed down by artists who had actually known Paganini and Liszt and Chopin and Brahms and the Schumanns. But then it became ossified, like nineteenth-century physics or one of those strict religions that forbid card games and dancing. "Johann Sebastian Bach, the great, austere Thomaskantor glowering down from the famous Haussmann portrait, he would *never* dance!" Now, of course, we know that almost all of Bach's music is *musique dansant* of one kind or another and, considering how much he liked beer, I'm absolutely certain the great Thomaskantor danced. Probably a lot. Over my long career, this has been one of my greatest joys, that music I've known and loved and played for half a century has been released from its conservatory cage and is dancing around the stage on springs. It's wonderful.

And there are many complexions of good "period" performers, as Trevor Pinnock and Malcolm Bilson would be the first to say. One was Sir Roger Norrington—a great musician, a penetrating intellect, and a compelling performer, but an absolute zealot about vibrato. That was his trademark thing, he *hated* it. As much as Pinchas Zukerman used to detest period instruments, Norrington detested vibrato. For him, vibrato was "sugar"—excessive sweetness without any redeeming nutritional value.

In my view they were both wrong, or at least partly wrong, just as any extreme position on anything is likely to be wrong, or at least incomplete.

Pinchas grew up when "period" performers were "the ones who couldn't play." I know, we're the same generation, I thought the same thing. And I'm guessing Norrington's dislike of vibrato came from a musical response to simply hearing too much of it from those who disliked period performers who couldn't play. On her pioneering cooking show, Julia Child accidentally dropped a freshly baked cake on the floor. Being Julia Child, she just shovelled it up with a spatula, reassembled the pieces into some facsimile of a cake shape, and liberally applied icing. Icing, icing everywhere. "They'll never know!" she chortled. That was Norrington's view on vibrato.

Or it could have come from his great care in achieving musical lines through phrasing and articulation and clarity and resonance, the essentials of music-making that you have to pay more attention to when you're not icing everything over with liberal applications of vibrato. In that sense Sir Roger, who, sadly, has recently left us, was a more honest cook than Julia Child. Perhaps his extreme position—and his fine performances—helped pave the way for the general acceptance of minimal vibrato in early music now, a huge advance in mainstream performing style.

I was lucky enough to have lunch with Norrington around the time he was doing his famous (or infamous) recording of Beethoven's Ninth Symphony. Personally, I love the recording, despite a few tempos that are, perhaps, a bit rhetorical. So I asked him the stupid question, "How come the best period performers—the ones who started the whole thing—how come they all seem to be from England and the Netherlands?"

"Easy," he said. "Hitler."

Cut off from inflexible European schools—"Do not play like the composer! Play what's on the page!"—young British and Dutch musicians had to figure things out for themselves. So they read up on the great musician-writers of those early periods—C. P. E. Bach, Leopold Mozart, Daniel Gottlob Türk, Joachim Quantz, et al.—and discovered a flexible, energetic way of playing that made the dry notes on the page come to life in a way that hadn't been heard for generations.

And not just early music. Take Rachmaninoff. His sensational playing captured on Ampico piano rolls made a century ago reveals the great romantic pianist and composer playing according to every single "revolutionary" idea in these centuries-old treatises. And here, after the Second World War created a diaspora of European artists fleeing catastrophe, we are figuring it all out all over again. How did we lose it?

Well, it seems to me that, like the Eleventh Edition physicists before the Great War, before Planck and Einstein, we thought we knew everything. Then impertinent, adventurous young artists began to do things differently and showed that we didn't know nearly as much as we thought. And Bach—and Rachmaninoff—came back to life.

Shall we dance?

Do You Believe What We Just Saw?

Music is the orphan whose father and mother no one can determine.

—Robert Schumann

I WROTE THIS ON ONE of those days where nothing works. Among other things, I was looking for my (official, purchased) VHS cassette of the New York City Ballet's original production of Balanchine's *Robert Schumann's "Davidsbündlertänze,"* choreographed to the glorious piano work of the same name by Robert Schumann. The heart-stoppingly beautiful music is played in its full forty-minute entirety by the New York City Ballet's superb pianist of that day, Gordon Boelzner, performing live on stage with the dancers.

Davidsbündlertänze is not the only time Balanchine had musicians actually performing onstage with the dancers. He choreographed Stravinsky's *Duo Concertant* for violin and piano with the two soloists onstage with the two dancers. In fact, *Duo Concertant* begins with the dancers just standing next to the piano and listening. This was a public gesture of respect for the music of Stravinsky, Balanchine's close friend and long-time collaborator, who had died just the year before. I had the pleasure of seeing *Duo Concertant* not long ago at the New York City Ballet, part of a brilliant all-Stravinsky program that redeemed my visit from seeing Peter Martins's *Romeo + Juliet* the night before. I relate that unsettling experience in "Movie Music." Balanchine's original staging of the Brahms *Liebeslieder Waltzer* also has the singers and pianists onstage. For Balanchine, who studied piano, music theory, counterpoint, harmony, and composition in his teens, music was never just an accompaniment to the dancing. It was the reason.

As an aside, Stravinsky dedicated *Duo Concertant* to the fine Polish-American violinist Samuel Dushkin and toured Europe with him during the early 1930s. Acknowledging the catastrophic history unfolding in that decade, Dushkin played a Guarneri del Gesù now named, appropriately, the "Dushkin," one of the greatest violins in the world. This gorgeous instrument has been owned for many years by Pinchas Zukerman, the NAC Orchestra's music director for almost two decades. On our many tours with Pinchas, he always played a concerto, usually Mozart or, spectacularly, Beethoven, with no conductor other than his phenomenal playing. These performances were the highlights of our many years of musical life with him. But, during all the unforgettable music-making, it was still impossible not to just gawk at that beautiful instrument being so masterfully played just a few feet in front of me.

Back to *Davidsbündlertänze*. The official website of the New York City Ballet has this:

> Poignant and purely poetic, *Robert Schumann's "Davidsbündlertänze"* takes audiences back to a time of refinement in an arresting series of dances intimating this brilliant composer's oft troubled psyche.

"Oft troubled" is a careful publicist's euphemism. Poor Robert Schumann was a poet, a fine writer, a fine pianist, and a great composer. He also fell like a ton of bricks for the young, beautiful, incandescently talented pianist Clara Wieke. Her domineering father took one look at her head-in-the-clouds suitor and promptly booked a year of concerts for her—out of town. *Davidsbündlertänze* was Robert's welcome home present for her, its eighteen movements were like eighteen love letters. He published it himself.

Back in the day, to see the official NYCB video of *Davidsbündlertänze* you had to buy a copy through the company, but now it's easy to find online. Gordon Boelzner's powerful playing is the performance to which Balanchine and eight of his closest dancers created one of Balanchine's most extraordinary ballets. And one of his last. To paraphrase Suzanne Farrell in her autobiography *Holding On to the Air*—essential reading, really—"If *Mozartiana* is Balanchine's idea of the next world, *Davidsbündlertänze* is his overwhelmingly powerful farewell to this one."

For a long time I couldn't find my copy of *Music and Dance in New York, 1973–1983* by the eminent critic Bernard Haggin. While looking for it I did find a book called *Working Stiffs*, about the life of a coroner, and two copies of *The Maestro Myth* by Norman Lebrecht (it must've struck a chord). But I finally found the excellent book by Haggin, which includes a chapter about *Davidsbündlertänze* as he observed it at its debut with its original dancers.

Bernard Haggin, a lifelong New Yorker, was a Juilliard graduate in piano but a writer at heart. He published his first piece of writing six years before the Great Depression and continued writing on music and ballet for the next sixty years. He told me that his earliest musical memories were of the Boston Symphony conducted by Karl Muck. Haggin's writing extended into the era of Daniel Barenboim (whom he didn't like) and Claudio Abbado (whom he did). He was one of the few critics to become personally friendly with Toscanini and was so respected by George Balanchine that he was the only critic allowed into New York City Ballet rehearsals. Haggin lived in a co-op just across Broadway from Lincoln Centre, his apartment notable for its modest forties-era furnishings, a narrow, monastic horsehair bed, and a vintage, single-serving Chemex coffee maker.

Typical of Haggin's dry, wry style and his love for semicolons is this:

> Ballet is not my field, I began in my first published statement, in 1935, on a subject of which I had no professional technical knowledge; but a few years later Balanchine validated my writing about it with his comment "You look; you see; you write what you see; and that's good."

Haggin wrote the following about the 1981 premiere of *Davidsbündlertänze*. I quote him, and later Suzanne Farrell, at some length, because I find it reassuring to read words of such intelligence, taste, and personal devotion about a contemporary work. And if I do go on about Balanchine, it's because, in addition to being arguably the greatest choreographer of the twentieth century, he absolutely lived and breathed music. He is known for saying, "Dance is music made visible." And of Balanchine's greatest ballets, his masterpiece *Robert Schumann's "Davidsbündlertänze"* is, for me anyway, at the top of the list. All I can say is to quote what an awestruck Bernard Haggin said to a friend as the curtain came down on its first performance, "Do you believe what we just saw?"

Haggin writes,

> Balanchine's major new work for the season was *Davidsbündlertänze*, to Schumann's set of imaginative piano pieces with that title. As he did with the waltzes of Brahms's *Liebesleiderwalzer*, Balanchine used the substance of the Schumann pieces for the purposes of

> his own dance imagination in the sequences he devised for his four pairs of dancers—sequences conveying the momentary states of mind and feeling of four pairs of lovers. And as with *Liebesleiderwalzer* he provided in the theatre program only the title of Schumann's musical work and the names of the dancers in his ballet—Farrell and Jacques d'Amboise, Martins and Watts, Ib Andersen and Kay Mazzo, Adam Lüders and Karin von Aroldingen. From this the spectator might infer that the absorbing dance invention he was seeing—from beginning to end, from the delightfully capricious first dance by Farrell with the for once baffled d'Amboise to the affecting conclusion performed by Lüders and von Aroldingen—was that of one of Balanchine's plotless pure dance ballets derived solely from that music, and that Lüders agitated last solo and his final duo with von Aroldingen were Balanchine's use of Schumann's music for the affecting end of the relation of this imaginary pair of lovers.
>
> But some spectators saw in these sequences an unexpected interjection by Balanchine's theatre sense of a stunning *coup de théâtre* in which it was Robert Schumann who performed what was a hallucinatory solo (during which five spectral Philistines in black, carrying enormous black quill pens, appeared briefly), and who, in the final duo, withdrew from a grieving Clara Schumann into the darkness of his insanity.

In other words, "Do you believe what we just saw?"

Haggin's masterly dissection of the ballet as he saw it is balanced beautifully by Suzanne Farrell's passionate description of it, coming from her respect and love for Balanchine and, as a great artist who danced in its premiere, her unique appreciation of the work:

Balanchine told some of the dancers, as well as the press, that the ballet was "about" Schumann and his wife Clara, but this was a biographical idea that he never mentioned to me. No doubt he told each of us as little—and as much—as was necessary to achieve his purpose. Because of the highly emotional nature of the music and dances, *Davidsbündlertänze* received enormous amounts of interpretive reaction.

It was without doubt a very profound, very moving ballet about love, but it had a tragic, tortured edge that made it significantly different from all other Balanchine ballets on the subject (which means most Balanchine ballets). Adam Lüders' final, slow disappearance was not so much the death of a beloved man as a metaphorical farewell to romantic love. In life, romance might be the foundation; in afterlife it definitely was not. One year later, in *Mozartiana*, Mr. B. explored what was.

I sincerely hope that anyone who's had the interest to read this far will, while waiting for Suzanne Farrell's book to arrive, watch the dark, evocative video of *Robert Schumann's "Davidsbündlertänze."* It was made under studio conditions with Gordon Boelzner and Balanchine's original cast of dancers, including Suzanne Farrell. The whole production represents the summit of Balanchine's creative power. And one heart-stoppingly beautiful love story.

You won't believe what you will see.

PART III

Composers: The gifted, and those who wish they were

What do I care about your damn fiddle?

—Ludwig van Beethoven

MOZAAAART!

Drop-dead gorgeous Adagio

"I heard it through the door . . . It started simply enough: just a pulse in the lowest registers . . . and then suddenly, high above it, sounded a single note on the oboe. It hung there unwavering—piercing me through 'till breath could hold it no longer, and a clarinet drew it out of me and sweetened it into a phrase of such delight it had me trembling . . . I called up to my sharp old God, What is this? . . . What? . . . Tell me, Signore! What is this need in the sound? Forever unfulfillable yet fulfilling him who hears it, utterly. Is it Your need? Can it be Yours? . . . I was suddenly frightened. It seemed to me I had heard a voice of God and it issued from a creature whose own voice I had also heard, and it was the voice of an obscene child!"

—Antonio Salieri, in Peter Shaffer's *Amadeus*

YES, THAT'S POOR SALIERI in Peter Shaffer's play *Amadeus*, hearing the music of Mozart through the wall and totally losing it.

Of course, the real-life Salieri and the real-life Mozart were not quite like that. Salieri was a successful and influential composer and Mozart was not an obscene child, he just enjoyed colourful language. And the villain in the play wasn't Salieri, the villain was God, as the fictional Salieri makes abundantly clear. But what was absolutely true to life was Mozart's miraculous music.

In the play, what drove Salieri around the bend was the oboe solo from Mozart's beautiful, sometimes even jazzy Serenade for Winds in B-flat, K. 361, "Gran Partita." This astonishing, one-of-a-kind piece was written in 1781. Or 1782. Or maybe 1784. Unless you're a musicologist, what does it matter? What we know for sure is that one Johann Friedrich Schink heard some of it, went home in a daze and wrote, "I heard music for wind instruments today by Herr Mozart. Oh, what an effect it made! Glorious and grand, excellent and sublime!"

I guess he liked it, and no wonder. The "Gran Partita" is one of the glories of all Mozart's music, and that's not just a convenient flourish of words. Bärenreiter-Verlag, publisher of the *Neue Mozart-Ausgabe*—the complete 132-volume critical edition of Mozart—says this:

> The *Gran Partita* is not only unique in Mozart's *œuvre*, but the largest work of the classic period scored for solo instruments. Although by definition a divertimento, it stands alongside the great genres of instrumental music—sonata, string quartet and symphony—with a richness of tone colour and a density of texture unheard of in the wind ensemble repertoire of its time.

Forgive them "*œuvre*" and "genre." There really is nothing else like the "Gran Partita."

And here I have to confess that the subtitle "Gran Partita" looks wrong to me, at least when put in quotation marks. When seen several times on a page, they start to look like scare quotes: "Gran Partita?" Really? Anyway, the history behind this famous subtitle is tangled and arcane (and entertaining) but the fact is that Mozart himself did not give this magnificent work any subtitle at all. On the manuscript score, a subtitle is written right at the top of the first page, almost cut off when the manuscript was trimmed: "gran Partitta." This odd mix of Italian words and German capitalization is clearly not in Mozart's handwriting and, as time has passed, "gran Partitta" is never used as the subtitle except in a priceless, scholarly work about the "gran Partitta" written by Dr. Daniel N. Leeson. And he hates it, too. He only uses it because, well, that's what it says on the title page of the manuscript.

So "Gran Partita" it is. Except if you look up a few paragraphs you see the quote from the publisher of the *Neue Mozart-Ausgabe*, the ultimate authority we have today, where "Gran Partita" appears as *Gran Partita.* Now that's more like it. Whatever the rules say, and whatever its provenance, *Gran Partita* became universally accepted as the subtitle of this grandest of all of Mozart's works for winds because it is, indeed, grand. It's monumental, it's one of a kind. It's wonderful. So I really dislike the "scare quotes." *Gran Partita* looks much more . . . grand. But rules are rules, "Gran Partita" it must be, even if the publisher of the *Neue Mozart-Ausgabe* distinguished the subtitle of this most distinguished work by setting it in italics. Sometimes, to paraphrase the famous epithet by Charles Dickens, the rule's an ass.

Some of us, if we live long enough, have the great good fortune to live, in a sense, several lives. Forty years ago, for a while, I was a conductor. Yes, my esteemed, beloved orchestra colleagues, I went over to the dark side. I was the music director of three orchestras—a fine amateur orchestra in Peterborough made up of wonderfully musical and kind people, a semi-professional orchestra in Oshawa that was game to try anything up to and including Mahler's Fifth Symphony (that was insane), and a professional chamber orchestra in Toronto that did first-rate work I'm still proud of decades later. And then there was the mid-life-crisis-going-back-to-university-for-pre-med-courses thing, which was really the only hard-core academic work I'd ever done outside of music and at which I was somehow successful. That crazy episode is detailed at heavenly length in "The Life It Brings." But then music, my true and patient love, caught me in a weak moment. I folded, auditioned for an opening in the National Arts Centre Orchestra and, by some total fluke, actually got in.

In the middle of all this, I was asked to conduct the Toronto Chamber Winds, a top-flight group of Toronto Symphony principals and guest soloists, for a commercial recording of the "Gran Partita." Yes, that's where this whole thing has been going. At every moment in that great masterpiece you think, "This is the best part. No, *this* is the best part." But the truly best part is the drop-dead gorgeous Adagio. You know it's the best part because, in the play, that's where Salieri realizes that the brat kid Mozart is gifted by God and he's not. I know the feeling.

We made the recording in the warm, friendly acoustics of Massey Hall, still the home of the Toronto Symphony in those days. The original LP got great reviews, it was nominated for a Juno award, and recently, four decades later, it's been re-released on CD and streaming and got yet another great review. That recording really is the gift that keeps on giving. Of course, the great reviews were really for Mozart. When the movie *Amadeus* won eight Academy Awards, the Academy Award for Best Original Score went to Maurice Jarre, for *Passage to India*. When Jarre accepted his Oscar, his first words were, "I was lucky Mozart was not eligible this year."

Our recording really was a special event, one of the greatest works of Mozart played by a group of terrific musicians who were remarkably patient being conducted by a former colleague who used to be in the fiddle section. And that former colleague was especially lucky because Daniel

Leeson (already mentioned with great respect above), who played second basset horn, was also the co-editor of the volume for wind instruments in the *Neue Mozart-Ausgabe*. Having Dan Leeson there was a very big deal. Dan Leeson knew everything there was to know about the *Gran Partita* including the literally hundreds of errors in the earlier editions. I was the conductor and I was pretty good at setting a tempo, but anything Dan Leeson suggested, my answer was, "Yes, sir."

You can search "mozart gran partita" and find a ton of distinguished recordings. The Netherlands Wind Ensemble with Edo de Waart was my favourite back then. But if I say so myself, few are as good as the recording my wonderful Toronto colleagues produced while putting up with me.

Bach's Little Black Book

He who sings, prays twice.

—St. Augustine (maybe)

LUTHERAN CHORALES, WHAT WE WOULD call hymns, were anywhere and everywhere in Bach's very Lutheran world. Calvinists thought music was superfluous (they thought anything fun was superfluous) but Martin Luther, like Salieri, regarded music as a gift from God. If you love something, you want to dress it up, so organists, being irrepressible improvisers with all that power under their itchy fingers, enjoyed dressing up their chorale tunes, perhaps to make their endless services more interesting. But none of them ever approached the skill J. S. Bach developed in this affectionate musical-theological-liturgical art.

J. S. Bach's *Orgelbüchlein* (Little organ book) is an exquisite but cryptic work. Scholars disagree on exactly why it was written or when, but all agree that the little two-minute-long chorale preludes in the *Orgelbüchlein* are among the most beautiful and precise music Bach ever wrote. Organists typically have teetering piles of music about to fall off their organ benches, but near the top is always the *Orgelbüchlein.*

All also agree that it's a little . . . odd.

For starters, it's odd that, for such great music, there is only one full-length book on the *Orgelbüchlein*, titled, not surprisingly, *Bach: The Orgelbüchlein.* It's by Russell Stinson, Ph.D., emeritus professor of music at Lyon College in Batesville, Arkansas. Batesville, pop. 11,539, may only have one high school, but it's got Lyon College and Dr. Stinson. He's had five books on Bach published by Oxford University Press, so don't get snooty.

Says Stinson:

> The *Orgelbüchlein* is simultaneously a compositional treatise, a collection of liturgical organ music, an organ method, and a theological statement. These four identities are so closely intertwined that it is hard to know where one leaves off and another begins.

Perhaps this musical multiple personality disorder has discouraged all but the most courageous scholars. In any case, good for Dr. Stinson. His excellent book is also on top of the teetering pile.

The *Orgelbüchlein* manuscript itself is also rather odd. The title page, stuck on at some point just before it was finished—or rather, abandoned—says that it's a pedagogical work, but that's probably more of an excuse. Bach originally planned it as a collection of 164 chorale preludes— short pieces for use during church services, each based on a Lutheran chorale. Since all the chorales are quoted complete, without interruption and have words to fit, it could almost be thought of as a highly embellished hymnal, but it would be hard to sing from. Bach never wrote a real one.

Following tradition, the preludes begin with "Nun komm, der Heiden Heiland," often translated as "Now come, the Saviour of the Nations." That's not quite precise, but precision in religion is often quicksand in disguise, so we'll let it pass. The forty-six—actually just the first thirty-three, the rest are sort of theological general purpose—cover the whole church year except, oddly, Epiphany. With this collection there are no straight lines.

Even more oddly, before he'd written a note, Bach "pre-assembled" his *Orgelbüchlein*-to-be as a little manuscript book—*really* little, roughly the size of a John le Carré paperback, but thinner. Nobody knows why Bach made it this small. Titles were written at the top of each page for each of the 164 planned chorale preludes but, when Bach quit working on it, he'd finished only forty-six. That's still eighty minutes of music, so it's substantial, but it's a strange feeling to look at all those empty pages with their lonely titles and wonder what might have been.

The great Alsatian organist, Bach scholar, physician, humanitarian, and cat lover Albert Schweitzer had this to say:

> Here Bach has realised the ideal of the chorale prelude. The method is the simplest imaginable and at the same time the most perfect. Nowhere is the Dürer-like character of his musical style so evident as in these small chorale preludes. Simply by the precision and the characteristic quality of each line of the contrapuntal motive he expresses all that has to be said, and so makes clear the relation of the music to the text whose title it bears.

"The relation of the music to the text . . ." There it is. In Bach's music, whenever there are words they are reflected in the music—sometimes subtly, sometime playfully, sometimes profoundly. If Bach writes something unexpected, it's because there's something big going on in the words.

The great French organist and composer Charles Marie Widor was *titulaire* of the great Cavaillé-Coll organ at Saint-Sulpice in Paris. Widor was only twenty-five when he got the most prestigious organ job in France after Notre-Dame (Cavaillé-Coll pulled some strings). Because of his youth, the powers-that-be hired young Widor for only one year, to see how it worked out. Despite his obvious talent, his next contract was also for just one year, and that insecure arrangement continued, one year at a time, for the next sixty-three years. Perhaps both sides were afraid of commitment.

Widor was Albert Schweitzer's revered teacher. Widor, then in his mid-fifties but probably already looking ancient, was puzzled by certain things in the *Orgelbüchlein*, so he asked his German-speaking student about them. A few weeks later, Schweitzer presented Widor with a copy of the *Orgelbüchlein* with the German words of each chorale translated into French and, in Schweitzer's meticulous handwriting, laid precisely under the related music. What a gift! Three generations later, Rolande Falcinelli, teacher of the recently retired *titulaire* of Saint-Sulpice, Daniel Roth, presented Roth (who revered Schweitzer) with Schweitzer's gift to Widor. *Omnes generationes.* She'd spotted it in a second-hand bookshop. It was pretty hard to miss, since it had WIDOR scrawled across the cover in thick blue pencil. Roth now displays it in a place of honour in his studio.

There's nothing in the historical record to indicate whether Albert Schweitzer converted WIDOR to the love of cats.

Ultimately, nobody knows for sure why, after all that planning Bach didn't finish the *Orgelbüchlein*. Best guess is that, after Weimar's short-tempered duke, Bach's employer at the time, threw Bach in the clink for wanting a better job (seems Bach got a bit snippy about it), Bach actually got the better job. In fact, he already had it, which really put the duke's nose out of joint. Says the official record: "On November 6 . . . the organist Bach was confined to the County Judge's place of detention for too stubbornly forcing the issue of his dismissal and finally on December 2 was freed from arrest with notice of his unfavourable discharge." No wonder he wanted to get out of there.

I make light, but I shouldn't. In the view of the eminent Bach scholar Christoph Wolff, Bach's month in jail "marked the absolute low point in Bach's professional life." In fact, according to a son of one of Bach's students, much of the first book of *The Well-Tempered Clavier* may well have been written "in a place where ennui, boredom, and the absence of any kind of musical instrument forced him to resort to this pastime." Melodramatic as that sounds, modern scholarship says it's surpassingly unlikely. More likely is that Bach spent his time locked up adding to the *Orgelbüchlein.*

We stand in awe of Johann Sebastian Bach the austere Thomaskantor, the forbidding figure glowering at us from the famous Hausmann portrait, in his hand a triple canon for six voices, in case you still didn't get it, but this same imperious personality now found himself locked up just for being rude. The only thing more terrible than being incarcerated must have been the blow to his pride. Bach had to endure the humiliation of not being able to leave for his new job when he wanted to while the duke got to flaunt his power over Bach by dictating when he could leave. On the other hand, today the whole world reveres J. S. Bach as the greatest composer who ever lived. Who remembers the duke?

Because Bach's new employer in Anhalt-Köthen was a Calvinist, his new job, strange as it sounds, did not include playing the organ. That meant Bach didn't need any more chorale preludes. That's really too bad, because, for all the *Orgelbüchlein*'s blank pages, what's left is gorgeous. One piece that haunts my nights is "O Mensch, bewein dein Sünde groß" (O man, weep for your grievous sin). That certainly wasn't for Christmas. "O Mensch" is without a doubt one of the most heart-rending things Bach ever wrote, and that's saying a lot. All those blank pages . . . But for Bach, always practical, the abbreviated collection was also *Gebrauchsmusik*—"useful music." In his new job, there was simply no use for it.

When Bach got around to adding a floridly-written title page, a translation reads:

> *Little Organ Book, in which guidance is given to beginning organists in how to set a chorale in all kinds of ways, and at the same time to become practiced in the art of pedalling, since in the chorales found therein the pedal is treated completely obbligato. For the highest God alone in his honour; for my neighbour, that he may instruct himself from it. Composed by Johann Sebastian Bach, p.t. Capellmeister to the Serene Reigning Prince of Anhalt-Cöthen.*

Beautiful. Except, obviously, almost all of it was actually written while Bach was still working in Weimar for the nasty duke. It would make sense that Bach would put off adding the title page until he could legitimately say he was somewhere else, *anywhere* else. And Anhalt-Köthen is 120 kilometres from Weimar (so was Anhalt-Cöthen, as Bach spelled it). In Bach's time it could take a week to travel that far by horse-and-carriage, so he was putting a healthy distance between his new home and his recent nightmare.

Despite that earnest title page, the existing entries show no planned technical progression. Some are "easy" enough for first-year students, a few are virtuoso showpieces for master performers only, and some, like "O Mensch," are priceless musical treasures. It's really all over the map. More important, this little book seems to have been the beginning of Bach's lifetime practice of collecting pieces of the same type all in one place. It wasn't a new idea, but even in their dreams none of Bach's predecessors could have come up with the fifteen two-part inventions and fifteen three-part sinfonias, the six *English Suites* and the six *French Suites*, the forty-eight preludes and fugues of *The Well-Tempered Clavier*, the six miraculous sonatas and partitas for solo violin, the six suites for solo cello, the Great Eighteen Chorale Preludes for organ, the masterful collection of organ pieces known as the *Clavier-Übung III*, and, not least, Bach's final, towering achievement, *The Art of Fugue*. Not even in their dreams.

Because the *Orgelbüchlein* is, obviously, organ music and, even worse, liturgical organ music, these short pieces are hardly known outside of churchy circles. That's sad, because the *Orgelbüchlein* was crucial to Bach's growth as an organist and as a composer. It's hard to imagine now, but Bach did not start out as Johann Sebastian Bach of the austere portrait. He had to start from the beginning and figure things out like everyone else. His talent was obvious from an early age, or at least his phenomenally energetic personality, but Bach still had to work hard at his craft. He said so himself later in life: "I was obliged to be industrious. Whoever is equally industrious will succeed just as well." Yes, Bach had a real passive-aggressive streak.

The title page said the *Orgelbüchlein* was "for my neighbour, that he may instruct himself from it." But it's entirely possible that Bach's "neighbour" needing instruction was Bach himself. The editors of the beautiful Concordia edition thought the small scale of the pieces was a clue to their purpose: "Just as the most intimate thoughts of a painter . . . are best observed in sketches and other small works, so the intensity of expression required in a short composition often shows the greatest dimension of a composer's technique and ingenuity."

It took Bach until he was thirty years old with seven children to come up with what Albert Schweitzer called "a complete musical catechism," what Charles Sanford Terry called "that miniature collection of masterpieces." The *Little Organ Book*, this small collection of big music, isn't where Bach suddenly became BACH. But it's where he found his wings.

Fleurs du Mal

How do you expect to play the oboe if you can't peel a mushroom?

—Marcel Tabuteau

THERE IS A SLIGHTLY STRANGE but beautiful piece for solo oboe and orchestra by Jean Françaix called *L'Horloge de Flore*, known in English as *The Flower Clock*. But that's not what the French name means. It means "The Clock of Flore," as if the clock belonged to someone named Flore. So, either the publisher made a mistake and the name should've been *L'Horloge des fleurs* or *L'Horloge fleurie*, or there really was someone named Flore who had a lovely clock made of flowers. Well, if the piece wasn't one of the few great virtuoso showpieces of the oboe repertoire, nobody would care. But because the piece is wonderfully well-written for the instrument and truly beautiful, it still doesn't matter. *Flower Clock* it is.

The idea of the piece is seven continuous movements portraying seven flowers planted in a "flower clock" as proposed by an eighteenth-century Swedish botanist with time on his hands named Linnaeus. His somewhat epic-sounding name is apt since he invented the binomial system of taxonomy, the way all plants and animals are given a genus name and a species name in Latin. It is still, three hundred years later, the scientific way of naming living things. You never know what you'll come across in a book on music, do you? In any case, each flower was supposed to bloom at a different time of day, hence the clock.

In fact, Linnaeus made a list of forty-three flowers that, he said, opened between 3 a.m. and 11 a.m. and closed, some of them, between 10 a.m. and 8 p.m. Theoretically, a judicious selection could be made into a clock, but you wouldn't depend on it to be on time at the dentist. Perhaps that's why Linnaeus never actually made one.

In fact, none of Linnaeus's forty-three flowers appear in *L'Horloge de Flore.* Françaix chose seven *different* flowers, which makes me think that his flower clock had nothing to do with the great botanist and everything to do with their beautiful, melodious names: Galant de jour, Cupidone bleu, Cierge à grandes fleurs, Nyctanthe du Malabar, Belle de nuit, Géranium triste, and Silène noctiflore. Just the names themselves form a soaring melody of language. Unlike, say, in English: poisonberry, blue batanche, torch thistle, Malabar jasmine, deadly nightshade, mourning geranium and, as if that wasn't gloomy enough, night-flowering catchfly. Nobody'd write a piece for *them.* All this beautiful music and these beautiful flowers, and they're all toxic. I somehow doubt that Linnaeus had such an arch sense of humour. Fortunately for us, it would seem that Françaix did.

En tout cas, the piece was written for one of the greatest oboists of all time, John de Lancie. John de Lancie the oboist was also father of John de Lancie the actor, who played both "Q" of *Star Trek: The Next Generation* fame and the pushy political operative who shows up in a white bathrobe next to Marlee Matlin in *The West Wing*. But, at least for musicians, John de Lancie the Younger will always exist in the shadow of his musically immortal father.

And our John de Lancie knew something about shadows, being the successor to the legendary Marcel Tabuteau, principal oboist of the Philadelphia Orchestra for four decades and a hugely influential teacher at the Curtis Institute of Music. Tabuteau was as French as they come, nevertheless, he single-handedly established what is now considered the American school of oboe playing. Unlike M. Tabuteau, John de Lancie was principal oboist of the Philadelphia Orchestra for only two decades. Perhaps he was appointed director of the Curtis Institute in compensation.

De Lancie began his career in the Pittsburgh Symphony before enlisting in the US Army in 1942. Everyone was either signing up or getting drafted for that all-out, all-in national effort (those were the days) but it was still a gutsy thing to do for a wind player, when one good knock to the face could end a career. He found a place in the US Army Band, eventually found himself in Germany and, in an unusually kind stroke of fate for those days, Corporal de Lancie knocked on the door of the last great European romantic composer still alive, eighty-year-old Richard Strauss—the New World literally knocking on the door of the old.

On the same day Hitler committed suicide and the city of Berlin was enduring several circles of hell, the US Army's 103rd Infantry and 10th Armored Divisions took control of the Bavarian region of Garmisch-Partenkirchen. The beautiful resort area had survived the war but hundreds of Allied bombers had orders to target it. Only a last-minute plea by a captured German officer saved the town. De Lancie's unit had been detailed to secure the area around Garmisch where Strauss lived—de Lancie now working in intelligence—and in a surreal example of the craziness of war, when de Lancie arrived at Strauss's house he shouldered his rifle, sat down with Strauss on his veranda (apparently posing for photos), and asked the great composer if he'd ever thought of writing an oboe concerto. Strauss said no, perhaps because he had just completed

Metamorphosen and couldn't think of anything but the end of the world. But obviously he recovered, because six months later Strauss did complete an oboe concerto, a masterpiece, thanks to de Lancie's presumptuous question. De Lancie read about it in a newspaper. Oboists the world over are forever grateful that Corporal de Lancie knocked on the right door.

For its entire first half-century (and now continuing into its second) the NAC Orchestra has had only two principal oboists: Rowland Floyd, for roughly the first twenty years, and Charles "Chip" Hamann for the next thirty and counting—two of the greatest oboists in North America. Chip is hugely admired, his playing is simply peerless. He's one of the best anywhere. But throughout his three decades in Ottawa, he has been haunted by the ghost of his colourful, eccentric predecessor. Seems great oboists cast long shadows.

Even now, decades after Rowland Floyd's retirement, people still tell "Rowland stories." The time he left his Gucci briefcase in a store in Paris with all his music in it, the store promptly locking up an hour before the concert (it would be Paris, it would be Gucci). The time on tour in Windsor, Ontario, when he couldn't sleep, got mad at the overstuffed motel pillow, cut it open with his reed knife and tried to flush the feathers down the toilet. Unsuccessfully. The time he was pulled over for speeding to make the next concert in Detroit and tried to explain to the officer that he was angry because he hadn't been able to flush all these feathers down the toilet and "please just let me go and tell me where's the damn bridge?" There are many.

During Chip's earlier days with the NAC Orchestra, the orchestra's founding conductor, Mario Bernardi, had returned after years of absence to conduct Mahler's huge song cycle *Das Lied von der Erde.* Lasting a full hour and concerned with nothing less than life and death, this great masterpiece is sometimes thought of as Mahler's "real" ninth symphony, he just didn't call it that because of "the curse of the ninth." Composers didn't like that Beethoven's last symphony was his ninth and that nobody since had completed more than nine before dying. Mahler's teacher, Anton Bruckner, didn't even make it that far, leaving his Ninth Symphony unfinished. And Mahler had many reasons not to tempt fate.

The huge last movement of *Das Lied von der Erde*, "Der Abschied" ("The Farewell"), begins with one of the most inexpressibly beautiful oboe solos in the repertoire. Considered the emotional centre of gravity of the entire work, the oboe's plaintively wandering musical line has been described as "the song of a soul caught between despair and acceptance in the face of mortality, like a cry from another world, as if from those who have already died." Yes, it really is all that. It's quite a piece.

Chip's playing was beyond compare—peerless sound, compelling, lyrical, heart-rending. And this was just the rehearsal. If it had been a concert, the audience would have been sobbing into their programs. After Chip's solo was over, Mario stopped the orchestra, looked at Chip with tears in his eyes, and said, "That reminds me . . . Did you know that Rowland Floyd has taken up painting?"

But seriously, folks . . .

I remember Rowland playing *L'Horloge de Flore* like it was yesterday—his plangent sound, his perfect intonation, his exquisite phrasing. And there was something else. When Rowland first auditioned for the then brand-new NAC Orchestra, a distinguished advisor to the audition panel, Lorand Fenyves, concertmaster for Toscanini before the war, said to the panel, "You should hire Floyd. He's a poet." He was and they did.

Rowland also had attitude. He found it entertaining that all the flowers in *L'Horloge de Flore* could kill you. Well, he was a poet from Huntsville, Texas, home of the Texas Department of Criminal Justice and five prisons, including death row. I think it damaged him.

As you must have surmised by now, Rowland Floyd was a dear, one-of-a-kind friend. He died eight years ago as I write this, at the age of eighty, and I miss him every day. And twice on Sunday.

An Adult Evening

Not your everyday loving

SOME BRITISH AND GERMAN MUSICIANS find their alternate selves in music from less corseted cultures, meaning music from places with nicer weather than Britain and Germany. During the same season we performed the suite from *Der Rosenkavalier* I rave about in "The Most Beautiful Music Ever Written by Anybody, Anytime"—Franz-Paul Decker did a more south-of-the-equator program with the deceptively chaste title "A South American Evening: Music by Alberto Ginastera, Astor Piazzolla, Juan José Castro, Heitor Villa-Lobos, and Manuel Ponce." But the high point of the program had nothing to do with evening, but with darkest night.

Astor Piazzolla, the hugely talented Argentinian composer and performer, single-handedly transformed the traditional tango into great art. He studied with a student of Rachmaninoff, played Bach on the bandoneon and, at the suggestion of Arthur Rubinstein, studied classical composition and counterpoint in Paris with Nadia Boulanger. His ability was obvious. It was finally Boulanger who told him that his unique talent was the tango. Thus encouraged, he proceeded to reveal the tango as an art form with few rivals. But how often is this noble music played on a classical stage? In fifty years in the business, this "South American Evening" was a first for me—the tango taken seriously by a great European conductor, a fine orchestra and one of the world's best bandoneon soloists, Daniel Binelli. You really had to hear it to believe it. A fine, live broadcast digital recording of this concert exists (I have a copy) but it has never been publicly released so I can't give you a link. Not for lack of trying.

Among other things, we played two pieces from Piazzolla's *Five Tango Sensations*: "Loving" and "Fear." Like the dark poetry of Pablo Neruda, it was hard to tell which was which. Piazzolla himself made a famous recording of *Five Tango Sensations* with the Kronos Quartet, one of his last, but Franz-Paul Decker and the NAC Orchestra's excellent music librarians found subtle, sophisticated arrangements for full orchestra. The audience didn't know what hit them. In a way, it was like that suite from *Der Rosenkavalier*, the highest possible compliment in my book. Music about passionate love is everywhere, but there is less music—at least sophisticated music—about dark love, ambivalent love, or frightening love (apart from Leonard Cohen). *Der Rosenkavalier* is about love compromised by time, *Romeo and Juliet* is about impossible love. But *Five Tango Sensations* is less about love than about torment. Like *Tristan*, only sweatier.

In fact, "Loving" was a real risk to perform, the risk being that nobody would hear it. The second of the *Five Tango Sensations*, it is eight minutes of music that never gets louder than very, very quiet, the kind of quiet where you don't hear it as much as feel the emotional ground shifting under you. It's all airless, moonless, ominous atmosphere, one of the most extraordinary experiences I've ever had in a concert hall. If it was available on a commercial recording, you'd have to listen to it in a quiet room, preferably late at night. And preferably alone. I'm not sure how that worked in a big hall with two thousand people, but it did. Those two thousand people were dead silent. Amazing, the way certain music can create the illusion of solitude in the midst of many.

"Fear"—the fifth "sensation"—is a fugue, of all things, revealing Piazzolla's studies with Boulanger and his admiration for Bach. The bandoneon, if you've never seen one up close, is a small, accordion-like instrument but with no keyboard, just thirty-three identical buttons for the left hand and thirty-eight for the right. Each button plays a different note depending on whether the bandoneon is compressing or expanding, so 142 notes to get mixed up, hence, perhaps, the title of the piece. Binelli did not mix them up.

Binelli then did a solo encore which he announced from the stage, *Adiós Nonino.* One of Piazzolla's most famous pieces, *Adiós Nonino* was written in memory of his father, Vicente "Nonino" Piazzolla. No avoiding the darkness of this piece, either.

Piazzolla was on tour far from home when his father died unexpectedly. The tour was not going well, there were financial problems, and then this black, black news. Piazzolla's son wrote later, "Dad asked us to leave him alone for a few hours. We went into the kitchen. First there was silence. After a while, we heard dad playing the bandoneon. It was a sad, terribly sad melody. He was composing *Adiós Nonino*." Online, there's an expanded, orchestrated version played by Piazzolla himself that will give you an idea of the piece—it's had fifteen million views. But what Binelli played that night with us was the original solo version, the unspeakably lonely version, just the bandoneon by itself. It was the music heard from the kitchen.

Piano Wars

I tell my piano the things I used to tell you.

—Frédéric Chopin

I'M HARDLY AN EXPERT ON Franz Schubert and can't even pretend to be an expert on the history of the piano, I just know what I've heard in five decades as a professional musician. I know what I've liked, I know what I've not liked, and usually it doesn't take me long to render a verdict from on high. But once in a while there's a surprise.

A decade ago, my dear friend Cynthia Floyd, long-time professor and former dean of the music department at the University of Ottawa and a fine pianist, having studied at the Universität für Musik und darstellende Kunst Wien for eight years and don't you forget it (I mean that only lovingly), brought in a colleague from Oberlin, David Breitman, as an academic and performing guest. The last piece in the generous selection of repertoire Breitman performed during his visit was the late Schubert Piano Sonata in A Major. It's big, impressive. In its way it should qualify as "public" Schubert just as much as the symphonies. But it has a slow movement that speaks to personal catastrophe more directly than any other music I can think of, except perhaps *Winterreise.* That slow movement is so personal it's almost embarrassing to hear with others. You avoid eye contact for sure. I know this, not from reading an erudite essay by someone who knows a lot more than I do, or from a performance by a famous pianist on a big Steinway in a big hall, but from that university performance by David Breitman.

To be sure, Breitman is a very fine pianist and well-known in academic circles, but he's not famous in the way that, say, Murray Perahia is famous. It was in a small hall in the music school that doubles as a classroom (it even has a telephone on the wall) and Breitman was playing, not a big shiny Steinway, but a reproduction of a piano of Schubert's time made by the Viennese maker Conrad Graf. Not big and shiny at all. Beethoven, Schubert, Chopin, Robert Schumann, and Clara Schumann played Graf's pianos, they were the best, but pianos of that time were half the size (and half the weight) of today's nine-foot concert grands. And they were more lightly strung, so they didn't need the heavy iron frames of today's pianos. The total string tension in a modern concert grand is roughly twenty tons. You don't want that letting go all at once, hence the iron. But the instrument Breitman played was made almost entirely of wood, like a fine string instrument. It was beautiful to look at but, compared to a modern piano, it had a sense of fragility to it.

When Breitman began the first movement of that big sonata on the small Graf piano, it was nothing less than a revelation. I play a "modern instrument" for a living. For piano concertos with the National Arts Centre Orchestra, as in most places, it's almost always a big-name soloist playing one of our powerful nine-foot Hamburg Steinways—as mainstream as you can get. Yet here, in this small, almost-a-classroom, it's as if I'd just heard Schubert for the first time. The reason that cliché's grown fuzz on it is because it can be true. It really was as if, for the first time, I'd really experienced the almost uncomfortably personal power of Schubert's music.

Then Breitman got down to the real business of the sonata, the slow movement, deceptively marked *Andantino* (little Andante). Nothing to see here folks. And indeed, the opening theme is as simple as it could be, just two notes moving down a half-step. But throughout the entire history of music, two notes going down like that has been the oldest, simplest, most powerful musical metaphor for grief. Brietman's small, historical reproduction piano sounded beautiful, not tinny or out of tune, but not "big shiny black monolith" either. There was something in the sound that was vulnerable, like the music. The piano was crying. Schubert was crying, you wanted to give him a Kleenex. You needed one yourself. By the end of the movement everyone in the audience was a wreck.

When the recital was over, after the obligatory smiles and handshakes, Cynthia, her husband Rowland, and I took David Breitman back to his hotel. Then the three of us went back to their house. Without even talking about it, we put on Murray Perahia's beautiful CD of that same sonata. We listened to it all the way through in silence, hoping to recapture the heart-stopping experience we'd just had. This was the great Murray Perahia on an excellent mainstream recording, on a fine Steinway piano, and he played beautifully. But the magic we'd heard, the sense of connection with, as Lorand Fenyves put it one time after encountering Clara Haskil, "the grief of the ages," no. It wasn't there, at least not in the same way, not the "avert your eyes" kind of grief that we'd just experienced with Breitman and the Graf. Murray Perahia is the best there is, but his was Schubert "in modern dress," as it were. With Breitman, on the small piano of Schubert's time, in the small room, it wasn't public Schubert. It was Schubert himself, sitting right next to us, with his head in his hands.

Only years later did I hear something approaching that evening. It was on a video by Malcolm Bilson, also on a piano of Schubert's time, playing two of Schubert's *Moments Musicaux*, only he wasn't playing in a classroom, he was in the august Brahms Saal of the Musikverein in Vienna. Just goes to show it's not where you play it, it's how you play it. I heard this special intimacy especially in the No. 2 in A flat, something about the essential fragility of the sound. And, of course, Bilson's superb musicianship. It's easy to find online. And perhaps it's not entirely a coincidence that David Breitman studied with Malcolm Bilson at Cornell.

But, another time, I heard David Breitman play the Beethoven "Appassionata" sonata on the same reproduction Graf that had sounded so exquisite in the Schubert. This time I thought he was going to break it. It was the same piano that had sung Schubert so beautifully, with such depth of humanity. It *spoke* Schubert. But for the athletic, almost violent "Appassionata," my biggest impression was fear for the instrument.

And that's where this "modern musician" is in trouble. I can't imagine Schubert's lyrical Impromptu No. 3 in G-flat, op. 90, the famous one with the gently rippling arpeggios often described as a song without words, on anything but a modern piano, with the modern piano's ease of tone production, its ability to suggest kindness, the roundness of its articulation in quiet dynamics, and its ability to sustain, or at least give a convincing illusion of sustaining. But, in the more virtuosic Impromptu No. 2 in E-flat, op. 90, with its flashes of impotent anger, I can imagine that very different music on a crisp, clear "period" instrument. It would portray so much better than most modern pianos the grace and articulation of all those runs, then the sense of helpless struggle in the middle sections. This is where other great modern pianos—Fazioli, Bösendorfer—with their transparency, their precise articulation and range of colour, would shine. I've realized, with considerable resistance, how much the ubiquitous

Steinway sound has seduced us. For all its beauty and power in so much of the repertoire, it's not the only convincing piano sound out there. David Breitman's Schubert recital in that small university classroom made the piano world a lot larger and more complicated for this "modern" musician.

The Gritty Affirmations of Basketball Courts

Sec. Sec! SEC!! SEC!!!!

—Arturo Toscanini

WORDS OF LARRY ROTHE, PROLIFIC author and, for many years, along with the superb writer Michael Steinberg, program annotator for the San Francisco Symphony:

The sacred, the profane, and the gritty affirmations of music . . . One of the ironies of our cultural scene is that concert music is often thought of as the province of the elite, as a super-sanitary adjunct of society's upper stratum, as the art form best suited to those who have little or no first-hand knowledge of what its critics think of as "real life." . . . How to dispel it? Not by the sort of "crossover" that brings us Pavarotti singing "Strangers in the Night"—that's not so much a meeting of sacred and profane as it is a convergence of opportunity and smart business. . . . The greatest

> Western concert music aims at the bull's eye, and the bull's eye is a representation of life as real as it comes, maybe not in a picture you can recognize . . . but of whose truth you're convinced.

Truer words were never spoken. The quotes are from their excellent book *For the Love of Music—An Introduction to Listening.* It's still in print and easily available. If you like music (and you wouldn't have hung in this far if you didn't), their book is essential reading. They both loved music with their whole hearts and, like loving anything with your whole heart, that means you're riding for a fall. Except it's never the music that lets you down.

Rothe's sobering words apply to all great music, but right now they remind me of Beethoven's gritty Overture to *Coriolan,* in particular a 1945 recording of Arturo Toscanini rehearsing (well, shouting at) the NBC Symphony, trying to get that first *fortissimo* chord dry and violent enough: *"Sec. Sec! SEC!! SEC!!!"* Yes, 1945. By that date, everyone knew what mattered and they weren't fooling around. Sacred, profane, and truthful. That's *Coriolan.*

You come into the concert hall and sit in a nice seat and open the program printed on that special shiny paper with that special shiny paper aroma that says you probably paid a lot for the seat. If you arrived early, you've probably read some stuffy program notes about the overture and how the music wasn't written for the famous Shakespeare play but for *another* play just *based* on the Shakespeare play, which was a flop, and how it's about a Roman general named Caius Marcius Coriolanus who defects to his arch-enemies the Volcians (no, not the Vulcans) to wreak vengeance on Rome for insulting him, but his mother talks him out of it and he kills himself. Based on that breathless synopsis, if you were a composer, would you then sit down and write one of the greatest concert overtures of all time? Of course not. And I'm sure Beethoven didn't, either.

When I'm onstage, playing this frightening piece, *not one word* of that story goes through my mind, nor, I'm sure, the minds of any of my sixty-some colleagues. Most likely what we're thinking is, "This is too goddam slow!" *Coriolan* is really the perfect piece to play when you're pissed off. That super-short chord at the beginning should be like a detonation that breaks windows. Carlos Kleiber said it should sound like a Rolls Royce hitting a brick wall.

So there's nothing of the pleasant concert hall or the shiny house program about *Coriolan*. Musicians know that it's unsurpassably great music but that it's almost never done well. Usually it's too tame, too much like "classical music." But, done right, it's one gritty affirmation after another.

For many years the National Arts Centre Orchestra toured small-town Canada every season, going either west or east for tours of two to three weeks. One year we toured the whole country for seven weeks, during which our fine principal clarinetist broke his big toe going down the waterslide in the Medicine Hat Holiday Inn. His screams were interpreted as fun. We've probably seen more of "real" Canada than any federal politician. Our small size (then) meant we could fit in small short-haul airplanes, and small halls, or churches, or cafeterias, or hockey rinks, or basketball courts—any place with a roof over it. And any touring artist will tell you it's in small towns, a million miles from nowhere, where you find your most appreciative audiences.

It was in a small but acoustically lively basketball court where we played *Coriolan* for the residents of Kirkland Lake, Ontario, pop. 7,981. The town was founded on gold mining but also punches above its weight in producing NHL hockey players. It is also notable for being the birthplace of the NAC Orchestra's founding conductor, Mario Bernardi, and for the nearby community of Swastika.

The eager citizens of Kirkland Lake were sitting not ten feet from us, wedged uncomfortably into metal folding chairs well over the foul line. In that small space, the first chord of *Coriolan* went off like a stun grenade. People literally jumped in their seats. It's a musical gut punch that leaves you gasping for air. *That's* what *Coriolan* is about. The gritty affirmations of music.

Movie Music

Women are not equal to men. They are better.

—George Balanchine

THE STORY OF *Romeo and Juliet* is so familiar, the Shakespeare play is so great, and there's all the movies—maybe an HBO series soon, who knows—and the fantastic ballet score by Prokofiev and the many choreographies. "The star-crossed lovers. Ah . . ." But these days we notice, more than before, that it was Juliet who caught hell for crossing the line in the family feud. The awful scene in the play (act 3, scene 5) where Juliet's father angrily shouts, "Young baggage! Disobedient wretch! My fingers itch . . ." In the theatre, those lines make your skin crawl, but at least he doesn't follow through and actually strike his daughter. Not until Peter Martins's controversial choreography for the New York City Ballet. Later for that.

There is an absolutely terrific performance of the Prokofiev score by Karel Ančerl and the Czech Philharmonic, recorded sixty years ago (heaven help us) with the vivid "sound stage" of the best early stereo: clarity, ambiance, weight, and presence all balanced and then beautifully pressed on top quality vinyl by the German Musicaphon label in the Prager Serie 10. It sounds best on the original LP, if you can find one, but it's easy to find online and sounds pretty good there, too.

Prokofiev's *Romeo and Juliet* is probably the favourite of all ballets for orchestra musicians, who've suffered through endless evenings of other scores where the assembly line music is just an excuse for the dancing, not the inspiration for it. So it was especially disappointing when the National Ballet of Canada's *Romeo and Juliet* was cancelled due to COVID. It was their excellent production with choreography by Alexei Ratmansky, whom the superlative former dance critic of *The New York Times*, Alastair Macaulay, called "the most gifted choreographer specializing in classical ballet today." Great music, great choreography and, knowing the National Ballet, great dancing. It was one of the most painful pandemic losses of the season.

The Prokofiev score is a curious mix. It's wonderful to play, it's very difficult (see "Death of Tybalt" in "Last Week Was Unacceptable!"), and, not least, it's beautiful. The music is downright cinematic in its variety and colour. We won't get into Prokofiev's miraculous ballet *Cinderella*. What a composer! Look at any photograph of him and he's looking straight into the camera, as if to say, "I'm Sergei Prokofiev and you're not."

The famous opening of the second suite from the ballet (act 1, no. 7 in the complete ballet) gives basically the whole story in thirty seconds. It starts with a grinding dissonance as the brass and percussion pile one "wrong" note on top of another, an apocalypse of sound that suddenly evaporates to reveal ethereal strings that have been playing underneath all the time, unheard. It's a shamelessly theatrical gesture, but one every musician looks forward to, night after night. How in the world did Prokofiev come up with it? That's why he was Prokofiev and we're not.

Macauley described Prokofiev's brilliant score as "almost movie music." Almost? In these days of fantastic film scores, that's not a criticism.

Macauley thought *Cinderella* had more actual *musique dansant*—"danceable music" or, more accurately, music that inspires dance—but between two such phenomenal scores, that's just splitting hairs. Besides, most great music well-played inspires dance, but that's another conversation.

During the National Arts Centre's grand opening festival in the summer of 1969, before the NAC Orchestra even existed, Prokofiev's *Romeo and Juliet* was the first classical ballet ever produced on the NAC's big stage. On the actual opening night a new ballet was premiered, *Kraanerg*, with music by Xenakis. The title is a creation of the composer, combining two Greek words *kraan* (κρααν) and *erg* (εργ) to mean "accomplished action." According to the composer, the accomplished action was "a biological struggle between generations unfurling all over the planet, destroying existing political, social, urban, scientific, artistic, and ideological frameworks on a scale never before attempted by humanity." Well, if nothing else, the brand-new National Arts Centre aimed high.

Prokofiev's *Romeo and Juliet* may have been the second ballet produced on the NAC stage, but it was the first to bless the house, as it were, because Lady Capulet was danced by the founder of the National Ballet of Canada, the spectacular, imposing, beautiful, inimitable Celia Franca. *The Guardian* certainly appreciated her:

> The world of dance has been a crucible producing visionary and indomitable women founders of what became major classical ballet companies at a time when few women ran any organisations at all, artistic or otherwise. Like [Dame Ninette] de Valois, who first recognised Franca's potential not only as a brilliant dramatic dancer and promising choreographer but also as a teacher, organiser and pioneer, Franca combined an unquenchable passion for ballet with the energy, sense of humour and practical

> savvy required to raise funds, keep her dancers fed and persuade recalcitrant boards of directors. She became what choreographer James Kudelka has called the icon of ballet in Canada.

I can't hear five seconds of *Romeo and Juliet* without thinking of Celia. For many, including me, her appearance that night as Lady Capulet consecrated the big National Arts Centre stage for great art forever.

The life it brings . . . I knew Celia a bit because she lived in Ottawa. Her husband, Jay Morton, was the founding principal clarinet of the NAC Orchestra and they were good friends with the NAC Orchestra's founding concertmaster Walter Prystawski, to whose house I was honoured to be invited to family Christmas dinners. One Christmas the company included Celia, Jay, the NAC's first publicity officer Tania Daniell, the Prystawski children and grandchildren, and the family Irish setter that got up on the table when people weren't looking and finished the leftovers. Later, grandkids put to bed, the conversation turned to Celia and Tania Daniell. As it happened, I found myself sitting between these two forces of nature.

For most of her life, Tania Daniell went by her unmarried name, Tania Long. Born a year before the Great War began, she was educated in Germany, France, and England, studying Russian literature and European history. At the age of twenty-eight she joined the *New York Herald Tribune's* London bureau and became a reporter for *The New York Times* a year later. When Allied troops landed in Europe, Tania followed them all the way to Berlin, becoming the first female war correspondent to file from defeated Germany. I don't think she met Richard Strauss on the way, although with her tenacity one can't be sure. After the war, she covered the Nuremberg trials as the only reporter who spoke all three official languages: Russian, English, and French. The charter of the trial did not include German as an official language, the intent being to emphasize that the Allied powers were the collective authority, not the defeated country in which the trials were being held. But, as a finesse, the charter also provided that *"all proceedings be translated into a language that the defendants understood."* Meaning German. Conveniently, Tania also spoke German. Around the time the National Arts Centre was first opening its doors Tania was retiring from journalism, so the NAC recruited her as its first music publicity officer. We did well, don't you think?

So there I was at Christmas dinner sitting between Tania and Celia as they told stories about living in London during the Blitz—something about hearing sirens, jumping out of the bath, and running to the shelter forgetting to put clothes on. That kind of thing. This has nothing to do with Prokofiev's *Romeo and Juliet*, but it does, because Tania came from an aristocratic Russian background and Celia danced Lady Capulet to inaugurate the NAC's big stage, so every time I hear Prokofiev's astonishing music I think of Celia and Tania and culture of such depth it makes me dizzy.

Now here we are, back to today, with the great dancer Peter Martins retired from dancing and his ballet based on *Romeo and Juliet* on the New York City Ballet stage, but now titled *Romeo + Juliet.* Apparently the "+" is supposed to signify an unusual, contemporary take on the story. There's at least one film by Baz Luhrmann titled that way and a later choreography by Matthew Bourne. Over the years there were, of course, many other choreographic takes on the music, including Leonid Lavrovsky (the original), Frederick Ashton, John Cranko, Sir Kenneth MacMillan, Rudolf Nureyev, John Neumeier, Alexei Ratmansky, Jean-Christophe Maillot, and Boris Eifman. (They all did fine without the "+").

Peter Martins was one of the finest classical dancers on the world stage and an overwhelmingly impressive interpreter of Balanchine. He frequently partnered Suzanne Farrell, and was Balanchine's heir apparent. After Balanchine's death, Martins became ballet-master-in-chief of the

New York City Ballet, a hugely distinguished position he held for twenty-eight years. If only that was the whole picture.

The last time I saw Prokofiev's *Romeo and Juliet* from the audience was at the New York City Ballet two years before the lockdown—a revival of an earlier production of *Romeo + Juliet.* I don't presume to have any great depth of knowledge of classical dance, I just appreciate what looks compelling and natural to me. I have been moved to tears when the doll appears to come to life in *Coppélia*, by Karen Kain's expressive hands at the end of *Swan Lake*, when Helena walks through the cheerful children wiping her eyes in sadness in Balanchine's *A Midsummer Night's Dream*, and when Robert Schumann desperately fights against his critics in Balanchine's *Robert Schumann's "Davidsbündlertänze."* These are great moments in dance, who wouldn't be moved? But in *Romeo + Juliet* even I could see that the excellent New York City Ballet dancers were having trouble making a convincing case for Martins's view of the story.

As Hercule Poirot says to a suspect in *Murder on the Orient Express*, "You feel warmly on the matter?" Yes, I do. And I was darkly gratified to have perceived what the distinguished critic Alastair Macaulay describes so much better than I could:

> If most of [Peter Martins's] one-acts fell out of repertory, they would not be missed. In an era when the ballet audience needs lures, however, he has given City Ballet three full-length productions that have drawn the throng.
>
> In the case of his *Sleeping Beauty* and *Swan Lake*, he drew on the work of previous masters. But *Romeo + Juliet*, which returned to repertory on Tuesday, is all Martins. (That "+" comes from the 1996 Baz Luhrmann movie.) There are worse versions of *Romeo*, but few so perfunctory or thin. Originally choreographed in 2007,

> Mr. Martins's featured an immediately notorious moment—Lord Capulet audibly slapped his daughter Juliet—that has now been excised. Instead of the slap, Lord Capulet now merely swipes the air in anger.
>
> Originally, at each performance of New York City Ballet's new *Romeo + Juliet*, numerous members of the audience gasp aloud in shock at the moment when Lord Capulet knocks his daughter to the ground with a highly audible slap. The slap occurs onstage; then, like an echo, the gasp occurs in the auditorium.
>
> At City Ballet, however, the feeling for many in the audience is not simple. In the many ballets made for it by its founder-choreographer, George Balanchine, women are glorified, shown as extraordinarily free and decisive, seldom content to be dependent on a man even in a loving relationship.

So why does an audience paying to see Balanchine's famous company have to endure seeing physical abuse onstage? I can only imagine it's because the uniquely expressive and athletic New York City Ballet dancers would be worth seeing even if they were just sweeping the floor. As for the other, I only know that Balanchine *loved* women. He was known for saying, "A stage full of men is a stage full of men, a stage with one woman is the world," and "Women are not equal to men. They are better." At least some echo of that attitude is what I hope to see when I visit the New York City Ballet, and I usually do. But that's not what I saw with *Romeo + Juliet.*

So it was even more disappointing not to have the National Ballet here with Ratmanski's celebrated choreography to this great music, and the National's celebrated dancers. Online there's a fine video from the Mariinsky of Ratmansky's imaginative and sensitive choreography for Prokofiev's *Cinderella.* That beautiful choreography respected women, too.

Love Is the Meeting Point of Truth and Magic

Every love story is a potential grief story . . . So why do we constantly aspire to love? . . . Because love is the meeting point of truth and magic.

—Julian Barnes, *Levels of Life*

FOR YEARS, LIKE EVERYBODY ELSE, I've loved listening to Puccini's *Madama Butterfly*. Just the music says so much, the rhythm of the words fits into the music so beautifully, it's such a compelling love story. But there's also Pinkerton's flawed character, Butterfly's tragic misjudgment, and the almost unbearably sad ending. A lot to think about.

As a dark companion to the glorious music, the story can also be heard to convey less glorious messages to us now. Puccini's librettists took their inspiration from original sources who were remarkably aware for their day, people who had seen first-hand the consequences of love between people of greatly unequal power and unequal morals. The passionate, PG-13 ending of the first act can be heard as some of the greatest love music ever written, or as one of the most elegantly concealed, most gorgeously sung, most subtly cruel #MeToo moments in all opera. Of course, Butterfly was not Tosca. This is worse.

Pinkerton sings, "Bimba dagli occhi pieni di malia, ora sei tutta mia" (Child with eyes full of witchery, now you are all mine). If we're just listening to the music, it's simply gorgeous and so perfectly written for the voice. But if we're paying attention to the words, we may start to squirm in our seats. Hear it one way, it's a breathless declaration of love. Heard another way, the American naval officer is already blaming the good-hearted teenager for everything. But I love this beautiful opera, everyone loves this beautiful opera. It isn't simple.

Butterfly describes how she would like to be loved: "una tenerezza sfiorante e pur profonda come il ciel, come l'onda del mare" (a tenderness gently caressing, yet vast as the sky and the waves of the sea). There is only one way to hear this beautiful line, our hearts melt for her. She is so far above him. And there's that wonderful Italian word *sfiorare*, which implies the infinitely tender way one caresses the blooms of flowers, *fiori*.

Unfortunately, the tenderness of *sfiorare* is not in Pinkerton's character. He's a young hotshot. Butterfly is head over heels in love with him but still has her wits, so she gets nervous and sings, "Dicon ch'oltre mare, se cade in man dell'uom, ogni farfalla d'uno spillo è trafitta ed in tavola infitta!" (They say that, overseas, if it should fall into the hands of a man, a butterfly is stuck through with a pin and fixed to a board!) And Pinkerton, thick as a board, replies, "Un po' di vero c'è: e tu lo sai perché? Perché non fugga più. Io t'ho ghermita. . . . Ti serro palpitante. Sei mia." (There's some truth in that, and do you know why? So that it shouldn't fly away again. I've caught you. . . . Quivering, I press you to me. You are mine.) Now she's really in trouble. And so are we.

"Sei mia!" are Scarpia's last words before Tosca, in self-defence, stabs him to death. And here are those words in *Butterfly*, already in the first act. But the music is so beautiful, it's how lovers have talked to each other forever. And, as if this isn't enough, when Butterfly and Pinkerton finally lose their inhibitions, Puccini puts the ambivalence of her situation into an unforgettable harmony called an augmented chord. It's so characteristic of this opera—and so unforgettable—some have called it the "butterfly chord." Yes, this seems like a sidetrack, but stay with me. It will take us into the heart of music, the heart of Puccini, and the heart of Butterfly herself.

It's not too much of a stretch to say that all of Western music is driven by a fundamental power of harmony, a sort of subconscious desire officially (clinically?) called "the dominant function." I talked about this idea way back in "She Sings as If She Doesn't Care If It Kills Her" but it's so important I'm going to go into it again, this time a little differently.

The "dominant function" is a stuffy music theory way of saying that a home key (thinking of Bizet's *Symphony in C* or Duke Ellington's famous "C Jam Blues") is established by relating it to the so-called "dominant" chord. (The basic tune for "C Jam Blues" is only two notes: the home key, C, and the dominant, G. It goes *GG . . . GG. GG. GG C.* There, now you can play it like Oscar Peterson.) Its name comes from the Latin *dominans*—ruling, governing, dominating. The dominant chord, the chord with such ineffable power over us, is a perfect fifth above the home key. If you have a keyboard, play a C-major chord. Then play a G-major chord (a perfect fifth higher). If you want extra sauce, add an F-natural. Then play the C-major chord again. "Home, away, home." "Tension, release." "Where are we? Ah, there we are." Amazing, isn't it? Like playing with a couple of magnets, you've just experienced an invisible but undeniable force, in this case the force behind four hundred years of Western music.

Historically, it's been observed that the fifth degree of the scale—**1** 2 3 4 **5**—**C** d e f **G**—is the first harmonic in the natural harmonic series, just as it's been observed that a major chord is composed of the first five pitches in the harmonic series. Pythagoras in ancient Greece discovered the math, Rameau in the eighteenth century linked the math to the music. As in grammar, music theory puts a shirt and tie on something that existed long before we made a rule about it.

The harmonic series is what you get if you twang a string, then twang a string half as long, then another a third as long, another a fourth as long, and so on. That explains where our musical pitches come from and how they're all mathematically related, but it does nothing to explain why they make us feel things. Leonard Bernstein described the dominant as a "questioning force" with the return to the home key as the answer. Aaron Copland called the dominant "the engine of tonal music." My teacher said, "For God's sake, forget music theory and play in tune." But nobody can say where our perception of "in tune" comes from, or why its violation sounds—and feels—so awful. So, as with the magnets, don't ask how the force happens. Nobody knows how it happens. It just is.

Evidence of this great secret is all over the place, starting with the fact that there is a "place" at all. Leaving aside the Big Question of Cosmology for the moment, part of that evidence is that, for some reason even the great neurologist Oliver Sachs couldn't figure out, *music makes us feel things*. It's an unarguable fact that a dominant chord "dominates" the harmony by making us feel a tension that can only be released by returning to the home key, thereby defining—"governing"—the home key and, in the process, somehow making us feel better.

And now back to our augmented chord, a chord that most definitely does *not* make us feel better. It's more like forbidden fruit.

The "butterfly chord" has power because it contains this ineffable harmonic tension all in itself, without reference to anything else. All by itself it makes us feel a sense of darkly pleasurable anticipation. Yes, it's a very adult chord. Technically (as I walk to the blackboard) this augmented chord is made up of two major thirds stacked on top of each other (scribble scribble), which means the outside notes are an augmented fifth apart, not the normal perfect fifth. See? No, you probably don't see. But that's OK, because that technical description would be meaningless if the chord didn't make you feel something. The theoretical description tells you nothing about *how* the chord makes you feel something, but it sure does. That's the great secret.

Getting into the machinery of the secret, all that has to happen to relieve the darkly pleasurable anticipation is for the top note to go up half a step. Easy. Take a pair of pliers, give it a half turn clockwise—*crink*—and the transformation from unease to total peace is instantaneous. If it was a drug it'd be illegal. And those are the transcendental harmonies to which these painfully sincere words of Butterfly are set: "Ah! dolce notte! Quante stelle! Non le vidi mai sì belle!" (Oh, sweet night! What a lot of stars! I have never seen them so beautiful!) Oh my . . . Toto, I've a feeling we're not in music theory class anymore.

The great writer Julian Barnes writes, "Every love story is a potential grief story . . . . So why do we constantly aspire to love? Because love is the meeting point of truth and magic." Yes. Oh, yes. But only Butterfly is seeking truth. Those dark augmented chords tell her whole story.

A dear friend read an early draft of this essay and told me I had ruined the opera for her forever. That was absolutely not my intention. I love this opera almost like a person. And so many operas are love stories with tragic endings. Why should *Madama Butterfly* be any different than, say, *Tosca*, which is about a powerful woman who has a fatal encounter with a rapist? Does it matter that in *Tosca* the encounter is fatal both ways, that Floria Tosca and Baron Scarpia are equally matched in strength and ferocity? Or can Butterfly's purity of spirit, despite the catastrophe to which it leads, be seen as a greater strength than Pinkerton's callous indifference?

When we bring this nineteenth-century story of unequal love and cultural arrogance into our own time, I like to think it does not discredit this great opera but deepens it. The same subject is at the core of Antoine de St. Exupéry's *Le Petit Prince*, the finest children's story ever written for *les grandes personnes*—grownups. There's a reason it's been translated into five hundred languages and dialects and sold more copies than any other book except the Bible. Because, as every child knows and many grownups have forgotten, when you allow someone to fall in love with you, you become responsible.

> Les hommes ont oublié cette vérité . . . Mais tu ne dois pas l'oublier. Tu deviens responsable pour toujours de ce que tu as apprivoisé. Tu es responsable de ta rose . . .
>
> (Men have forgotten this truth . . . But you must not forget it. You become responsible, forever, for what you have tamed. You are responsible for your rose . . .)

How beautifully, beautifully said. As in *Le Petit Prince*, Pinkerton has forgotten his responsibility. In return for enjoying the unearthly beautiful music of *Madama Butterfly*, we must not.

PART IV

Music: Can you live without it?

I love this stuff and I'll explain it to you
if you want to come along for the ride.

—Heather Cox Richardson

You Can't Be Too Rich or Too Thin

"Valse triste," "Valse romantique," "Canzonetta," "Scene with Cranes"
—Jean Sibelius, incidental music from *Kuolema*

IT'S SAID THAT YOU CAN'T be too rich or too thin, but it's certainly possible for a piece of music to be too popular. In 1903, not long before an overconfident Europe fell apart, thirty-eight-year-old Jean Sibelius wrote six pieces of incidental music for a now-forgotten play by his brother-in-law called *Kuolema* (Death). Yes, how Finnish. One of them, "Valse triste" (Sad Waltz), became a warhorse of pops concerts the world over. Sometimes there's just no sense in these things. Anyway, the runaway popularity of "Valse triste" led to so many bad performances of it that the work got an unfair reputation as "light music"—unfair, because the rare, good performance of it is an extraordinary experience. This strikingly original "pops music" was in the repertoire of no less a conductor than Wilhelm Furtwängler.

In the play, the music accompanies a dying woman who is dreaming about her life. She hesitantly begins to dance, then becomes possessed with manic energy until death suddenly claims her. The play was not a success, even in Finland. Richard Strauss dealt with basically the same subject in his early tone poem *Tod und Verklärung* (*Death and Transfiguration*), which takes twenty-five minutes to deal with mortality. Twenty-six years later, Strauss dealt with the same subject, metaphorically to be sure, in *Eine Alpensinfonie* (*An Alpine Symphony*), which can take upwards of an hour. Well, Strauss was older. By way of contrast, "Valse triste" takes five minutes, but then the Finns never were much for talking. Give it five minutes of your time. There's a reason it's so popular.

Another of the six pieces, "Valse romantique"—a lighter piece, thank heavens—accompanied another dance in a revival of the play. Sibelius himself was rather dismissive of it, but it still contains expressive gestures that are deeper than just incidental music and is the most fully scored.

"Canzonetta" is on an altogether different level. It begins hesitantly, like someone who has something difficult to say. The melancholy theme returns against a two-note motif that repeatedly tries to rise but fails, like someone speaking through tears. The piece impressed Stravinsky so much that he made his own arrangement of it.

Sibelius combined two of the other original pieces into "Scene with Cranes." This astonishingly atmospheric piece is, if anything, even more original than "Valse triste." In fact, it's downright creepy. Sibelius said, "Every day I have seen the cranes . . . their cries echo throughout my very being." Sibelius saw a flight of cranes shortly before he died. He said he found it comforting, so perhaps I should not be quite so offhand about it. The upper strings begin with a bleak passage of utter desolation. When great music gets serious, there's just no getting around it. Against startling, massive chords, unsettling cries of a pair of cranes are heard in the clarinets, followed by an almost surreal shiver of recognition in the strings. A solo violin asks an uneasy question over an almost inaudible note in the timpani, a haunting sound unique to Sibelius, much like the strange opening of his First Symphony. True to the spirit of the play, the answer is only somewhat reassuring.

Say *Zazpiak Bat* Three Times Fast

Maurice Ravel, *Piano Trio in A Minor*

RAVEL WROTE, "GREAT MUSIC . . . must come from the heart. Any music created by technique and brains alone is not worth the paper it's written on." But Stravinsky called him "a Swiss watchmaker" and, indeed, Ravel usually took great care composing. But both are true of Ravel's spectacular Piano Trio in A Minor, written in a white heat of creativity during the portentous summer of 1914. Said Ravel, "I have never worked so hard, with such insane heroic rage." Composing near his Basque hometown, Ravel was haunted by the approach of the cataclysm that would still be echoing in the world a century later. Even though he was nearly forty, Ravel knew that he would want to enlist in the war effort, so he worked feverishly to finish the work. The result was a masterpiece of concentration and astonishing intensity, one of the glories of the chamber music repertoire.

Ravel himself said that the unusual rhythm in the lyrical first movement, marked *Modéré,* was related to a Basque dance called a *zortziko,* but it's even more Basque than that. Ravel took the movement's uneven 3 + 2 + 3 rhythmic pattern from an early, never-completed piano concerto he had named *Zazpiak Bat*, after a Basque nationalist motto meaning the seven (traditional Basque provinces) are one. But, despite its irregular rhythm and modal tonality, the movement is cast in classic sonata form and has one of Ravel's gentlest themes as its opening. It's just fabulous music.

The second movement, "Pantoum: Assez vif" is constructed on the outlines of a complex Malay poetic form called a *pantun berkait*, in which stanzas are repeated and interwoven. But again, like the first movement, this exotic pattern is written within a traditional form, in this case a scherzo. Throughout the work the piano writing is highly virtuosic but especially so in this movement, where the piano part is comparable to the notoriously difficult solo piano work "Scarbo" from Ravel's *Gaspard de la nuit*. Here the pianist needs the reflexes of a cat. And the claws.

The third movement, "Passacaille: Très large" is exactly that. Originating in Spain as the *pasacalle* but developed in Italy as the *passacaglia*, this time-honoured form is invoked by a solemn eight-bar motif stated in the piano. Nine variations follow, creating a towering musical arch. Many other great compositions—Bach's *Passacaglia* and *Fugue* in C Minor for organ, Bach's mighty *Chaconne* for solo violin from the Partita in D Minor, and the last movement of the Fourth Symphony of Brahms, for example—have been based on this simple but powerful idea.

Ravel's Spanish influences are vividly on display in the last movement, "Finale: Animé." Using irregular rhythms, a brilliant orchestral style of writing for the strings, and exploiting all the resources of the piano (and the pianist), Ravel finishes the trio in a blaze of colour and sonority unique in the trio repertoire.

There are many recordings you can hear online. Personally, I think there's nothing to compare with the incandescent performance of

Rubinstein, Heifetz, and Piatigorsky. There is Ravel's "white heat" like nothing else. Or, if you've already had too much coffee, there's an exquisite live performance on video by Inon Barnatan, Augustin Hadelich, and Efe Baltacigil. An added dimension to that performance is that Hadelich is playing the gorgeous 1744 Guarneri del Gesù owned for many years by the late, great Henryk Szeryng. It is clearly in good hands.

Mom Always Liked You Best

Felix Mendelssohn, *String Quartet in D Major, op. 44, no. 1*

IF MENDELSSOHN EVER WANTED TO drop names at a party, he'd have been insufferable. "When I played for Goethe, he said I was *way* more talented than Mozart." Robert and Clara Schumann? Robert kissed sixteen-year-old Clara for the first time on her father's doorstep after returning from a party where Mendelssohn danced with her. At the end of his short life Mendelssohn was working with Robert Schumann on what would have been the first complete edition of the organ works of J. S. Bach, a name that drops with the weight of a house. Mendelssohn's mother studied piano with a student of Bach's, Johann Kirnberger, so when young Felix had his first piano lessons with her, she could say, "My teacher heard Bach play it *this* way." Not quite the original tablets of the Ten Commandments, but close. Moses Mendelssohn—famous philosopher, the "German Socrates," and friend of Immanuel Kant? Felix's grandfather. Abraham Mendelssohn—wealthy banker, philanthropist, and political activist, who, when Felix was two, had to escape French-occupied Hamburg in disguise for using his wealth to equip two Prussian battalions and help his fellow countrymen avoid a blockade? Felix's father.

Fanny Mendelssohn, Felix's older sister? An astonishing prodigy on the piano considered by her parents to be even more talented than Felix, a first-class case of "Mom always liked you best." At a house concert, young Felix impressed the guests by playing a piece from memory only to be upstaged by his sister playing, from memory, all twenty-four preludes from the first book of *The Well-Tempered Clavier*. Still, somehow, they got along. In short, the Mendelssohn household, really a salon, was a gathering place for the brightest lights in the intellectual and artistic life of Berlin. Anyone who was anyone went there. And young Felix impressed them all.

Is it possible to be too talented? Well, what some hear as a certain shallowness in Mendelssohn's music others hear as just astonishing and sometimes, frankly, annoying facility. Young Felix is clearly having the time of his life writing down the torrents of perfect notes that pour from his imagination. The opening of his String Quartet in D Major, op. 44, no. 1 is sheer, uninhibited musical energy. It's wonderful, it's amazing. It just shouldn't sound so easy.

But the man Mendelssohn was more than just his prodigious talent. Unlike, say, Beethoven and Debussy, who knock over furniture (see *Wingardium Leviosa*, and "Listen to Me! I'm Amazing!"), Mendelssohn was, by nature, conservative. He guided his talent by the light of his much-admired predecessors. He put the furniture back in place. For Mendelssohn (and all great composers), head and shoulders above them all was the towering figure of Johann Sebastian Bach, who was also, perhaps not coincidentally, a conservative. Unlike Beethoven or Stravinsky, for instance, Mendelssohn did not divide music history. He tried to reconcile it.

But Mendelssohn was a conservative in a time of change, a man from a highly cultured Jewish family that had largely converted to Christianity, a painful concession to the practical and personal difficulties of professing their faith surrounded by antisemitism. Abraham Mendelssohn had Felix baptised as a child, but as an adult Felix was a driving force behind publishing his grandfather Moses Mendelssohn's complete works. Felix, married and the father of five, also had a lengthy relationship with the great Swedish soprano Jenny Lind. He wrote the aria "Hear Ye Israel" in his oratorio *Elijah* for her. Mendelssohn's love for Jenny Lind was genuine and generous. A critic who was with Mendelssohn at her London debut remarked on Mendelssohn's beaming smile, that his "attachment to Lind's genius as a singer was unbounded, as was his desire for her success." Many passionate letters to her from Mendelssohn were discovered after her death and prudishly destroyed. What a loss.

So underneath Felix's polished appearance must have been a much more complicated and conflicted person than the steady, sunny disposition his music suggests. And the irony wasn't lost on Mendelssohn that he, the grandson of one of Germany's most famous Jewish philosophers and the son of a famous Jewish banker, should be the one to resurrect, literally, J. S. Bach's greatest sacred work, the immense *St. Matthew Passion*.

For his fourteenth birthday, Felix's grandmother had given him a hand-copied score of the *St. Matthew Passion*— it must have been one of the only scores in existence then. Bach's own densely written manuscript score covers 186 pages. It's impossible to overstate the importance to music history that the score and parts for this great work—much of it dispersed since Bach's death to who knows where—should have reappeared in the hands of such a talent as Felix Mendelssohn.

The great Bach scholar Christoph Wolff wrote:

> . . . the *St. Matthew Passion* is the first monumental work of music history still shining in a splendour undiminished by the passage

> of time. No opera, no other sacred work can occupy this unique place.

So it's hard to imagine today that, when Mendelssohn's grandmother gave him one of the few existing copies of this immortal work, Bach's music had been virtually forgotten. It was a measureless service to music when Mendelssohn, at the august age of nineteen, edited the score and parts, hired, coordinated and rehearsed the huge double orchestra, double chorus, and six soloists required and conducted the first performance of the *St. Matthew Passion* since Bach's death over sixty years earlier. It is beyond doubt that none of the musicians, none in the audience, and certainly not Felix Mendelssohn had ever heard a note of the *St. Matthew Passion*. Just imagine the first rehearsal. *Et resurrexit.*

Bach himself, obtuse and stubborn to the end, died without a will. Despite the confusion, one of Bach's sons, Carl Philipp Emanuel, managed to hang onto the score and parts for the *St. Matthew Passion.* When he died, the priceless manuscript score went to his musical successor in Hamburg, but somehow the performing parts . . . walked away. Eventually somebody wanted money for them and put them up for auction in Hamburg. There, they were spotted by someone with a more discerning eye, none other than Felix's father, the banker Abraham Mendelssohn. Abraham later willed the *St. Matthew Passion* parts to the Berlin Sing-Akademie, a pioneering group devoted to the performance of early music, and it was this group that his son Felix conducted in his historic performance.

Felix earned the right to drop all the names he wanted.

What Does It Mean When a Church Burns?

Arvo Pärt, *Fratres*

KENNETH CLARK, AT THE BEGINNING of his famous television series *Civilisation,* is shown standing on the left bank of the Seine. He says, "What is civilisation? I don't know, I can't define it . . . yet. But I know it when I see it, and I'm looking at it now." And the camera pans up to show the cathedral of Notre-Dame de Paris, usually referred to in English as just Notre-Dame, by any name one of the great sacred places of the world.

People have always looked at this magnificent building in different ways: as a holy place, as an astonishing architectural achievement, as a symbol of, for lack of a better word, civilization, or, perhaps more often now, as a destination to check off a bucket list. How we have progressed.

Before that terrible day of April 15, 2019, of the thousands of tourists who stood taking selfies in front of the cathedral, how many really knew what they were looking at? Turns out maybe more than we thought. Watching live streams of the horrendous fire, countless millions around the world looked at the flames with a unique kind of horror, a sickening sense of desecration, perhaps the most acute attack of existential anxiety since 9/11.

What does it mean when a church burns? If this immense holy place that has lasted eight hundred years can come close to destruction in an hour, what can possibly be depended on? As Kenneth Clark went on to point out, not much, because, for all its outward appearances, civilization is remarkably fragile. The outpouring of emotion after the Notre-Dame fire showed how deeply people feel the need for something that lasts, something permanent. Something sacred.

At a critical point in his life—after criticisms and rejections by Soviet authorities, among other things—the Estonian composer Arvo Pärt went back to the origins of Western music in the medieval liturgies of the Church: the simple, reflective patterns of Gregorian chant and early polyphony. Two of the greatest composers of this early music were members of the so-called Notre-Dame school, based at the then new cathedral. So Arvo Pärt began composing music of similar simplicity and stillness, music that also reflected the liturgy of his newly confirmed Orthodox faith. Popularity would've been the furthest thing from his mind, but despite that—or perhaps because of that?—his new serene style of music became hugely popular anyway.

Back in the Middle Ages, John of Salisbury, bishop of Chartres, said the music of the Notre-Dame school ". . . drives away care from the soul and the solicitudes of life, confers joy and peace and exultation . . . and transports the soul to the society of angels." At least, the bishop said, when it was good. Apparently much of the time it wasn't. But today, clearly enough people want to hear music of this kind of reflective character to make Arvo Pärt one of the most often performed living composers in the world.

Many might be reluctant to perceive such a frankly religious effect except, perhaps, in a safely secular space, like a concert hall. But perceive it we do, perhaps because of the obvious sincerity of Arvo Pärt's music, perhaps because of his fame, or perhaps just because we need to. However it happens, and despite many who might deny it, the perception is real and people treasure it. It will keep Arvo Pärt on top of the classical charts for the foreseeable future, and it will rebuild Notre-Dame for the next eight hundred years.

That's One Way to Die for Your Country

Edvard Grieg, *Holberg Suite*

"I CAN SEE IT NOW . . . Snow, hail, storm and thunder, and me conducting in a raincoat, boots, and umbrella. Then I'll catch cold or God knows what. Well, that's one way to die for your country!"

Unhappy Edvard Grieg had been asked to write a celebratory cantata for the bicentenary of Ludwig Holberg, Norway's most famous playwright. As Norway's most famous composer, Grieg could hardly refuse, but his heart obviously wasn't in it. The grandiose and noisy result made no mark on the world, it's not even on YouTube, surely today's definition of oblivion. But, perhaps as a reward to himself for doing his civic duty, Grieg also wrote a series of dances for piano that he titled *Fra Holbergs tid, Suite i gammel stil* (*From Holberg's Time, Suite in the Olden Style*), op. 40. This more personal tribute to Holberg was instantly successful, capturing Holberg's personality far more vividly than the official cantata. In Grieg's own arrangement for string orchestra, overnight it became one of Grieg's most popular works, now known everywhere simply as the *Holberg Suite*.

Grieg's string writing is brilliant, often dividing the sections to enrich the harmony and doubling the parts in octaves, creating a rich sonority that makes even a small string orchestra sound bigger than it is. Grieg's idea was a suite of dances, modelled loosely on the Baroque dance forms of Holberg's day, but the style is entirely his own.

The work begins with an energetic and virtuosic "Praeludium." The vitality of this movement is unforgettable, doubtless mirroring that of Holberg himself. A highly expressive "Sarabande" follows. Then a gentle "Gavotte"—correctly beginning in the middle of the bar—which follows the form by also including a "Musette," evoking that Baroque bagpipe-like instrument. The nostalgic "Air," clearly modelled on the air from J. S. Bach's D major orchestra suite and including many written-out ornamentations, expresses a depth of feeling unusual even for Grieg. A jaunty "Rigaudon" ends the piece, comically recalling the fact that Norway's immortal playwright Ludwig, Baron Holberg, once earned his living as a fiddle player.

Listen to Me! I'm Amazing!

Claude Debussy, *String Quartet in G Minor, op. 10*

TODAY, PEOPLE WHO GO TO concerts are used to hearing all kinds of crazy things. Compared to even a few decades ago, we are more open to new sounds and new talent, we are more likely to enjoy the adventurous and the unusual. There is little now that truly astonishes us. But with centuries of great music available for free on YouTube, we're also, perhaps, less likely to be astonished.

In its day, astonishing doesn't even begin to describe the new musical language that Claude Debussy introduced into the world with his shimmering, and frankly erotic, orchestral masterpiece *Prélude à l'après-midi d'un faune*, and his harmonically off-the-wall but achingly beautiful string quartet. Unlike Haydn, Debussy wrote only one quartet, but it did the job.

No less a judge than Pierre Boulez declared that Debussy's new harmonic language marked the beginning of modern music. But when Debussy began his studies at the Paris Conservatoire, the Western musical conventions his austere professors drilled into him were based on the "common practice" harmonic system, the harmonic language of everything from Bach's *Coffee Cantata* to Mahler's Ninth Symphony to Happy Birthday that had defined Western music for over three hundred years. From the spectacular but harmonically basic music of the early 1600s—think Monteverdi's *Vespers*—to the lush, disorienting chromaticism of the 1800s—think *Tristan*—all Western music was based on the idea that there should be, no matter how sophisticated the writing, only one harmony going on at a time.

That system produced the miracle that is Western art music: Monteverdi, Bach, Handel, Haydn, Mozart, Beethoven, Brahms, Wagner, Strauss, Mahler . . . the lot. With such music, the music history equivalent of the Himalayas, what truly new thing could possibly be desired, or even imagined? In the strict French conservatory system of the late 1800s, not much.

It took the marvel of the Exhibition Universelle in Paris, with nearly sixty-two thousand exhibitors from thirty-five countries and its centrepiece, the brand-new—and controversial—Eiffel Tower, to awaken an idea in Debussy's frustrated mind. This dizzying display of art, architecture, and especially music from non-Western cultures, what is now somewhat patronizingly called "world music," was a breath of fresh air. And a shock.

When Debussy first heard the evocative and, to our ears, wildly exotic music of a Javanese gamelan, the history of Western music changed. The gamelan's unsettling non-Western tunings (scales made of different numbers of notes than ours), complex, non-Western harmonies (and several going on at the same time, *quelle horreur!*), and sophisticated rhythms fascinated him. It was a completely alien musical culture. It was Debussy's genius to mix some of it into the techniques of Western "common practice" and come up with something totally original. The invention of a new and compelling musical language out of whole cloth like that is surpassingly rare, but Debussy achieved it. What's more, it was astonishingly beautiful.

"People call what I'm trying to write 'impressionism,' but that's totally wrong, especially when used by art critics who like to stick that idiotic label on Turner!" complained Debussy, loudly. He didn't want his music linked with the soft-focus style of painting named after Monet's *Impression, soleil levant,* which had caused such a stir. And Debussy was right to object. The clear, concise, resonant and powerful style he introduced with his quartet had nothing in common with paintings of indistinct light and washes of colour.

Debussy's new musical style (which, despite his strenuous objections, is still called impressionism) had an immense range of expression. And it was no one shot wonder. Parts of the style were picked up by composers as diverse as Lili Boulanger, Delius, Scriabin, de Falla, Respighi, Puccini, and even Sibelius. Hold onto your hats, or whatever you're wearing. Debussy's string quartet grabs you by the lapels from its very first notes and says "Listen to me! I'm amazing!"

The Other One

Maurice Ravel, *String Quartet in F Major*

OF THE MANY "SUCCESSFUL FAILURES" in music, both Ravel's String Quartet and Ravel himself are colourful examples. Ravel was expelled from composition class at the Conservatoire after failing at fugue writing, his five attempts to win the Prix de Rome were all unsuccessful, and his beloved teacher Gabriel Fauré described the last movement of his new string quartet as "badly balanced, in fact, a failure." To be fair, this was more about conservatory intrigue than talent, but it must've hurt.

Ravel, at age twenty-eight, was still a student at the Conservatoire when he wrote his quartet. After failing to win the Prix de Rome, the most prestigious composition prize in France, he quit. His rejection by the prize jury created a scandal—"*L'affaire Ravel*"—that actually enhanced his reputation. Debussy, in a gesture of support, wrote to Ravel, "In the name of the gods of music and in my own, do not touch a single note you have written in your quartet." Now, of course, the work is universally acknowledged as a masterpiece. So much for politics.

Both Debussy and Ravel were pioneers in a new "impressionist" harmonic language, using polytonality, extended chords, exotic scales, and complex cross-rhythms to create an entirely new sound world. Ravel's quartet, like Debussy's written ten years earlier, introduced these new techniques into chamber music and added a whole textbook of special string effects. This suave, complex, and expressive harmonic language is familiar to us now, but in its day it was completely original, one of the great creative leaps in music history.

But Ravel was conservative when it came to formal construction and thematic development. He said, somewhat defensively, "Stravinsky is often considered the leader of neoclassicism, but don't forget that my string quartet was already conceived in terms of four-part counterpoint . . ."

True to Ravel's conservatism, the first movement of the quartet is in classic sonata form, with a distinctive and difficult-to-play second theme with violin and viola playing two octaves apart (actually, not very conservative). The second movement is a complex scherzo, making extensive use of pizzicato to create polyrhythms and exotic sonorities that reflect Ravel's encounter with the Javanese gamelan at the Exposition Universelle—yes, the same thing that happened with Debussy. That exposition must've really been something. The strange, reflective third movement breaks the mould, it's almost like an improvisation. But the fourth reverts to form as a rondo, full of unsettling tremolandos that, oddly, recall Sibelius, another great composer who was influenced by "impressionist" ideas. This final movement is in such a hurry to say what it has to say that it lasts barely five minutes. Ravel's famous teacher may have had a problem with that, but time has shown Ravel to be right.

Wingardium Leviosa

Ludwig van Beethoven, *String Quartet op. 59, no. 2*

IF THE DEBUSSY QUARTET WAS "the beginning of modern music," the three Beethoven quartets op. 59, were, if not the beginning of the romantic period, well, they were sure banging at the door. In Beethoven's time, even the most sophisticated listeners were used to the balanced, civilized quartets of Haydn and Mozart—the very essence of the Classical Style. As expressive and complex and surprising as these works could be, and they include some of the greatest music ever written, where these quartets started out told you pretty much where they were going to end up. The listener always felt safe.

But what would Beethoven's listeners have made of a quartet that begins with two loud chords like someone barging into a room, slamming the door, and then nothing? Into this gaping silence a theme pokes its head up, as if from behind a piece of furniture, but then thinks better of it and hides again. Another brief look also evaporates into nothing. Finally, the quartet finds the courage to stand its ground and say something, only to be shocked into silence by the loud chords again. This isn't safe and predictable, it's as bizarre as a scene from *Harry Potter*, with Latinate charms sending things flying off in all directions.

Still, being "classical," this bizarre scene eventually settles down and Beethoven begins speaking in complete sentences. But the potential for strangeness in all three op. 59 quartets, especially no. 2, marks a brave new world in Beethoven's thought, just as much as his Symphony No. 3 ("Eroica")— "Where did *this* come from?"—did in his symphonies, and the darkly personal "Appassionata" did in his piano sonatas. That puzzled audience in Vienna over two hundred years ago couldn't have known it, but these "middle" Beethoven quartets would force a fundamental change in Western music, from the highly sophisticated but "civilized" works of the so-called Classical period toward the less predictable, more dangerous world of the Romantics. Just as the Enlightenment had in it the seeds of revolution, the Viennese Classical Style was the foundation for Beethoven's norm-busting Fifth Symphony and the incredible roller coaster ride of musical expression that followed in its wake.

Demain fera un an

Lili Boulanger, *D'un matin de printemps*

OF ALL THE GREAT COMPOSING talents whose gifts were lost to music at an early age, the loss of Marie-Juliette Olga "Lili" Boulanger at the age of twenty-four has to be one of the greatest. A person of charm and grace but frail from an early age, at the outbreak of war in 1914 Lili and her older sister Nadia both volunteered for war work. Lili, just out of her teens, took the lead in organizing ways to help musicians who had become soldiers serving at the front. That selfless effort was a credit to her character but it did little to help her health.

Lili Boulanger wrote no less than four versions of *D'un matin de printemps*: one for flute and piano, one for violin and piano, one for large orchestra and, the version I prefer, one for piano trio. The last work she completed in her own hand due to her failing health, ironically this brief piece is full of vitality and virtuosity, an exuberant glissando in the piano ending the piece with great energy and style. But much of her beautiful, sophisticated, and highly personal music is quite different, and there's a reason.

It's an injustice that the memory of Lili Boulanger, for all her talent, is eclipsed by the great fame of her older sister Nadia. Nadia was phenomenally accomplished as a pianist, organist, composer, music critic, conductor (she was the first woman to conduct the London Philharmonic, the BBC Symphony, the Royal Philharmonic, the Boston Symphony, the Philadelphia Orchestra, and the New York Philharmonic) and, absolutely not least, the most influential music teacher of all time. A list of Nadia Boulanger's students during her seventy-year career reads like a *Who's Who* of twentieth-century music, among them Leonard Bernstein, Daniel Barenboim, Elliott Carter, Aaron Copland, John Eliot Gardiner, Philip Glass, Quincy Jones, Dinu Lipatti, Igor Markevitch, Astor Piazzolla, and Virgil Thomson. And this is a *very* incomplete list. Virgil Thomson described her as "a one-woman graduate school so powerful and so permeating that legend credits every US town with two things: a five-and-dime and a Boulanger pupil."

The Boulanger sisters were born into an unconventional household. Their father, Ernest, had studied composition at the Paris Conservatory and won the Prix de Rome. His compositions were popular in his day and they paid the rent. Later, he became a professor at the conservatory, was made a Chevalier of the Legion of Honour and, after lobbying hard, was appointed to the Académie des Beaux Arts. His friends included Fauré, Gounod, Massenet, and Saint-Saëns.

Not to be outdone, their mother, Raïssa Myshetskaya, a professional singer, was a Russian princess. She didn't like to talk about it, but if her story was true, her great-great-great . . . grand something or other was Michael of Chernigov, who was, at one point, among many other things, Grand Prince of Kiev. When the Mongols invaded the Kievan Rus' (this was a very long time ago), Michael was captured and executed by the grandson of Genghis Khan. Beat *that.*

To make things even less conventional, Ernest was forty-one years older than Raïssa. He was teaching voice in Saint Petersburg when they met. True love would not be denied, so, despite the fact that she was Ernest's student and that he was almost old enough to be her grandfather, they married and moved to Paris. They had a daughter, Ernestine Mina Juliette, who died in infancy. Then came Nadia, who was born on her father's seventy-second birthday. Five years later, when Ernest was seventy-seven, came Marie-Juliette Olga, known as Lili, a birth that would change the history of music.

The intellectual environment Nadia and Lili grew up in was ridiculously accomplished. Their parents were cultured to within an inch of their lives and they moved in the loftiest Parisian musical circles, the great French composers of the day (great now, too, not just then) were frequent visitors. The house was constantly full of music at the highest level. Which, until she was five, little Nadia hated with a passion.

Whenever her parents played music, Nadia would run and hide. Sometimes she would scream before she ran and hid. Her behaviour was so bizarre that her parents (affectionately) called her *l'enfant du diable.* But when Raïssa became pregnant again, suddenly little Nadia wanted to know *everything* about music. She claimed to have heard the bell of a passing fire engine and was seized with a desire to imitate it on the piano. For a century now, amateur psychoanalysts have had a field day trying to figure out five-year-old Nadia Boulanger's musical road to Damascus. A credible biographer believes little Nadia was simply afraid she would be replaced in her musical parents' affections by the new arrival, so she figured she'd better get with the program. Whatever the truth, what's important to the musical world—and to the once-in-a-lifetime talent who was about to be born—is that it happened.

The great composer and family friend Gabriel Fauré recognized Lili's extraordinary talent early on when the two-year-old sang one of his songs from memory. And in the right key. By the age of five she was attending classes at the Conservatoire with her older sister, still only eleven, good grief, where little Lili eventually studied composition, singing, piano, violin, cello, and harp, and studied organ with Louis Vierne, one of the principal organists of Notre-Dame. How a child could do all this, I have no idea. Her little hands and feet couldn't reach the pedals or even most of the keys on the huge console of the organ at Notre-Dame, but all the biographies say she did. And she was tough. Despite nearly constant illness, in her short life she composed over fifty musical works and, at nineteen, won the prestigious Prix de Rome, just like her adored father. Lili was the first woman ever to win that high distinction, an honour that her sister Nadia and, famously, Maurice Ravel, never achieved. And Ravel tried five times.

Lili's compositions were influenced by Fauré and Debussy—how could they not be?—but her music has a sense of imagination, colour, and depth of feeling that can only be achieved one way. It's tempting to hear in her music a great talent grappling with a tragically shortened lifetime in which to express itself. Not surprisingly, much of Lili's music is dark, such as the large choral work *Psalm 130*, "*Du fond de l'abîme,*" dedicated to the memory of her father, and the song "Demain fera un an," the last in the cycle *Clairières dans le ciel*, which ends, "Plus rien. Je n'ai plus rien, plus rien qui me soutienne." (Nothing left. I have nothing left, nothing left to sustain me.)

The extraordinary thing among many extraordinary things is that, when her parents and distinguished visitors fell all over themselves in awe of Lili's precocious talent, ten-year-old Nadia was not jealous at all—at least not that she showed—and took her little sister under her wing, just as her father had asked her to do. What took Nadia years to accomplish in her music studies Lili accomplished in months, but Nadia persevered.

The two sisters became inseparable, even travelling to Rome together on the funds from Lili's Prix de Rome, where they helped each other work on their compositions. It's really one of the great love stories in music that, as one great musical talent was silenced prematurely, another great musical personality took up the cause. In her grief, Nadia wrote to her departed sister, "I place this new year before you, my little beloved Lili. May it see me fulfill my duty towards you so that it is less terrible for Mother and that I try to resemble you." And for the next sixty years—sixty years!—Nadia Boulanger devoted herself to doing exactly that.

Frantic, Fierce . . . and Hopeless

Bryce Dessner, *Aheym*

HOW DO YOU EVEN BEGIN to get your head around a piece written by a rock guitarist, but for string quartet, that most "conservative" of ensembles, but a rock guitarist with a master's degree in classical music from Yale who, in his time off from his rock band, writes for some of the biggest names in classical music and, in this case, writes a piece inspired by the poetry of one of the few child survivors from the Warsaw Ghetto, a survivor of the nightmare of nightmares? Listen to the warm, lyrical sounds of Dessner's band, then look at *Children of a Vanished World,* a book of photos of the Warsaw Ghetto taken secretly in the late 1930s by Roman Vishniac, if you can. I can't. Clearly, Bryce Dessner has an unusually wide outlook on life.

Like Arvo Pärt's *Fratres*, Bryce Dessner's *Aheym* could be called "minimalist"—saying the most with the simplest material. Some breezily call Arvo Pärt's music "holy minimalist" because of its reflective and religious nature. But one would never call Dessner's very different music "unholy minimalist." If Pärt's music can be heard as devotional, Dessner's

Aheym can be heard as devotional also, but to a very different sacred object and with a very different result.

"Homeward" is the usual translation of the Yiddish title. It comes from the title of the poem "Di rayze aheym/The journey home" by the Polish-American poet Irena Klepfisz, born in the Warsaw Ghetto in 1941, eighty-four at the time of this writing and living in Brooklyn. In the poem, home can never actually be reached but the journey is attempted anyway. In *Aheym*, according to Bryce Dessner's music, this journey homeward is frantic, fierce . . . and hopeless.

The poem's intense expression of estrangement is printed here, and heard, with almost unbearable intensity, in the music. Dessner dedicated the piece to his grandmother, who survived the war and eventually made her way to America. Astonishing and frightening, what can be said by the formerly oh-so-civilized string quartet.

Di rayze aheym/**The journey home**
Ziflit
she flies
vi a foygl
like a bird
vi a mes
like a ghost
Ziflit
iber di berg
over the mountains
ibern yam
over the sea.
Tsurik
tsurik **back**

back

In der fremd

among strangers

iz ir heym

is her home.

Do

here

ot do

right here

muz zi lebn

she must live.

Ire zikhroynes

her memories

will become monuments

ire zikhroynes

will cast shadows.

The Finest Theories Are the Last Things That Come to Mind

Jean Françaix, *Cinque piccoli duetti*

THROUGHOUT HIS LONG LIFETIME, Jean Françaix composed over two hundred elegant and stylish works, many of them for wind instruments. A protégé of Ravel and a student of Nadia Boulanger from the age of ten, Françaix lived almost into the twenty-first century, but not for him any experimentation with atonality or other modernisms: "When I am composing, the finest theories are the last things that come to mind." His lifelong influences were the so-called impressionism of his early mentor Ravel and the neo-classical side of Stravinsky.

Flute and harp form one of the great instrumental pairings in music, recall the beautiful concerto Mozart wrote for that combination. But *Cinque piccoli duetti* is the only work for flute and harp by Françaix. Its five movements are indeed small. The shortest lasts barely a minute and the longest not quite three, but together they form a coherent and substantial musical structure. The highly chromatic and virtuosic "Preludio" is followed by the lyrical "Pastorale." The short "Canzonetta," a delightful interlude of *musique dansante*, leads to the musical high point of the work, an exquisite slow movement titled "Sogno" (Dream). *Cinque piccoli duetti* concludes with the brilliant "Rondo," prickling with technical fireworks for both instruments.

Round Up the Usual Suspects
Richard Strauss, *Enoch Arden*

IN THESE STRANGE TIMES, the days pass . . . well, as someone said, "We don't pass through the days, the days pass through us." When things are strange, certain composers just "do it." Front of the line are J. S. Bach (always) and at times, oddly, or perhaps not so oddly, Richard Strauss.

I've already mentioned Strauss's brilliant music for chamber orchestra, *Le bourgeois gentilhomme*, in "The Most Beautiful Music Ever Written by Anybody, Anytime" near the beginning of this book and in "Canon" near the end—Strauss's music does have a sort of "alpha and omega" feel to it. Strauss has a way of almost persuading you that he, not J. S. Bach, was really the greatest composer ever. According to Glenn Gould, Strauss actually didn't like Bach that much. Perhaps that's where he got his confidence.

Easily found online is Glenn Gould's excruciatingly erudite, annoyingly unselfconscious spoken introduction to the music of Richard Strauss—part of an old black-and-white film of a much-shortened version of *Le bourgeois gentilhomme*. Much better is Glenn Gould actually playing Strauss, since Strauss was one of Gould's great loves. Perhaps that's because Strauss didn't write all that much for the piano.

Which brings to mind, at least to my mind, one of the most compelling of the few piano works of Richard Strauss, *Enoch Arden,* written for the unusual combination of piano and reader. Gould recorded it sixty years ago with the exceptional, one-of-a-kind actor Claude Rains, famous for his role as Captain Renault in *Casablanca.* It's Renault who orders, "Round up the usual suspects!" Yes, just after shooting the Nazi.

Rains was seventy-two when he read *Enoch Arden* for Columbia Records's microphones, but he sounded not a day older than eighty-two. The actor Richard Chamberlain once described Rains's voice as "honey mixed with gravel." Plus the world-weariness of years. Rains's "marvellous, unmistakable voice" as Chamberlain described it was the result of endless practice, since Rains grew up with a Cockney accent and a speech impediment. As if this weren't enough, while he was serving with the London Scottish Regiment in the First World War, his voice was damaged during a gas attack at Vimy during which he lost almost all the vision in his right eye.

Since Rains and Gould went into a studio all those years ago, many fine actors have recorded *Enoch Arden*, but none of them bring to it the sheer weight of the world like Claude Rains. Nor would they want to.

I last listened to *Enoch Arden* on a Sunday, not entirely inappropriate, since the poem is really a thinly disguised Christian allegory couched in a not so thinly disguised soap opera love triangle couched in an even less thinly disguised Christian allegory. But don't give up on it yet. So is *Harry Potter.*

The poem *Enoch Arden* is a lofty melodrama "of heavenly length" (to misquote Robert Schumann) written by Queen Victoria's poet laureate Alfred, Lord Tennyson. I could tell you why the comma, but best to just let it pass. Tennyson is still one of the most popular poets in the English language, or at least the most respected, or at least the most *English*, and still one of the most frequently quoted: "Theirs not to reason why/ theirs but to do and die." That sort of thing. And yes, one of the most sentimental, which makes *Enoch Arden* a strange choice for the famously unsentimental Glenn Gould. But there are lots of notes for the piano and it's wonderfully evocative music, so maybe Gould went along with all the *poetry* in return for all the Strauss. Sadie Stein said this in *The Paris Review*:

> Most people probably know Claude Rains best as the blithely unscrupulous Captain Renault in *Casablanca*, or maybe as the gleefully unscrupulous Prince John in *The Adventures of Robin Hood*, or even as a wholly unscrupulous senator in *Mr. Smith Goes to Washington*. No question, Rains brought particular *élan* to a certain kind of villain, yet nowhere did he commit as fully to a performance as to *Enoch Arden*.

Luck had something to do with it, too.

Back in the glory days of Sputnik and the Beatles, Glenn Gould was barely thirty, still in the spring of his career. He'd recorded his famous *Goldberg Variations* just a few years before. But Claude Rains, who'd appeared in countless productions in England and Hollywood since his debut at the Haymarket Theatre at age ten (and six marriages), was in the autumn of his.

Schuyler Chapin, a producer at Columbia Records in between stints managing Jascha Heifetz, Lincoln Center, and the Metropolitan Opera, wrote this about the recording:

> Ormandy wanted to record it. He'd just had Claude Rains as a guest doing an orchestral version in Philadelphia and they wanted

> to record it, and *NO WAY* was I interested in that. But Glenn was in my office and he heard the conversation and he said "*Enoch Arden*, it's really a lot of fun. I'd love to do it." So this was the moment. Claude Rains had just finished it. Why not? I said, "I can't pay you." He said, "I understand, just union scale." So then I got hold of Rains and he was a great admirer of Gould's, so all this was tickety-boo.

That's how it's done.

You can find the recording easily online. The most recent post I've seen of the complete recording has had a grand total of 224 views in two years, so you may well ask, how far from the pack have we strayed? Never mind.

There's no point in re-telling the story of *Enoch Arden* here (square-rigged ships, storms, bad food, no email, the lash) because Tennyson and Strauss do a great job of that, except to say it's the classic tale of a faithful, hard-working sailor, Enoch Arden, who signs on to a long, risky voyage to earn money to support his young family and is never heard from again.

Except . . . he is.

The story is so famous that, in some jurisdictions, laws under which a missing person may be presumed dead for legal purposes after a lengthy absence are called Enoch Arden laws. Of course, the story of Enoch Arden is a little more complicated than that. And then there's Tennyson's fabulous use of the language. It's easy to forget what beauty there can be in precise, meaningful, musical, *truthful* use of words, especially now that our sublime English language has been so debased by, well, all the things that debase it these days. Iambic pentameter is nice, too.

As you'd guess from all this, *Enoch Arden* is serious stuff. It's not for "background" listening. It deserves the investment of about an hour of uninterrupted time, quiet time, preferably late at night, with the lights low, and, nice but not absolutely necessary, rain coming down. That's how I first heard it.

A Toronto Symphony colleague was in a chamber music group with me, way back when, and one evening after a rehearsal he asked if I'd ever heard *Enoch Arden*. No? "*You've never heard Enoch Arden???*" He had one of the original LPs, a collector's item even then. The powers that be at Columbia Records had thought, "Who the hell is going to buy an hour of Tennyson?" and, forgetting Glenn Gould was on it, pressed only two thousand copies. They instantly sold out, attained cult-like status, and sold on the Tennyson black market for $2,000 in today's dollars. So much for the wisdom of Columbia marketing execs. So . . . my colleague played it for me on that dark and stormy night all those years ago, and I thank him every time I hear it.

Imagine, in some elegant, public establishment, an actor of genius reading aloud this deceptively deep poem while a pianist of genius, having had a few, improvises. That's *Enoch Arden.* Night or day, rain or shine, if you can let it in, it's unforgettable. Then you can ask your friends and exclaim in astonishment, "*You've never heard Enoch Arden???*"

I'll Take That One!

Maurice Ravel, *Introduction and Allegro*

THE TWO GREAT PARISIAN PIANO manufacturers of Ravel's day, Erard and Pleyel, were commercial rivals. Both made fine instruments that differed somewhat in construction and playing qualities. Some players preferred the Pleyel for its lightness of touch and delicacy of sound, others preferred the Erard for its greater power and the rapidity of its double escapement action. With some adjustments of touch (and expectations) a player could go from one to the other. But both companies also made harps, and there the competition was cut-throat. Their harp technologies and playing setups were completely different, so whoever eventually won would get the whole market.

Pleyel commissioned Debussy to write a piece to promote their new chromatic harp, a harp with one string for every note of the chromatic scale. A *lot* of strings. A year later, *en riposte*, Erard commissioned Ravel to write a piece to display the wider capabilities of their double-action pedal harp, a harp tuned to the diatonic scale but with pedals that changed the pitch of each string to make the entire chromatic scale playable but using fewer strings. That rivalry is long over (Erard's pedal technology won hands down, as it were) but Debussy's *Danses sacrée et profane* and Ravel's *Introduction and Allegro* both survived to become standards of the harp repertoire, a coincidental reward to music for what was otherwise a corporate fight to the death.

Arguably, Ravel's work is the more original. In fact, it is a tour de force of idiomatic, colourful writing for an unusual combination of instruments. Perhaps Ravel chose to accompany the harp with flute, clarinet, and string quartet because that combination offered more potential colours than the plain string accompaniment Debussy chose. In any case, it worked. Ravel obtains a wealth of compelling effects from these few instruments and an astonishing depth of sonority.

The brief introduction displays Ravel's genius for orchestration from the very first entrance of the flute and clarinet. Well-played, it's hard to tell the instruments apart, such is the singular colour they create together. By the time the entire ensemble is playing in the Allegro it could be a full orchestra. The sound is simply amazing. The writing for all the instruments is ingenious, including many orchestral effects in the strings, but it is the virtuoso writing for the harp that stands out. Sometimes considered almost a short concerto for harp instead of a chamber work, Ravel's *Introduction and Allegro* displays virtually everything that's possible on the pedal harp. Surely, potential customers hearing the harp's dramatic first entrance would have instantly said, "I'll take that one!"

Mendelssohn in a Bad Mood

Johannes Brahms, *Piano Trio No. 2 in C Major*

"BRAHMS PLAYS MORE AND MORE abominably. It is now nothing but bump, bang, and scrabble!"

Most likely Clara Schumann was affectionately overstating the decline in Brahms's piano technique when she wrote this in her diary, but Brahms was about to endure his fiftieth birthday and was probably paying less attention to his piano playing than he was to something that might last a little longer. Notorious as a merciless critic of his own work, Brahms had just completed this drop-dead gorgeous trio and he was uncharacteristically—and justifiably—proud of it, writing to his publisher, "You have not yet had such a beautiful trio from me and very likely have not published its equal in the last ten years!" And he was right. Indeed, this trio shows Brahms at the height of his creativity, handling the classic sonata, variation, and scherzo forms with masterly confidence and freedom. The powerful, independent writing for the violin and cello allows them easily to be heard against a piano part of immense emotional scope and technical difficulty. Perhaps Clara was commenting on an unsuccessful attempt by Brahms at playing it himself?

The strength of spirit in this music is evident right from the beginning, with the violin and cello announcing the theme in powerful octaves, without piano. Throughout the first movement, Brahms's trademark rhythmic complexity keeps the attention of both players and listeners. The plain vanilla triple time gives no hint that the strings often play in three while the piano plays in two, or that the soaring musical line often totally ignores the neatly spaced bar lines.

Brahms takes the listener on a vast musical journey though the theme and five variations that make up the second movement, showing why Brahms is considered one of the greatest masters of the variation form. The vivid character of the theme is one of many examples in Brahms of his lifelong love of Hungarian music. The fourth variation, with its surprising and gentle shift into A-major and the heartbreakingly beautiful final variation, are extraordinary.

The scherzo surprises. Marked *Presto, pianissimo sempre e leggiero* (very fast, always soft and light), it sounds more like Mendelssohn in a bad mood. But the clouds part with a lyrical second theme marked *Ben legato, espressivo* (very connected and expressive)—one of those special musical moments that are as enjoyable to play as they are to listen to. Surprisingly, this is the only part of the trio that Clara Schumann really didn't like, writing to Brahms that she thought it was "not quite important enough and seems rather manufactured." History has not agreed with her, but that candid professional assessment shows just how close their working relationship was, surely one of the most productive and complex collaborations between two great artists in the history of music.

The open-hearted good cheer of the last movement disguises a highly sophisticated treatment of the sonata form, including visits by variation and rondo forms as well. The string parts sing out over virtuoso piano writing of almost orchestral complexity and power. And alert listeners will note that the intervals in the main theme sound oddly familiar. It's the theme from *The Simpsons*.

The Only Thing They Had in Common Was Crazy Hair

Ludwig van Beethoven, *String Quartet op. 18, no. 6*

FROM THE EARLIEST TIMES OF Western written music, that's nearly a thousand years ago now, composers have inspired each other, stolen from each other and, more often than they would admit, intimidated each other. Brahms was famously intimidated by Beethoven, putting off writing his First Symphony until Clara Schumann told him to just get on with it. Debussy painted Ravel into a corner by writing his spectacular string quartet first, Beethoven was so intimidated by Haydn's mountain of masterful string quartets that he put off writing any himself until he had first struggled with everything else. And everyone was intimidated by Johann Sebastian Bach. At least they had good taste.

When Beethoven was still just a ridiculously talented teenager stuck in provincial Bonn, he was given an all-expense-paid trip to Vienna to meet Mozart. Is it even possible to imagine Beethoven as a teenager? Is it even possible to imagine meeting Mozart? Well, Beethoven had to imagine it, too, because as soon as he got to Vienna his mother got sick and he had to turn right around and go home. So it meant a lot to him when he got a second sponsorship to Vienna just a few years later, and this time for more than just a visit. But young Beethoven's renewed hopes fell into one of the blackest holes in music history. Mozart, only thirty-five, had died. The toweringly uninformative death certificate read "miliary fever"—basically fever and rash—so the only thing we really know is that music's brightest light died a dark, untimely, and unpleasant death. One can understand Salieri's attitude about God.

The revised plan was for Beethoven to study with Haydn, hence the beautiful parting words from Beethoven's first real supporter, Count Ferdinand Ernst Gabriel von Waldstein: "May you receive the spirit of Mozart from Haydn's hands." Isn't that lovely? And he did. Beats even getting into Juilliard.

Mozart, Haydn, and Beethoven in the same place at the same time is almost too much coincidence and talent to take in. The rational, humane values of the Enlightenment, the overlapping lifetimes of three composers of genius, a high point in the cultural life of Vienna—whatever else, always the ultimate musical city—plus something in the spirit of the times, all conspired to create balanced, civilized, conversational music now known, for better or worse, as the Classical Style. It also gave Western art music its stuffy and inaccurate popular name, "classical music," but that's a rhetorical disaster for another time.

Heroic! Revolutionary! Transcendent! Larger-than-life words always seem to attach themselves to Beethoven's music. But early in life Beethoven was just a talented, annoyingly confident, somewhat coarse but well-dressed young man who was already admired and successful, the life of any party, and always in love with women impossibly far above his station. Bach's employers were abusive, Mozart spent his short life basically as an insecure freelancer, Haydn, luckier, found an enlightened and humane patron but, though Haydn was highly respected, he was still considered one of the servants. But Beethoven? Ha! In his opinion, royalty should be grateful for the chance to support *him*.

Beethoven's six early quartets, op. 18, fine as they are, don't storm the heavens. The scowling plaster bust, larger-than-life Beethoven is already lurking in the background, but the composer of the frighteningly intense "Eroica" Symphony, the otherworldly late piano sonatas, the indescribably deep late string quartets? Not yet. His String Quartet, op. 18, no. 6 is one of the last and greatest statements of the Classical Style—the most civilized music for the most civilized ensemble, just before it all went off the rails. Only three years after Beethoven died, Hector Berlioz wrote his hallucinatory *Symphonie fantastique*. The only thing they had in common was crazy hair.

We're Joyful Already

J. S. Bach, *Cantata BWV 51, Jauchzet Gott in allen Landen*

A CANTATA IS A PIECE IN several sections for singers and instruments, often on sacred texts but not always. The word comes from *cantare,* the Italian verb "to sing." Johann Sebastian Bach wrote at least two hundred of them for the church during his unbelievably productive life, which is impressive enough. They can last for fifteen to twenty minutes and contain chorales, arias, recitatives, more chorales . . . They're big pieces. But even more impressive is that he composed half of them during just the first two years of his tenure as Thomaskantor in Leipzig, a new one for every Sunday. I guess time was different then.

Michael Steinberg, program annotator for the San Francisco Symphony and the Boston Symphony and the author of some really good books on music, said:

> Bach's church cantatas are sermons in verse and music, beautiful and intense supplements to the sermons preached by the pastor in his pulpit. Like the pastor's sermon, they take their point of

> departure from the Gospel or Epistle for that particular Sunday or festival. These cantatas are the works in which Bach delves most deeply into those matters of faith that concerned him so pressingly and faces the most important spiritual and intellectual questions in his life. Thus they are the repositories, overall, of his most exploratory and intense music.

One every week.

Bach's cantatas are usually written for several solo voices, and most include a chorus, if only to sing a chorale at the end to keep his choir from falling asleep. But he also wrote a few cantatas for just one solo voice. Perhaps the choir was on vacation? Anyway, Bach's great solo cantata for soprano and trumpet, *Jauchzet Gott in allen Landen* (Shout for joy to God in all lands) is by far the most famous of them. And for good reason.

The opening aria bounds out of the gate with a display of astonishing virtuosity, literally shouting for joy. It's really an amazing piece. In his enthusiasm, Bach throws in a high C for the voice before the aria is even half over. Why not give away the whole show? We're joyful!

A quieter section calms things down with the words "Kreuz und Not" (affliction and distress), just as clouds can darken the brightest day. But the bright-eyed and bushy-tailed opening music bashes right back in, with yet another high C. Bach was irrepressible. Hard as it is to believe, this stunning vocal part may have been written for an exceptionally gifted twelve-year-old boy, a member of Bach's choir. And Bach's long-time virtuoso trumpet player, Gottfried Reiche, likely played the hugely demanding (meaning really high) solo part. Reiche was old enough to be the boy's grandfather. Bach took talent where he found it.

The brilliance of the opening aria sets off the deeply affecting section that follows, an accompanied recitativo with the words "Wir beten" (we pray) that could easily be from one of the great Bach Passions. At one point the orchestra strings suddenly disappear, Bach's way of portraying "ein schlechtes Lob" (imperfect praise), a technique he used in the *St. Matthew Passion* for the crushing moment when Jesus believes that God has abandoned him. A solo aria follows with gently rising triplets in the bass line, Bach's symbolism for prayer "to the highest." As people said to Sherlock Holmes, "Well, it's obvious, now that you point it out."

At the end, instead of something short and simple to cheer his listeners who'd probably been sitting in a cold church for an hour already, Bach indulges in a complicated chorale prelude in trio sonata form. His shivering listeners, and likely his musicians, hated when he wrote tricky things like that, but it's absolutely amazing music. And, lacking the usual chorus, the final chorale is sung by the soprano soloist alone, accompanied by two solo violins that dance around the voice like happy children. The trumpet also joins in for a joyful celebration of "Alleluia!" to conclude this much-loved cantata. Bach was going to have a good time writing the ending no matter what anyone thought. Unrepentant to the end, just for show, he made it a fugue, of course.

Is So Beautiful!

Giacomo Puccini, *Crisantemi*

TOSCANINI AND PUCCINI WERE SITTING in a provincial Italian opera house (no, this isn't the beginning of a bad joke) listening to a provincial performance of *La Bohème*. Toscanini saw tears streaming down Puccini's face and said sympathetically, "I know, is so terrible!" Puccini replied, wiping his eyes, "No, is so *beautiful*!"

Puccini knew how to push our buttons like no other composer. Yes, Wagner knew how to do it too, but his operatic subjects are monumental figures, larger than life, as is his monumental music. Sometimes we just don't like being monumental, at least I don't. But with Puccini, everything is human. When Rudolfo discovers that Mimi has died, we weep for the poor guy. When Cavaradossi declares his ardent love for Tosca, every man listening feels hopelessly inadequate—at least when Giuseppe Di Stefano sings it. When the unknown prince defies death and sings "Nessun dorma!" we feel like we could conquer the world. And at that moment, we probably could.

Puccini wrote three short pieces for string quartet that are never played, but *Crisantemi*, written in one night after learning of the death of Amedeo of Savoy, the former king of Spain, has held the stage. *Crisantemi* is usually played in a larger version for string orchestra, which is beautiful, but the original quartet version is more intimate, more powerful, and reveals deep musical roots. Suddenly, is that Debussy? As with the compelling, unique *Il tramonto* by Respighi, also highly influenced by Debussy, it seems as if there's really nothing the string quartet can't do.

Seven Last Words

Franz Joseph Haydn, *The Seven Last Words of Our Saviour on the Cross*

TO START WITH, WE'RE ALREADY in the weeds with the title of this profound, much-loved sacred work. The title on the first published score was in German: *Die sieben letzten Worte unseres Erlösers am Kreuze*. That's translated, accurately, as "The Seven Last Words of Our Saviour on the Cross," and that's one way it's seen in English. But, as with anything about religion, there are issues. Concert presenters and recording companies sometimes avoid the explicit religiosity of the words "Our Saviour," especially because of the possessive. Some concertgoers may even be offended by that presumption, even though the work was written over two centuries ago. So the work is often listed as *The Seven Last Words of Christ* or even *The Seven Last Words.*

Myself, I have no problem any of those alternatives, especially if the shorter, less categorical titles help more people feel comfortable approaching the work. As the dean of King's College, Cambridge once said of the hundreds of thousands of tourists who walk through their famous chapel every year, "It matters less why they come here. It's more important what they find when they get here."

And what listeners find with *The Seven Last Words*, presented as originally intended, has to be one of the most emotionally overwhelming experiences in all music.

How did this unique work come about? The story goes that one Padre José was a poor Spanish priest in Cádiz whose chapel—which later became the Oratorio de la Santa Cueva—was exactly what that name implied, a cave, basically a hole in the ground. But then Padre José inherited a title and a fortune and became Don José Sáenz de Santamaría, Marquis of Valde-Iñigo. And don't you forget it.

Newly wealthy Don José engaged an architect to build a magnificent edifice over the cave and later commissioned Spain's most celebrated painter, Francisco Goya, to decorate the interior. It still exists. But most important, he commissioned Franz Joseph Haydn, then the most famous composer in Europe, to write a sacred masterwork the likes of which had never been heard before.

For the Good Friday service of his dreams, Padre José (Don José in his day job) specified a work consisting of seven slow sonata movements, each of which would be a musical reflection upon words spoken by Christ from the Cross—actually seven sentences. The movements were to be framed by an introduction of a weight and intensity appropriate to the subject and concluded with a graphic depiction of the earthquake that shook the earth upon the death of Christ. Padre José wasn't fooling around.

Nothing in Haydn's immense output of string quartets is anything like op. 51. No quartet by *any* composer is anything like op. 51. Each sonata illuminates, embraces, kneels before, the most profound words of Joseph Haydn's Christian faith. In fact, the words were so central to Haydn's inspiration that he wrote the theme of each movement to fit the Latin version of the texts and had his publisher include the words in the first violin part at the beginning of each movement.

Haydn's music was never intended to stand alone from words. This music creates a sort of electric charge that seems to attract words. Padre José's original intention was to read a reflection on each of the seven sentences, followed by music each time, but many other texts have been used since. For a famous recording by the Aeolian Quartet, the distinguished tenor Peter Pears selected poems by John Donne, George Herbert, Robert Herrick, Edith Sitwell, Edwin Muir, and David Gascoyne. To hear a performance of this music accompanied by a reading of these powerful verses, at the right time of year, in the right frame of mind, will change your life.

Actually, *The Seven Last Words* is not "performed," at least not in the usual sense. The seven last "words" are not like any other words. The music is not like any other music and the experience of hearing it together with great poetic reflections, as intended, is not like any other concert experience. Haydn's unique work is probably the only other composition in music history that breathes the same rarified air as the great Bach Passions, but compressed into an intense act of devotion lasting just over an hour.

The mechanism of the benefit of Christ's suffering and death remains an ineffable and terrible mystery, even to the most devout. For the hour occupied by Haydn's *Seven Last Words* it is enough, in the words of St. Matthew, to hear with our ears and understand with our hearts.

PART V

Remembrance Day

In the world of Brahms, it is, above all, always late.

—Alex Ross

Dark Was the Night, Cold Was the Ground

Tragedy is sacred. Peoples' suffering is sacred.

—Stephen Colbert

THE LOCKED-DOWN OCTOBER WEEKEND when I wrote most of this essay was Canadian Thanksgiving. Canadian Thanksgiving is basically the same as the American one, only it's at the right time of year, without snow, without dubious paintings of Pilgrims (or, these days, paintings of dubious Pilgrims), and no Santa Claus parades. Canadian Thanksgiving is exactly what it says it is. It's wonderful. Not sure Santa parades happened anywhere that strange year.

It goes without saying that most of us have much to be thankful for. Given the state of politics in the US, more than a few Canadians might add, "We're thankful we're not American." But we're all grateful. Unfortunately, as the days got shorter, for many of us that lockdown year there was more darkness than usual.

OCTOBER 12, 2020

As the Thanksgiving weekend approached, musicians' social media in Canada was overwhelmed with sadness at the untimely death of our close colleague and friend, the magical soprano Erin Wall. Cancer, age forty-four, two children. If it weren't for the miracle of great music and the miracle of great talents like Erin's that give a hint there might be some greater good out there somewhere, however well hidden, one could be forgiven for looking for the nearest bridge. One musician wrote to Erin posthumously:

> Dear Erin,
>
> Making music with you was such an incredible gift to my heart. . . . I weep every day.

We all did. The news of Erin's death hit the musicians of the NAC Orchestra like a truck.

Such gratitude and such grief, so a sombre and even deeper than usual Thanksgiving. Where to turn? For me anyway, the composer who speaks most personally to these kinds of things, who speaks to everything human, is always Schubert.

But there's public Schubert and private Schubert. Public Schubert would be his many works for the church, his eighteen (!) operas and other music for the stage, the big piano sonatas, his overtures, and his seven symphonies—thirteen including the ones he didn't finish, including the famous Symphony No. 8 ("Unfinished") and especially the big C-Major Symphony No. 9 ("The Great"), with its "heavenly length" as Schumann charitably described it. It lasts almost an hour. If you're a violinist, add fees for your physiotherapist. This is all "big" music, meant for a big hall and a big audience, or at least what passed for big in Schubert's day. Mendelssohn conducted the first performance of the "great" C-Major Symphony for a packed house of five hundred, the most that could fit in the first Leipzig Gewandhaus.

But it's the private Schubert we love, the Schubert who somehow wrote six hundred miraculous songs, almost as many piano pieces, twenty string quartets and other chamber works and, *primus inter pares*, the cello quintet, which has to be the most beautiful chamber music this side of heaven. And he wrote all that in fourteen years! How on earth did he write a lifetime of music in fourteen years? Even more, how did he survive the emotional territory?

Let's go all the way. *Winterreise* (Winter Journey) is a cycle of twenty-four songs that's about as personal as it gets. Only a very great composer—and a very troubled composer—would dare go as far into grief as Schubert did in these intimate, starless songs. They're part of a powerful repertoire that, in my view anyway, is borderline dangerous, so dark are the places they take the listener. For instance, Schubert's *Winterreise*, Schubert's String Quartet in D Minor ("Death and the Maiden,") Schumann's *Frauenliebe und Leben*, Tchaikovsky's Symphony no. 6, ("Pathétique"), Strauss's *Metamorphosen*, Elgar's Cello Concerto, Britten's *War Requiem* and his violin concerto, Mahler's *Kindertotenlieder*, "Der Abschied" ("The Farewell"), of Mahler's *Das Lied von der Erde*, the last movement of Mahler's Ninth Symphony—well, a *lot* of Mahler—and, of course, the great Bach Passions, but those take grief to a whole other level.

On a much smaller scale, but no less intense, there's also the "Cavatina" from Beethoven's String Quartet, op. 130. Beethoven was said to have composed the "Cavatina," "truly in the tears of melancholy." What a heavy responsibility such music places on performers, and for performers to place on their audience. And, countless years into the future, the audience for Beethoven's "Cavatina" may be a non-human intelligence we can't possibly imagine, because the "Cavatina," performed by the Budapest Quartet, is the final track on the Voyager Golden Record.

For those too young to remember (ah, lucky people) the Voyager space program was two interstellar probes, each about the size of a small car, launched into space almost fifty years ago to take advantage of a rare alignment of Jupiter, Saturn, Uranus, and Neptune. The plan was for the two spacecraft to "fly by" these planets to send scientific data back to Earth, and then continue on into interstellar space for, well, eternity. And that's exactly what they're doing.

As of this writing, both Voyager nuclear-powered spacecraft are roughly twenty billion kilometres from earth, still operating and travelling away from home at sixty thousand kilometres per hour. Taking Earth's velocity around the Sun into account, that is escape velocity from the Solar System. Roughly a decade ago, the two Voyager spacecraft were the first human-made objects to reach interstellar space. This isn't a movie, those spacecraft are really way, *way* out there, leaving far behind, at incredibly high speed, everything we have ever known. And they are taking the "Cavatina" of Beethoven with them.

The Golden Record is exactly what it says, a twelve-inch, gold-plated copper phonograph record. A Golden Record, containing twenty-seven tracks of sounds and music of Earth, plus 116 images and greetings in fifty-five languages, is mounted on the outside of each Voyager spacecraft. The record cover, also gold-plated, has line drawings of a man and a woman (controversial at the time because they are nude), scientific information including the location of Earth with respect to nearby stars, and symbolic instructions for playing the record. A drawing of a hydrogen atom showing the transition between its two fundamental states is used as the unit of time. Yes, the recording technology is already hopelessly dated, but that was bound to happen. In the vacuum of space, the expected lifetime of the golden records is trillions of years—longer than our sun, our planet, and our solar system will even exist.

The musical tracks include Bach (of course), Mozart, Beethoven and Stravinsky, Guan Pinghu, Chuck Berry ("Johnny B. Goode"), Kesarbai Kerkar, Valya Balkanska, and Azerbaijani folk music. And the second-to-last music track, just before the Beethoven "Cavatina," is the inexpressibly sad gospel blues song "Dark Was the Night, Cold Was the Ground" by Blind Willie Johnson.

Engraved on the cover of each Golden Record is this message:

> This is a present from a small, distant world, a token of our sounds, our science, our images, our music, our thoughts, and our feelings. We are attempting to survive our time so we may live into yours.
>
> —President Jimmy Carter

I find it deeply moving—and nostalgic—that American scientists of a half-century ago and their American president would create such a thoughtful multicultural recording and write such a humane message to send into eternity. And that the same record that contains "Johnny B. Goode" and sounds of steam engines ends with two of Western culture's most intense, most personal, and most honest expressions of grief. In my view, with these two final tracks the Golden Records truly fulfill their purpose. Because whatever form of extraterrestrial intelligence finds these tracks of Beethoven and Blind Willie Johnson, even after our sun and the planet we live on have ceased to exist, they will learn that grief was the most basic, the most universal part of the human condition. It may not be the most basic condition of theirs, if they're lucky, but we want them to know.

Kenneth Clark says, in his book *Civilisation*, that when he looked at a beautiful ancient sculpture he was reminded of the most famous lines of Virgil. Clark writes:

> . . . Virgil's hero Aeneas has been shipwrecked in a strange country that he fears will be inhabited by barbarians. Then, as he looks around, he sees some figures carved in relief and he says, "These men know the pathos of life, and mortal things touch their hearts." And he is reassured.

I heard a consummate, mid-winter performance of *Winterreise* some years ago at the St. Lawrence Centre in Toronto, performed by the excellent Canadian baritone Russell Braun and his superb collaborator, pianist Carolyn Maule. It was, well, a dark and stormy night, and the audience desperately needed reassurance, but Aeneas was made of sterner stuff than we were. On that cold, forbidding evening, with these two great artists, the songs were simply overwhelming. After the last song, "Der Leiermann," where the hero of the songs literally loses his mind with grief, the audience couldn't move.

Drüben hinter'm Dorfe	There, beyond the village,
Steht ein Leiermann	stands a hurdy-gurdy player;
Und mit starren Fingern	with numb fingers
Dreht er, was er kann.	he plays as best he can.
Barfuß auf dem Eise	Barefoot on the ice
Schwankt er hin und her;	he totters to and fro,
Und sein kleiner Teller	and his little plate
Bleibt ihm immer leer.	remains forever empty.

Oh dear God . . . Only Schubert would dare go there. And if the songs weren't so beautiful we would wish he hadn't. And bless dear Russell—a great guy, a great father, a great husband, and a great singer, in whatever order is needed at a given time—Russell comes out again after several calls and, with a polite gesture, quiets the applause. He thanks everyone for coming out on such a miserable night and for being so appreciative, then says he can't stand to let us go out into the snow with only the final song of *Winterreise* to keep us warm, because it won't. So, after a respectful pause to let things settle down, he sang three lovely encores. All were respectful of the tone of the evening, but they gently released the audience from the unbearably bleak spell of *Winterreise,* so we would at least be able to breathe.

I think conductors who perform Tchaikovsky's "Pathétique," which is also usually performed in the bleak mid-winter, should follow Russell's example and play something else afterward, just so the final desolate notes of that symphony are not the last thing the audience hears before trying to dig their cars out. That may or may not be respectful of the music, but it certainly would be respectful of the audience. Some conductors—the great German conductor Christian Thielemann is one—find the "Pathétique" so emotionally devastating to perform that they rarely program it. But I've never experienced a conductor to be so thoughtful, like Russell, to consider the audience's re-entry afterwards. It would be a singer!

In an episode of *The West Wing*, screenwriter Peter Noah describes the Voyager record like this:

> Voyager, in case it's ever encountered by extraterrestrials, is carrying . . . a collection of music . . . including "Dark Was the Night, Cold Was the Ground" by '20s bluesman Blind Willie Johnson, whose stepmother blinded him at seven by throwing lye

> in his eyes after his father beat her for being with another man. He died penniless of pneumonia after sleeping bundled in wet newspapers in the ruins of his house that burned down, but his music just left the Solar System.

Some clear, dark night, go out somewhere where you can see the stars. Take out your phone, go on YouTube and search "golden record dark." Then look out into the universe and listen to Blind Willie Johnson's music, now voyaging through interstellar space, carrying the heart of humanity with it. Until the end of time.

"When Will You Pay Me?" Say the Bells of Old Bailey

Thou knowest, Lord, the secrets of our hearts.

—Book of Common Prayer

A CENTURY AGO, IN A DARK, damp corner of the City of London, a ten-year-old boy made his way up the aisle of the gloomy church of St Sepulchre without Newgate, squeezing his way past the Newgate Prison execution bell mounted on a pillar in the south aisle, trying hard not to look at it. He would likely have preferred to be anywhere else, but he wanted organ lessons and his father sang in the choir so . . . there he was.

St Sepulchre's has quite the history, even by the grisly standards of old English churches. The church was named after the Church of the Holy Sepulchre in Jerusalem, like St Sepulchre's, located on the west side of the city and outside the gates, and even gloomier. The Jerusalem church contains the tomb of Christ and is the focus of rivalry between no less than six Christian denominations, so it's not really set up for coffee hour. The London church is somewhat friendlier.

"The bells of Old Bailey" in the nursery rhyme "Oranges and Lemons" refers to the bells of St Sepulchre, located near The Old Bailey courthouse. The bells were rung to mark each execution in Newgate Prison across the street. The "execution bell" itself, a grim-looking handbell, was rung twelve times at midnight outside the cell of the condemned prisoner. The idea was to wake the prisoner so that he might reflect on his sins before meeting his Maker. He would be further encouraged to do so by this solemn invocation, read by the Vicar:

All you that in the condemned hole do lie,
Prepare you, for tomorrow you shall die.
Watch all, and pray, the hour is drawing near,
That you before Almighty God will appear.
Examine well yourselves, in time repent,
That you not to eternal flames be sent.
And when St Sepulchre's bell tomorrow tolls,
The Lord above have mercy on your souls.

And we think *we* live in tough times.

Early churches on the site were dedicated to St. Edmund, who was killed by the Vikings. Long ago, a Protestant vicar of St Sepulchre's, John Rogers, was burned at the stake for the sin of translating the Bible into English. The selection committee for his successor must have been interesting. Later, a parishioner named John Smith travelled to the American colonies where he was captured by the Powhatan tribe. His life was saved by none other than Pocahontas, but, unlike the Disney movie, Pocahontas did not marry Smith but another man named Rolfe. Smith came back to England, met Pocahontas again (no record of how Rolfe felt about that), and is buried in St Sepulchre's south aisle, not far from the executioner's bell. And built into the railing just outside the church is London's oldest public drinking fountain. It was funded by a member of Parliament named Samuel Gurney, who went on to found the Metropolitan Drinking Fountain and Cattle Trough Association.

Anyway, the frightened young organ student was one Master Henry Wood, later to become Sir Henry Wood, founder of the immensely successful Promenade concerts—"the Proms." He started the Proms during the reign of Queen Victoria and conducted them for fifty years without a break, almost until the end of the Second World War, when sheer exhaustion caught up with him. He was a good conductor—the Boston Symphony and the New York Philharmonic offered him positions— but he felt an obligation to promote great music in his native land. And so in England he stayed, all seventy-five years of his life. Obviously, he meant it.

When the estimable Sir Henry passed away, Ms. Granger Kerr, a well-known singer, created what she called the Carnation Fund to memorialize him, because Sir Henry always wore a carnation when he conducted. They really don't make them like that anymore. Because the great Sir Henry had such a long history at the gloomy St Sepulchre's, the proceeds of the fund were used to establish the Musicians' Chapel in the church. Fortunately, it was built in a separate side aisle that is not gloomy at all. Everything in the chapel is related to musicians: the stained glass windows, the chairs, over one hundred embroidered kneelers, a Book of Remembrance, and, not least, in a place of honour, the ashes of Sir Henry Wood himself.

Every summer, the bronze bust of Sir Henry that normally resides at the Royal Academy of Music is brought to the Royal Albert Hall and placed in front of the great organ for the duration of the Proms, so that the great man can oversee the festivities. For the traditional Last Night of the Proms, a chaplet is placed on the bust and, the next day, is brought to St Sepulchre and placed on the tomb of Sir Henry in the Musicians' Chapel. Isn't that wonderful? Only in England!

At its founding, the Musicians' Chapel was dedicated by the Dean of St. Paul's Cathedral, Walter Robert Matthews, who also blessed the Book of Remembrance in which the names of British musicians who have died the previous year are inscribed and read out during an annual service of Evensong—over a thousand names to date. All this was inspired by the formidable personality of Sir Henry Wood, who, among his many positive attributes, really liked musicians.

Full disclosure: in 2016, I had my father's name inscribed in the Book of Remembrance. He was born in 1895, studied organ at Coventry Cathedral, and died in 1961. Better late than never. For the Evensong that year, the Magnificat and Nunc Dimittis were in the venerable settings by Sir George Dyson. My father would have approved. His name now appears in the book between the superlative British organist John Scott and Sir David Willcocks, the revered director of the Choir of King's College, Cambridge—2015 was not a good year for organists. My father is in distinguished company.

After the names inscribed that year were read, the Reverend Canon Michael Hampel, then Precentor of St. Paul's Cathedral, delivered a thoughtful and actually interesting homily. I thought Canon Hampel's words were wise, timely and beautiful:

> The Christian faith has at its heart the concept of memory. It is something which the Church articulates in liturgy and prayer and in its Calendar of Holy Days. We celebrate the faith often by commemorating the saints. Tonight's holy men and women are the saints of the Musicians' Chapel—people who have been blessed with gifts from God and used those gifts as talents, not

to be buried in the ground but to be invested in the hearts and minds of other people, young and old alike, to build on God's divine work of creativity with little echoes of the divine in their own human creativity. And we're here commemorating them and giving thanks to God for them by singing what is often described as that most Anglican of services, Choral Evensong.

The pianist Stephen Hough described Choral Evensong on his blog as the liturgical expression of Christ's *Noli me tangere*—"do not touch me, for I have not yet ascended to the Father." And that's an interesting comment about Evensong, coming, as it does, from a good Roman Catholic. He says, "Most religious celebrations gather us around a table of some sort. They hand us a book, or a plate, or speak a word demanding a response. They want to 'touch' us. Choral Evensong . . . reminds us that thresholds can be powerful places of contemplation, and that leaving someone alone with their thoughts is not always denying them hospitality or welcome."

That's not a bad image for us as we, God's faithful people, contemplate, in awe and wonder, the power of the divine majesty, conscious that our exchanges with God can't always be as close up and personal as we might like, not least because, to presume that they will always be like that, is to run the risk of feeling let down by God and of consequent disappointment that our encounters with God are rare and brief, but all the more profound and affecting for that.

Of course, Evensong has its detractors, partly because it is so undemanding of its worshippers, and I'm reminded of John Betjeman in his verse autobiography, *Summoned by Bells*, in which he recalls a bicycle journey through the lanes of Cornwall, with his one-inch map, chancing upon St. Ervan and its priest "in their small hollow, deep in sycamores." The priest sees young Betjeman by the churchyard gate: "Better come in. It's time for Evensong." Which Betjeman describes as being said "rapidly among discoloured walls, impatient of my diffident response." Tea in the Rectory follows where the Rector talks of poetry and Cornish saints and of his apiary and the cow he keeps.

Betjeman takes up the story. "He asked me which church service I liked best. I told him Evensong. 'And I suppose you think religion's mostly singing hymns and feeling warm and comfortable inside?' And he was right, most certainly I did." Against the backdrop of our anxieties about declining church attendance, perhaps we're not honest enough about what we like and what makes us tick, about what is in that room into which Jesus told us to go and shut the door and be still and know that God is God. So, I'm grateful to that Roman Catholic pianist for giving me permission to love this service.

I remember a fellow precentor in another cathedral telling a musical conference that he reckoned that Evensong should be prescribed on the NHS. I remember a judge in my previous cathedral who came to Evensong straight from the bench because he couldn't go home until the tension in his muscles and the anxiety in his brain had been released by centuries of choral music offered honestly and sincerely to God. I remember a note in a pew of a great northern cathedral describing Evensong being as if you were dropping in on a conversation already in progress, a conversation between God and his people which began long before you were born and which will continue long after you are dead. Now there's a thought. A liturgy strong and confident, outlasting me.

Now, of course, our worship of God does not revolve around

Choral Evensong. But it's a thread in the great tapestry of Christian devotion, a strong thread, a lengthy thread, and, perhaps you'll permit me to suggest, a golden thread. For the worshipper it is undemanding, and that may be no bad thing in what is otherwise a very demanding world. But, at the same time, it is only one language amongst many, one conversation amongst many, one mood amongst many, one line of thought amongst many. One prayer amongst many.

But Stephen Hough goes on, "It is a service into which all can stumble without censure, a rambling old house where everyone can find some corner to sit and think, to listen with half-attention, trailing a few absentminded fingers of faith or doubt in its passing stream."

If Stephen Hough is right, then Evensong says something about what our churches should be—places into which all can stumble without censure, where everyone can find some corner to sit and think. And, if they do, they might look up and see people like us, worshipping God by making music, our faces shining and our hearts burning within us because our precious encounters with God in Christ have changed us, for the better. And they, too, might step gently but confidently into the circle of faith, and our circle of faith will be all the better for that.

All this is the kind of thing the British do supremely well. This is not the place to describe my own adventures and misadventures in the Christian faith, and besides, who would care? But the Church of England has a unique place in my heart that has stood me in good stead in this world and, who knows, perhaps in the next. So, being Anglican, a musician, and the son of a British musician, I'm thrice blessed.

The Deep Difficulty of Excellence

Falling short of perfection is a process that just never stops.

—Wallace Shawn

FORTY YEARS AGO, BEFORE COMPUTERS and CDs and iPhones and generally the end of civilization as we knew it, the strings of the NAC Orchestra and our one-of-kind Sicilian conductor, Franco Mannino, recorded a simply astounding work for twenty-three solo string players. The piece was *Metamorphosen,* one of the last works of Richard Strauss, a great nineteenth-century romantic composer who found himself living halfway into the most un-romantic twentieth. Composed at his Bavarian home in early 1945 as his world collapsed around him, *Metamorphosen* is without a doubt the most extraordinary piece ever written for string orchestra, the most skillfully constructed, the most brilliantly contrapuntal, the most beautiful. And by far—*by far*—the saddest. On the other side of the record is Schubert's "Unfinished" Symphony, and I suppose something could be made of that.

After Strauss finished *Metamorphosen*, he mourned to his diary, "The most terrible period of human history is at an end, the twelve-year reign of bestiality, ignorance and anti-culture under the greatest criminals, during which Germany's two thousand years of cultural evolution met its doom."

It's one of many great sadnesses of music history that the composer of "the most beautiful music ever written by anybody, anytime" had to write something so tragic near the end of his life. And Strauss never really explained the title. Why *Metamorphosen*? The word comes from the Greek metamorphosis (μεταμόρφωσις), meaning transformation—from meta (μετα), "after" and morphe (μορφή), "form." So, "after-form" Essentially, something unrecognizable from its origins.

The classical idea of metamorphosis is a transformation from a lower form to a higher, as in nature: a wormy-looking pupae transforming into a beautiful butterfly. Maybe Strauss saw his great culture, his art, his own life, as having undergone a metamorphosis, but in the wrong direction. He also wrote about Goethe, about a kind of personal metamorphosis:

> I am reading him as he developed and as he finally became . . . . Now that I am old myself, I will be young again with Goethe and then again old with him, with his eyes. For he was a man of eyes—he saw what I heard.

Why in the world would I want to write about our recording of a piece that so explicitly describes utter despair, as explicitly as the last movement of Tchaikovsky's "Pathétique" Symphony, but (heaven help us) with a wider view? It's not for any maudlin reason, but for the reason contained in the title: a personal encounter, a risky encounter (see the next chapter) with what Spinoza called "the deep difficulty of excellence."

Excellence, oh please. . . . How many motivational speakers insult their audiences with platitudes like "We must go from excellent to outstanding!" Back in our darker days, the incoming chair of the board of trustees—a second-rank executive of an oil company—sought to motivate us by standing on our podium and appealing to us to "go from excellent to outstanding" while toying with our music director's baton. Right away we knew this could go nowhere good, and we were right.

All this might sound impossibly lofty—first I cite Greek etymology, then quote Spinoza—but as a performing artist, or as close as I can come to being an artist, I can tell you that the pursuit of excellence is our life. Even in these populist days there is, in fact, such a thing as excellence, and it's no joke trying to achieve it. If you're shooting for the real thing, your patron saint is Don Quixote.

Meanwhile, for anyone who cares to submerge themselves in a great and shatteringly sincere piece of music that tries to express nothing less than the end of the world, played by twenty-three members of the NAC Orchestra doing their damnedest to play it well, you can hear it on Spotify. By the way, the courageous, somewhat strange cover art for the original record jacket (not what you see on Spotify) was by the Czech painter Miro Malish. If you search around, you can find an image of it. Born in 1944, he would have been a young artist working in Prague in 1968. Another metamorphosis in the wrong direction.

OK, I have a confession. A long time ago, in a galaxy far, far away, I was a seemingly faithful young member of the Toronto Symphony. I was thrilled to be there, we had great conductors and played great music, but I secretly loved another. I'd hear the then-brand-new National Arts Centre Orchestra on the CBC and unfaithfully think, "I wish we played like that."

The NAC Orchestra was unique. Its small size—forty-six members then, half the size of most orchestras—gave it the clarity and edge of a chamber orchestra, but it was big enough to sound like a *real* orchestra. And one hell of a good real orchestra, with a unique vitality in the sound you'd recognize instantly. Even today, when the group is reduced to its original size for Haydn, Mozart, et al., its huge sound will knock your socks off. The TSO was a good orchestra then and it's a great one now, but when I first heard the NAC Orchestra on the radio it was like the stranger across a crowded room.

Naturally, the course of true love never runs smooth. I may not have been Cary Grant waiting for Deborah Kerr at the top of the Empire State Building, but it was close. As I said before, I'm not famous so who would care, and I'm for sure not Cary Grant, but if you want to know anyway, I describe the interrupted but passionate courtship in the next chapter, "The Life It Brings."

The Life It Brings

Any idiot can be a doctor!

MY LOVE-FROM-AFAR FOR the National Arts Centre Orchestra stayed from afar for a long time. Just out of school I had landed a dream job in the Toronto Symphony—a fine orchestra—but after seven years (classic) the dream had become like working in a musical factory, though admittedly a very good one. It wasn't just that I was turning thirty. Musicians in big orchestras, even in great orchestras, can soon feel like a small cog in a very big set of gears.

For years I had thought about going back to school for pre-med courses and making a try for that unique, professional gold ring. Yes, the mid-life side of this is banal, but the ambition was long-standing and genuine. Music had never been the only thing I'd wanted to do, but it was by far the best thing. I just didn't know it yet. My age said it was now or never, so I made a break for it and was accepted at the University of Toronto as a mature student, not an easy get. I sold my instrument to pay the tuition and kept my conducting jobs to pay the rent. Yes, it was totally crazy.

A few years earlier, I'd interviewed for the conducting program at Juilliard. They asked me what I was doing, I said I was music director of three orchestras. They said, "Our graduates would be glad to have just one." They suggested I study privately with Juilliard's head of conducting at the time, Sixten Ehrling. I already knew Ehrling because he was also the music director of the Detroit Symphony, my hometown orchestra. I'd heard him conduct there several times, including his party piece, Stravinsky's *Rite of Spring*, which he did from memory (very annoying). So I called him and he accepted me. For two years I flew to New York once a month, had private lessons in his Juilliard studio, discussed how I might progress in my conducting career—"Whatever you do, *never* conduct ballet!"— and heard unrepeatable stories about his extra-musical life. After each lesson I walked over to Central Park, found a place to sit, and studied scores. It all felt *very* serious. Looking back, I can't believe I did any of this.

At the University of Toronto I signed up for the standard pre-med curriculum—calculus, physics, biology, general chemistry, physiology (doing terrible things to cockroaches), and organic chemistry (the washout course). And I learned that the old joke was actually true: if it's green it's biology, if it stinks it's chemistry, if it doesn't work it's physics. The courses were well-designed and well-taught and the students (almost all pre-meds) were desperately attentive. In those pre-internet days, exam results were posted on the walls outside the lecture halls—reams of dot-matrix printer paper filled with tiny numbers that held the key to your future.

One of the perks as a student in the chemistry department was sitting on the floor outside the office of Nobel Prize winner Prof. John Polanyi while waiting for your lecture to start. It was a very special floor. As soon as exam results were posted the pre-med students descended on them like a school of sharks. I have to say it felt good to be one of them, even being a decade older. And, back then, I could sit on the special Nobel Prize floor and actually get up again. The lectures and labs were quiet, advanced, and intense. I loved it.

I did the usual pre-med hospital volunteering at Toronto General, in my case in peritoneal dialysis and in the ICU waiting room. That was real. And I was accepted as a summer research fellow at the Ludwig Institute, then connected to Princess Margaret Hospital, to assist a well-known cancer epidemiologist. That work resulted in an actual published paper in the *Journal of the National Cancer Institute* (*JNCI* 1986; 77: 397–404). If you actually look it up, I'm listed as first author but my supervisor, Dr. Norman Boyd, was the real first author. I just did the legwork in the library stacks, but he listed me first as a leg up on my med school applications, which was kind.

The professional side of the hospital cafeteria was full of white coats talking non-stop about their research projects. I sat with them, just surfing on their enthusiasm. This was the thing, at least as I saw it then. The best of music was in the past. Medicine—all of science—was the future.

Following the first-year biology finals, a good chunk of it genetics, the whole class of a hundred or so met in a big lecture hall to get the answers to the thirty exam questions. Each answer was met with groans and cheers, it was fun. But there were also five bonus questions. Did anybody get any of them? Silence. The answer was, if anybody had actually got a correct answer, there's a Nobel Prize waiting for you. Because nobody knows the answers. The lesson was, the bonus questions looked exactly like all the rest. There was the future. I loved that.

But my friends and family, who had been with me through all my years studying music, did not love my change of course. Even worse for them, I think, was how much I was enjoying it. In the middle of the second year of pre-med courses, I accepted an invitation to conduct the Calgary Philharmonic. I did well, but the only friend who came to hear me was an airline pilot who happened to have a layover in Calgary that night. My musical friends felt I had betrayed myself and there was some uncomfortable truth in that. And it would catch up with me.

After the Christmas holidays, I was in the Royal Conservatory of Music building on Bloor Street waiting to meet a friend when I spotted a notice of audition on the bulletin board.

VACANCY
National Arts Centre Orchestra
VIOLIN

Damn. Damn! Now I was in trouble. My courses were going well, I had volunteered in scary parts of the hospital, I had published research, I'd even received an encouraging letter from the medical school at Queen's University, inviting me to apply. They found my background interesting. But here was an advertisement for a rare opening in this wonderful orchestra I had loved for years. What to do?

It was a party full of doctors that did me in. It was at a friend's house who was a senior researcher at the Banting Institute, a pathologist working with state-of-the-art electron microscopes. In his early days he had made the first electron microscope photograph of the centriole, a vital part of the cellular machinery responsible for cell division. In other words, life. His photograph is in every cellular biology textbook, he even gave me a signed copy. He invited me to look through one of his multi-million-dollar electron microscopes at the Institute. I wore a suit and tie for that, like he did, none of this sitting on the floor student stuff. I was in his world now.

Well, not so fast. A doctor at the party (he was a dermatologist, which makes no difference at all) asked me what I was doing. I proudly told him about my pre-med courses and the research paper and how I was going to apply to med school. He squinted at me over his Scotch. "You look a little old for a pre-med student. What did you do before?" When I told him I'd been a member of the Toronto Symphony he almost threw his drink at me. "What? You have to have talent to be a musician! Any idiot can be a doctor! How the hell can you throw that away?" I knew he'd had a few and that not any idiot could be a doctor, but I didn't have a good answer for him. How *could* I throw that away? And suddenly the whole thing felt shaky. Maybe my family and friends were right. I'd worked incredibly hard to win that position in the Toronto Symphony. You actually did need talent to do that. And here was an ad for a position in the National Arts Centre Orchestra, my true love. And that's not just literary license.

Via viatores quaerit. I had been sought. So I applied for the position.

Turning my back on two years of hard science courses and a possible, perhaps even likely career in medicine was insane. I didn't even have an instrument. All the time I'd been taking courses I hadn't played at all. So I borrowed a violin from the fine instrument dealer across the street from the conservatory, Michael Remenyi, who said with a generosity that still astounds me, "When you get the job, you can pay for it." As I held a violin in my hands for the first time in two years, I replied, "When? You mean if!"

University-level science courses move fast. Miss a week and you're lost. I started practicing for the audition, missed some classes, went to my physics lecture section and suddenly didn't understand a thing. It was over.

The Toronto Symphony hired me for some concerts, whew, which was nice and some income. My first week back playing was an all-Strauss program with Andrew Davis, plus a recording. Talk about in the deep end. I practiced like mad, did an application tape in a conservatory classroom right next to The Bulletin Board and marked the April NACO audition date in my now-blank calendar. I arrived in Ottawa a day early, holed up in a hotel room and kept practicing, now just down the street from the promised land. I wasn't going to let a delayed train mess *this* up. I got so frustrated with my playing that I threw my little windup metronome out the window. It landed on the roof of the building next door. It's probably still there.

The NAC Orchestra's concertmaster, Walter Prystawski, ran the audition. I didn't know him at all then except I was in awe of him, since he had basically founded the orchestra. He gave me a tempo for a Brahms excerpt and, before I could think, I said, "That's too slow." I honestly don't remember anything after that, I knew I'd blown it. After the audition, for lack of anything else to do, I went across the street to the National Gallery and walked around the French Impressionists in a daze. Maybe I could drive a taxi.

A week later, the National Arts Centre Orchestra personnel manager called me and said a contract for the following season would be arriving in the mail. Was I still available? *Was I still available?* It was four in the afternoon. After the hyperventilation and dizziness passed, I took a cab straight to the airport and caught the next flight to Ottawa. I can remember like yesterday standing in line at the NAC box office, getting a seat for that evening and hearing the forty-six musicians of the NAC Orchestra play an all-Beethoven program: the Overture to *Coriolan*, the Piano Concerto No. 5 ("Emperor") with André Watts, and the Seventh Symphony. That small orchestra on that huge stage . . . how in the world do they sound so big? So perfect, so musical, just like on the radio, only better. And next fall, I'll be on that stage with them.

What can I say? When you're young, stupid, and very lucky, these things can happen. It's not until years later that you realize how close you came to the abyss. I had dropped the dream of a medical career in favour of a one-in-a-thousand chance of winning an audition on a borrowed instrument. And yet here I was. In the years following I would play Beethoven's Seventh many times with the NAC Orchestra. For years it was NACO's party piece, the way we play the last movement can break things. It's what George Balanchine called an applause machine, it always brought down the house and we deserved it. And later, we played *Metamorphosen,* just like on the record.

The life it brings.

Canon

Mathematics is one of the most efficient means of approaching the great secret, of considering what lies past all that we can see or presently imagine. Mathematics doesn't describe the secret so much as it implies that there is one.

—Alec Wilkinson

LIKE MOST MUSICIANS, I HAVE music going through my head all the time. Not like listening to a recording, sometimes behind other things, but it's always there. And there's often a cue. I hear someone speaking Italian and I think of Rossini's effervescent overtures, full of sunshine and olive oil and hopeless dramas that aren't serious. Or something sad happens, perhaps the death of a friend, so, privately, perhaps the slow movement of Bruckner's Eighth, when you need the kind of reassurance that this world cannot give. Or a musical colleague has to play the solo piano part to Richard Strauss's difficult but hugely funny suite from *Le bourgeois gentilhomme*, so I think of our terrific recording with Eduardo Mata, made forty years ago now, and I feel cheerful all day.

For the most intense human situations it's Schubert, it's always Schubert. But there are times when one doesn't so much need a friend, even a best friend. One needs a priest. And this is Beethoven of the late quartets. Since we're in this far, let's go all the way, the Beethoven String Quartet in B-flat Major, op. 130.

Op. 130 has one of those openings sent straight from heaven. The very first bar as much as says, "It will be all right. You are in the presence of kindness"—much like the first phrase of Beethoven's Piano Sonata, op. 110, a benediction that brings tears of gratitude. Or the first four bars of Schubert's late Piano Sonata in B-flat, D. 960, quietly conveying, in the words of Bernard Haggin, "profound lessons learned, inner illumination achieved." Everything the soul needs to know, in four bars of music.

My dear Viennese friend Greta Kraus, sadly no longer with us, once told me how, after the Anschluss, just before she fled Vienna, she was invited to a gathering of her Jewish friends to say goodbye, hoping not to be noticed by the Gestapo. They were all fleeing for America, going their separate ways, hoping to meet up eventually at the Mannes School in New York. But Greta was leaving for Canada, because she'd obtained a visa to America's friendly neighbour through an offer of employment as an au pair for a family in Quebec. Crossing the Atlantic they were travelling independently, who knew when they'd see each other again, if ever, so one of them sat down at the piano (in Vienna, there's always a piano) and said to Greta, "Come sit next to me." As a consecration of their friendship in the face of the unknown, he played for her the first four bars of the Schubert B-flat Sonata. Then he said, "The next time I play this for you, we will all be together again in America."

Greta made it to Canada but she was refused admission to the United States because she was already safe, at least that was the stated reason. So it wasn't until many years later, after the war, that she was finally able travel to New York and reunite with her Viennese musical colleagues. More of Hitler's gifts to America. When she walked into the room, the same friend from all those years ago was there. Without a word, he sat down at the piano (in New York, there's always a piano) and played for her the first four bars of the Schubert.

There's a certain controversy about the "canon" of Western music, about what some might call its cultural baggage. I wouldn't dream of venturing into such politically sensitive territory.

Yes, I would.

The canon of Western high art music—sometimes referred to with a sideways look as "the great masterpieces"—now stands accused of being culturally biased. Since it's the product of a culture—mainly European culture of the eighteenth and nineteenth centuries, the culture of the *Encyclopaedia Britannica*, Eleventh Edition—of course it's biased. Where some see focus, others see narrowness, where some see greatness, others see exclusion. But none of that invalidates the reasons why the works became "canonical" in the first place.

They're canonical because something about them has spoken to millions of people over centuries of time, and still does. And, despite many sins of commission and omission, of which we're becoming painfully aware, the selection was not made in a backroom somewhere. The selection was made over time by countless listeners, the great majority of whom had no interest in selecting their listening for any reason other than that it gave them greater energy of spirit. Therefore, one of its biases was a bias towards truth. Incomplete truth, as we are learning, but truth, nonetheless.

For instance, the four canonical Gospels. Please don't run away, this won't hurt.

I haven't darkened the doors of a church for a long time and nobody official at any of the several churches with which I was once associated has ever asked me why that is, and that's neither here nor there. But it always impressed me that the four Gospels, indeed every chapter in the Bible, are such a chaotic, inconsistent, confusing, uneven collection of work. Some are inspired to the level of great literature, some definitely not, and by seemingly countless different writers, a number of whom are now thought to be women. I'm not sure Charlton Heston was aware of that.

And of the four canonical Gospels—Matthew, Mark, Luke, and John—the first three more or less line up but the fourth is from a different planet. What?

Ask any professing Christian "What is the foundation of the Christian faith?" and they will say, or should say, "The reality of the Resurrection." They will quote Paul, "If we do not believe in the Resurrection, then we are most to be pitied of all people." Or words to that effect, I haven't looked it up. And yet the Resurrection—this fundamental, miraculous, frankly unbelievable event—is not actually described in any of the canonical Gospels. In fact, the oldest and shortest of them, Mark, ends before the Resurrection even happens. It ends abruptly with ". . . and the women ran from the tomb." Unfortunately, there's no security camera footage.

So, here's the central belief of the Christian faith, over two millennia the faith of billions, but none of the canonical Gospels say what the actual event looked like. There were other gospels that were not included in the canon, quite a few actually, between thirty and fifty, depending on what you call a gospel. And at least one, the Gospel of Peter, describes the Resurrection as literally as a video, ready for YouTube: the stone rolling itself away (I'm sure it made an impressive noise), Jesus coming out on the arms of two other men—or at least one man being supported by two others—and so on.

Why is no such made-for-television scene found in any of the four canonical Gospels? You'd think the early fathers of the church (and they were all actual fathers, they weren't celibate yet) would want to encourage membership. What better to do that than a Cecil B. DeMille epic movie scene showing the central event of the faith? But they didn't. They certainly rejected at least one. To be sure, the literal account in the Gospel of Peter is distinctly weird: voices are heard, including the cross itself, moving and talking on its own, and other supernatural, almost hallucinatory descriptions, more like the book of Revelation. But it was explicit and unsettling, like the vivid, literal description of the raising of Lazarus in the Gospel of John. Apparently, the church fathers didn't like the supernatural side of the Gospel of Peter. As if rising from the dead wasn't supernatural enough? No, they preferred the four Gospels that threw a discrete veil over things. In such discernment, such restraint, such respect for the truth as they saw it, not what would sell, the canonical Gospels were born. Truth, not Technicolour.

Which is a long-winded way of saying that a canon of anything—literature, art, music, or cookbooks—really tells us something fundamental about ourselves. Because we chose it.

Finally, if you're still here, the now-disputed canon of Western music.

The forty-eight preludes and fugues of Bach's *The Well-Tempered Clavier*, one of the most astonishing achievements in all of art, are sometimes referred to as the Old Testament of the Western musical canon. The thirty-two Beethoven piano sonatas, no less monumental (turn out the lights, listen to op. 111, and see if you ever come out the other end) are the New Testament. The parallel with Scripture is not accidental.

Is this saying that, compared to such an impossible standard, other music is not as good? I'm sorely tempted to say yes. There's bad, there's good, and there's great. We make value judgments all the time—how was that new restaurant? Western high art music is, undeniably, a product of a particular culture. But it's also undeniable that this music has been "vetted" through countless generations of listeners, just as the canonical books of the Bible were vetted through a critical, albeit opaque, process over centuries. We don't know as much as we'd like about that process, but the result is still, by far, the best-selling book in history.

We can love and revere the canon of our art while also recognizing that the culture that created it was flawed. We can widen our horizons and find that there is excellent work out there that should've been included, but was overlooked for cultural reasons. We can learn. But while we're doing this good work, listen to Beethoven's String Quartet, op. 130. It's canonical for a reason. Listen and, among many other good things, hear Abraham Lincoln's better angels of our nature. They're getting harder and harder to find.

Scripture

Don't be discouraged if your deepest inmost feelings don't match Beethoven's.

—Donald Francis Tovey

AS I SAID A FEW pages earlier, musicians sometimes refer to Bach's forty-eight preludes and fugues of *The Well-Tempered Clavier* as the Old Testament of music and Beethoven's thirty-two piano sonatas as the New Testament. To be honest, I haven't actually heard them called that very often, but we sure think it. Violinists have the six Bach solo sonatas and partitas as a form of Holy Writ, but to find true salvation a violinist has to climb the sacred mountain with three other string players and play the sixteen Beethoven string quartets. It's a pilgrimage.

In the bleak mid-winter, long, long ago, when the strings of the NAC Orchestra came onstage with Pinchas Zukerman to perform Beethoven's String Quartet, op. 95, arranged for string orchestra by Gustav Mahler, no less, it was very much "Remove your sandals, for the place where you are standing is holy ground." Beethoven's op. 95 is as close as it gets to the burning bush that is not consumed. (Yes, there's also op. 127, op. 130, op. 131, op. 132, and op. 135—a lot of burning bushes—but you get the point.)

The weight of the occasion also seemed to preoccupy the host for the live broadcast, the CBC's distinguished, long-time presenter Eric Friesen. Eric was still describing Pinchas Zukerman walking onto the stage, Pinchas Zukerman bowing to the audience, Pinchas Zukerman stepping onto the podium, Pinchas Zukerman picking up his . . . *WHAM*! The explosive opening of op. 95 made the producer lunge for his mixing board. The radio audience must've wondered why the music suddenly came out of nowhere, but disruptive music like this *always* seems to come out of nowhere, and not just because a conductor was making a point. No mere mortal who'd had too much for dinner last night could possibly have created such music.

Much is always made of op. 95's extreme mood swings, between overwhelming power and calmness, between frightening aggression and gentleness, and for good reason. The piece is almost pathological in its range of expression. And part of the package is its technical difficulty, like Beethoven's famous brush-off: "What do I care about your damned fiddle?"

With its "Get out and *stay* out!" opening, op. 95 certainly earns its name, "Quartett Serioso." It's written by Beethoven himself in the manuscript. The tempo marking *Allegro con brio* (literally, "cheerful and with spirit") is at odds with the deadly mood, but then no less a musician than Arturo Toscanini dumped on heavy thinking about the opening of Beethoven's Fifth Symphony, yelling in rehearsal, "Is not fate! Is Allegro con brio!" I think he was just saying, "Keep it moving." In any case, fair warning. When Beethoven writes *Allegro con brio,* watch out.

Playing this overwhelming music in a quartet is hard, but playing it with an entire string orchestra is magnitudes harder. Of course, you never want to make mistakes, but this particular evening there was a paying audience that had come out to hear us despite the cold and a threatening weather forecast. As a performer, all you can do is put your brain in high gear, turn around three times and spit (or curse, or both), and give it everything you've got.

There's much less "inspiration" than many think. As Thomas Edison supposedly said about his amazing inventiveness, "It's ten percent inspiration, ninety percent perspiration." Actually, most of what you feel onstage playing music at this level isn't inspiration, it's responsibility. Pinchas himself expressed it succinctly that same night. The opening work on the program was Beethoven's Romance in G Major for Violin and Orchestra, a gentle, lovely piece that, of course, Pinchas played. The solo violin begins alone, very softly, playing double stops that sound easy but they're not, because they must be absolutely steady and dead in tune. Any microscopic inaccuracy in the left hand, the slightest unsteadiness of the bow, everyone will hear it—"He's nervous!"—and the whole concert will get off on the wrong foot. As he walked out, Pinchas looked at the microphones, then looked at us and muttered, "Who the hell decided to start with *this*?" We loved it when he said stuff like that.

Op. 95 is not quite "late Beethoven" officially, but it might as well be. It navigates the same "strange seas of thought" as J. W. N. Sullivan wrote, quoting Wordsworth. I got that unsettling quote from Bernard Haggin's notes on all the Beethoven quartets that come with the complete recording by the Guarneri Quartet. One of the greatest music writers ever, one of the greatest quartets ever, another great English writer, and a poet laureate of the United Kingdom who was succeeded by Alfred, Lord Tennyson. For Beethoven, I bring out the big guns.

Writes Bernard Haggin:

> . . . the vehemently, abruptly, even explosively dramatic and powerfully concentrated writing of the first movement . . . the

> first part of the third movement that is like a fierce scherzo . . . but contrasting with these is the expansive slow movement, whose poignant opening section is followed by a fugal development of a strange and affecting theme . . . also, the fierce first part of the third movement alternates with a lovely, consoling middle part . . . and utterly dumbfounding is what happens at the end of the finale . . . a last climatic reference to the chief idea of the movement, which subsides into a poignant comment that ends in a pause, and then, for no reason in what has happened up to this point, a dazzlingly swift, light, and gay coda.

I'm not the only one who likes long sentences.

I don't usually write literal descriptions of pieces, at least I try not to. I like to think that, at least most of the time, people can hear for themselves what's going on in the music. If the music speaks to them, words aren't needed. If it doesn't, words won't help. But Haggin's vivid language gives a perspective on op. 95 that might well be missed on first hearing. And in a live concert, a first hearing is all you get.

The brilliant, seemingly fearless political commentator Rachel Maddow was once asked by a colleague what she thought of a political speech they had just heard. Honest as always, she said, "I'm sorry. Sometimes watching a speech live on TV I get distracted by the camera angles and the production values and it all just goes in one ear and out the other. I catch much more when I see it again at home." Thank you, thank you, thank you, Rachel Maddow, it's not just me. Maybe the speech was controversial and Maddow was playing for time, but I don't think so. If a great journalist can't get everything the first time through a political speech that's largely predictable, let's cut some slack for a winter concert-goer who maybe ran out of the house without a sweater after a rushed dinner, couldn't find a parking space, forgot to go to the washroom, and is now confronted with a grizzly bear of a piece like op. 95. The first time I heard it, all I could think was, "Please don't hit me, gosh that's gorgeous and a lot of notes, and what the hell just happened there, and wow that's fast." Applause, applause.

What B. H. Haggin's brilliant writing will do—what I'm trying in my own way to do—is just tell you ahead of time that, with Beethoven's String Quartet, op. 95, you will be encountering a huge piece of music that will take you to places not of this world, better places, and therefore unfamiliar. It's the highest of high art, like the paintings you can't see for the long lines at the Uffizi, but at the same time it's the most human. Everybody's dazed the first time.

Because, with Beethoven in live performance, high art and being human are one and the same. It's the greatest of great music and those sweaty musicians are performing right there in front of you, with microphones ready to carry each wrong note across the country to anyone running a recorder so they can play back your wrong note for all their friends. Those musicians onstage are talented, they've worked incredibly hard, they're led by one of the world's greatest musicians, and they're playing beautifully. And they're scared shitless. Take off your sandals.

A Death in the Family

You are the music while the music lasts.

—T. S. Eliot

NOVEMBER 1, 2020

THE MEMBERS OF THE NAC Orchestra learned yesterday, between the morning dress rehearsal and our live-streamed concert last night, that Yehonatan Berick, international violin soloist, beloved teacher of many grateful students world-wide, and partner of our beloved principal cellist Rachel Mercer, had died just that morning at age fifty-two. I use the word beloved twice because it's so appropriate. He had been diagnosed with terminal cancer just two weeks before. It was so fast. It was surreal. It was horrible.

We had been asked not to post anything on social media until his family had been notified but, of course, the news got out anyway. At least there was a short space for private shock. And, as it happened, our concert that night was already dedicated to the memory of the stellar Canadian soprano Erin Wall, who was such a great friend of the orchestra and had died just three weeks earlier. This is not just professional talk, we really were that close to these two wonderful human beings. He was only fifty-two, she was only forty-four. Again, cancer. Where is God when you need him?

Many remarked about the intensity of our playing that night and the overwhelming power of the music. There were many reasons for that, but first among them was our recognition of Erin's untimely death and, that very day, Yehonatan's. But even in shock at such a loss, we played anyway. We had a live online audience waiting for us. It was a gesture of professional respect to the superlative musicians we were grieving. And it's where great music really comes into its own.

This was sent to the orchestra by our concertmaster, Yosuke Kawasaki:

> We are all devastated and saddened by the sudden passing of Yehonatan Berick. He was truly one-of-a-kind as a human being and artist and touched all of our lives either directly or peripherally. Yehonatan succumbed to an advanced stage of stomach cancer that he and Rachel only found out about a few weeks ago. They were very private with the diagnosis and some of us became aware this past Wednesday, but it was an exponential decline from that point.
>
> Yehonatan was a terrific violinist and a popular teacher at the university. He would come to our concerts—back when there were actual concerts—and have dinner with Rachel in the Green Room before the performance, like many NAC Orchestra musicians, and chat with colleagues and friends. He was part of the NACO family.
>
> His was one of those health catastrophes that happen so fast it takes your breath away. A few of us knew he was being treated

in hospital and that it was serious, but nobody expected it to be this fast. It feels unreal.

It was indeed unreal. Online there's a remarkably candid conversation between Stephen Colbert and Anderson Cooper about grief. Cooper's mother had died just months before, Colbert, in his day life, is an observant Catholic and a diligent student of religion. Colbert is also a lifelong reader of Tolkien, having escaped into *The Lord of the Rings* at age ten as solace after the deaths of his father and two brothers in a plane crash. As they were talking, Stephen handed a quote from Tolkien to Anderson Cooper to read. Cooper looked at it and was visibly shaken, but he read it anyway, controlling his voice as best he could. "What punishments of God are not gifts?" After a pause to collect himself, Cooper asked Colbert, "Do you really believe that?" It was obvious that Cooper did not.

Neither do I. I admire the attempt to find something positive even in the face of terrible, senseless loss. It's the subject of the arcane word "theodicy"—the attempt to justify the existence of an all-good and all-powerful God with the reality of bad things happening. In fact, the Greek roots of the word literally mean "justifying God." It's the subject of a bestselling book by a popular rabbi, *Why Do Bad Things Happen to Good People?* The painful question is as old as time, but good answers are thin on the ground. Colbert, through Tolkien, found an answer that worked for him: "I am grateful for the thing I most wish had not happened." But obviously that did not work for Anderson Cooper. Colbert had the good grace not to press the point.

Once, in a hospital, I caught a really good priest with that question. His answer was simply, "Sometimes these things just happen." Cooper did not believe Tolkien's lofty philosophical construction, the rabbi who wrote the book could only conclude that, if God was good, he was not, in fact, all-powerful. But my priestly friend probably came closest to the truth by not trying to answer the question at all.

I believe that, indeed, sometimes bad things happen just because they do. They are nobody's fault and they have no meaning. All we mortal humans can find in them is bottomless grief. So all we can do as survivors (for the moment) is to be human and embrace the wisest words in the Bible, in my view, from Paul's letter to the Romans: "When your friend rejoices, rejoice with him. When your friend weeps, weep with him."

And *that*, my friends, is truly all the law and the prophets.

So tonight, we weep with Erin Wall's family. We weep with Rachel and Yehonatan's family. We wept for them backstage last night before the concert, embracing each other despite COVID. Then we played for them, live-streamed to the world, but nobody watching would have seen our backstage tears. All the online audience saw was musicians playing their very best. All they heard was music full of heart. And that was the original point of the program anyway.

On the night that Dr. Martin Luther King, Jr. was assassinated, Robert Kennedy was giving a speech to his supporters in Indianapolis. Many in the crowd had not yet heard of Dr. King's death, so Kennedy had to break it to them. As his shocked listeners tried to absorb the news, Kennedy read to them a quote from Aeschylus, words that are now engraved on Robert Kennedy's own memorial, words the truth of which he knew only too well:

> Even in our sleep, pain which cannot forget falls drop by drop upon the heart until, in our own despair, against our will, comes wisdom through the awful grace of God.

Chaconne

Study Bach. There you will find everything.

—Johannes Brahms

SOME YEARS AGO, *The New York Times* senior music critic Anthony Tommasini decided to put together a list of "the top ten composers in history." Of course, this was ridiculous from the start, a dinner party game, and he admitted that, but because it would be in the pages of the national newspaper of record, written out of a lifetime of musical experience . . . well, it wasn't totally stupid. He got tons of letters saying the whole thing was pointless, *outrageous*. One well-known composer called it "a horror" (perhaps because he knew he wouldn't be in it). Another wrote "Don't you dare leave off Mahler!"

But Tommasini pressed on and did his list, relating to his readers the intellectual and personal gauntlet he endured in the process. No matter how much dodging and weaving he did, somebody still had to be number one. With all the great composers of the past four hundred years, how in the world do you choose "the greatest?" But it turned out that wasn't a problem at all, probably the biggest discovery of the whole project.

The problem turned out to be deciding who was the *second*-greatest composer in history. Because the overwhelming opinion was that the greatest of all composers, ever, was Johann Sebastian Bach. By a mile. No contest.

Given the awesome competition—who could ever think of Mozart or Beethoven being in second place for anything?—why J. S. Bach? Was it the incredible range of his compositions, from short, bouncy dances for keyboard instruments to his monumental *St. Matthew Passion*? No opera composer of his time wrote anything close to that huge musical drama. Was it the sheer amount of music he wrote, so much that it would take a lifetime just to copy it all out? Perhaps his total mastery of the craft of composition, the fluency and sophistication of his counterpoint, the creativity of his orchestration, his infinitely expressive harmonic invention—that Bach was both a great artist and a consummate craftsman? Or that he was a famous and successful teacher? Many of his students went on to become fine players and composers, including several of his sons. Or that, on top of all this, he was the most famous virtuoso performer of his day, astonishing his audiences with the rapidity and accuracy of his technique, that when he played the organ, "his feet were as agile as the hands of anybody else." Or that his astonishing personal vitality had been constantly challenged during all sixty-five years of his life by adversities of every type: losing both his parents at the age of nine, brutal schoolmasters, tough schools (Bach once got in a knife fight), ignorant or outright abusive employers—at one point actually resulting in a jail term—the sudden death of his first wife while he was away from home, the deaths before adulthood of ten of his twenty children, and his own painful end from a stroke after having had two eye surgeries by a quack. Life in Bach's time was difficult for everyone, but Bach endured way more than his share of pain and grief. Hard to believe when his music is so full of joy.

Tommasini decided that Bach was the greatest composer because of all these things, Bach as the composer who did it all, but also because of something else. Because Bach's music, more than the music of anyone else, speaks from the highest place to the deepest place, because no other composer saw so deeply into the heart of music, was so obedient to the foundational laws of music. Because Bach seemed so intimately connected to the ineffable source of music itself.

The *Chaconne* is the last movement of Bach's Partita in D Minor for unaccompanied violin. To hear the *Chaconne* played live by a masterful performer is a rare and marvellous thing. The music itself is obviously beautiful and the sheer technical feat of its performance obviously impressive. That's a lot right there. But there are a few more things that are good to know.

A chaconne is a slow, austere Baroque dance. Its foundation is a short, solemn bass line or harmonic pattern repeated over and over, usually written in groups of three beats. It actually started as a quick, even sexy dance in South America that then somehow migrated to Europe where, of course, it got darker. It was this serious chaconne that captivated composers as different as Bach, in the monumental solo violin chaconne we're talking about here and the great Passacaglia in C Minor for organ; Purcell, in the famous aria "When I Am Laid in Earth" from his opera *Dido and Aeneas*; Brahms, in the finale of his Fourth Symphony; and Nicolas Hooper, in "Dumbledore's Farewell" in *Harry Potter and the Half-Blood Prince*. That last isn't just for a popular culture reference. The scene is tremendously affecting, due in large part to Hooper's sensitive use of this ancient form. A chaconne even appears in a ballet, appropriately titled *Chaconne,* by George Balanchine. The music is the lyrical finale of Gluck's opera *Orfeo ed Euridice*. All of these can be heard online.

But among all examples of the form, Bach's *Chaconne* is unique in conception, scale, complexity, and emotional power. It is one of a kind.

Bach wrote an endless number of Baroque dances, not just as named dances in the obvious places like his dance suites for orchestra, keyboard, solo cello, and solo violin, but dance forms appear unnamed all over the place in his music. The monumental opening of the *St. Matthew Passion* can be heard as a slow sicilienne but without the lilt. People will argue, but I love the metaphor.

For some reason Bach wrote only three chaconnes in his entire life: the final movement of the first cantata he ever wrote (an early, workmanlike piece) and the two, massive, famous ones—the Passacaglia for organ (a chaconne by any other name) and the *Chaconne* for solo violin. Since the form obviously inspired his best work, why only two mature examples?

And there's an extra mystery with the violin *Chaconne*. Bach wrote three suites of Baroque dances for solo violin, he called them partitas. Usually, Bach's suites of dances for any instrument ended with a jaunty gigue, sending everyone out happy. There's no reason he couldn't have ended his D-minor Partita likewise and, in fact, the first four movements are like any other typical suite: "Allemande," "Courante," "Sarabande," and yes, a "Gigue." But that's not the end. The D-Minor Partita for solo violin is a bit like walking along a familiar street—I know this, I know that—then rounding a corner and OMG, there's Chartres.

The theme of the *Chaconne* lasts four measures, nothing unusual about that. But the rhythmic stress in a typical chaconne is on the second beat, not the first, leaving the music a bit off balance. Since Bach never did anything without a reason, choosing a chaconne with its off-balance rhythm might well reflect how Bach himself felt when he wrote it. I'd even speculate that it was intentional that the whole, huge piece begins with an absence, the missing first beat, like the missing man formation performed by aircraft for military funerals. If you've ever seen one in person, you never forget it. As a form, the chaconne is a time-honoured way to express grief. Is all this going too far? We haven't even started.

The Bach *Chaconne* is built from sixty-four groups of four measures, each growing from, commenting on, contrasting with the preceding one. All together they form a massive three-part, arched structure: the first part severe, the second part gentle and consoling, the third part solemn. A virtual musical cathedral.

The whole piece should have 256 measures (64 x 4) except Bach adds a measure, so the total is one more, an odd number, 257. Again, why? Is this just part of a variation or is it like the secret flaw church architects build into their designs, since only God can be perfect? Or is this something more personal? Bach always felt a connection with numbers and number patterns, he sought their guidance and their inspiring limitations. And, sometimes, he used them as a way, again like a church architect, to invisibly sign his name somewhere.

If you put numbers on the letters of the alphabet, starting A = 1, B = 2, C = 3, and so on, the letters of Bach's name add up to 14. Add up the digits in the number of measures in the *Chaconne*, 2 + 5 + 7, and they equal 14. This isn't just playing with numbers, Bach did this kind of thing all the time in his work, invisibly signing his name using 14 or its inversion, 41, or repeating themes an exact number of times to signify something important. In the *St. Matthew Passion*, after Jesus says, "Wahrlich, ich sage euch: Einer unter euch wird mich verraten" (Truly I say to you: one among you will betray me), in a panic one disciple after another asks "Herr, bin ich's?" (Lord, is it I?). But Bach writes "Herr, bin ich's?" only eleven times, because one disciple already knows it's him.

Nobody will be counting the entrances. Nobody will shout out "Hey! It only happened eleven times!" The counterpoint is complex, even looking at the score you have to pick it apart to see that, yes, it happens only eleven times, there they are. Bach didn't intend for anyone to notice. But Bach noticed. And, by the way, this brief chorus lasts exactly eleven seconds.

So, did Bach really add a measure to the *Chaconne,* this otherwise perfectly symmetrical masterpiece, just so he could, in this totally obscure way, sign his name? Personally, I'm sure of it. So in this masterpiece that stands out in so many ways—it's as long as the rest of the D-Minor Partita put together, so big and so serious as to seem out of place—why should including a symbol of Bach's name in a way nobody would ever notice unless they got out a calculator matter so much to him?

The long-time first violinist of the great Guarneri Quartet, Arnold Steinhardt, spent a lifetime studying and playing the *Chaconne*. In his beautifully-written book *Violin Dreams*, Steinhardt asks this:

> Perhaps cathedrals are grand in order to hold the powerful emotions that grip us, lofty so that we can more easily reach out to our mysterious universe and its creator, and artful and personal in detail to enable us to slip into the recesses of our own souls. "Grand," "lofty," and "personal" are words that also describe the *Chaconne,* but what, if any, was the reason for this mighty cathedral of a work?

In the year Bach wrote his sonatas and partitas for solo violin, or at least the year when he signed the exceptionally beautiful original manuscript, Bach's employer Prince Leopold decided to travel to Carlsbad to visit the spa and asked Bach to go along with him. It was a long trip. Finally Bach returned home only to find that, while they were away and out of touch, his wife Maria Barbara had died unexpectedly at age thirty-five. The funeral had already happened, she was already buried in the churchyard. From the suddenness of her death and her young age, it's reasonable to speculate that she died of eclampsia, making her death tragic several times over. Poor Johann Sebastian, shocked and profoundly bereaved, suddenly found himself a single father of four. So, a natural question: did Bach compose the *Chaconne* as a *tombeau*, as a memorial to his wife?

Composers in Bach's time did not usually write music to express themselves, but as a way to fill a need, such as court entertainment, something for the Duke to play after dinner, or for the liturgy of a church service. *Gebrauchsmusik*, "useful music." But German musicologist Helga Thoene finds the *Chaconne* full of references to Bach's sacred works, works about death and sorrow, references Bach's circle of friends would have recognized. Thoene's analysis extends into speculation and controversy, but she is only one of many who have listened to this great work and wondered what in the world is going on here?

When we imagine Bach's situation we are deeply moved, the poor man, but we'll never really know why he wrote the *Chaconne*. But we do know that a fine performance of it can move us in ways that surpass understanding. In his book, Steinhardt talks about the time he was asked to play for the funeral of a close friend who, like Maria Barbara, had also unexpectedly died young. Without a moment's hesitation he knew that he had to play the *Chaconne*. Nothing else would do. He felt this as a great responsibility and studied and practiced as much as he could. But somehow, perhaps because of the weight of the occasion, the harder he worked the more the great piece eluded him. He was close to despair that he could ever play it well enough to do justice to his friend. Then one night he dreamed that he was practicing the *Chaconne* when, out of nowhere, Johann Sebastian Bach himself appeared in front of him. "Herr Bach, I am having so much trouble. What is the right tempo? How should

I play the rhythm at the beginning? What is the right bowing in this place? Please help me." Bach didn't answer. Then Bach held out his arms and said, "Dance with me."

Edinburgh

Judge of the Nations, spare us yet,
Lest we forget—lest we forget!

—Rudyard Kipling

AT SOME POINT IN A room somewhere, it was decided that the National Arts Centre Orchestra should do a tour of the UK with Pinchas Zukerman, who was shortly to step down after almost two decades as our music director. A gesture of respect for his long tenure was likely one reason, another that it had been two decades since the last time we were there, only that time with Pinchas's brilliant opposite, the early music specialist Trevor Pinnock. We loved the best parts of both of these brilliant musicians, it's just that those best parts were different.

But another reason, the best one, was that 2014 would mark the grim centennial of the First World War and the arrival of thousands of brave, young, frightened Canadian troops on Salisbury Plain in southern England. There they would train for what turned out to be endless, deadly, unimaginably horrible trench warfare. The tour would be to honour their courage and sacrifice. Lest we forget.

The tour was five cities—Edinburgh, Nottingham, London, Salisbury, and Bristol.

Nottingham was notable for having a raucous street fair the same night as the concert, which made walking back to the hotel interesting.

Bristol is notable for being the embarkation point five hundred years ago of the Italian explorer Giovanni Caboto—John Cabot—whose next port of call was (probably) Newfoundland. Wherever he actually landed, they hadn't seen Europeans since the Vikings who got there a thousand years ago, though not before Indigenous populations who had been there forever. Anyway, Caboto's sponsor King Henry VII named the island "New founde lande," thereby claiming North America for England and all that's happened since as a result. Wherever it was, for sure Caboto's sailors were more than grateful to get there. Do you know how long it takes to get from Bristol, England to North America by wooden square-rigged sailing ship? I don't either, but the Vikings did and clearly kept it to themselves.

London was notable for, well, being London, and for our performance of Beethoven's Ninth Symphony sitting side-by-side with the Royal Philharmonic. Yes, almost two hundred musicians packed onto the groaning stage of Royal Festival Hall, plus the two hundred singers of the London Philharmonic Choir up in the choir loft. And up in the Royal Box was the Royal Patron of the tour, His Royal Highness Prince Charles. His presence was notable for making the concert start late, then causing a backstage traffic jam at the end because of security, and for HRH himself looking, according to the obviously anti-colonial *Globe and Mail*, "resplendent as a piece of expensive furniture." Actually, I thought having Prince Charles there was pretty neat.

But Salisbury—to be precise, its glorious medieval cathedral—was the heart of the tour. And our CEO Peter Herrndorf, who had used his considerable networking skills, distinguished name, and Harvard MBA to inspire the necessary funding, was just as awed by the place as the rest of us. I attempt to describe the indescribable in the final chapter, "Remembrance Day."

Which leaves the first for last, Edinburgh. Unfortunately, our arrival in the beautiful, ancient capital of Scotland was notable for, first, a nightmare.

It would be breezy and accurate to describe the travel arrangements to get us from Ottawa to Edinburgh as an endless itinerary averted, thanks to a pilots' strike at Lufthansa. The original schedule had called for a five-hour layover in Frankfurt before finally dragging our sleep-deprived, jet-lagged sorry behinds to Scotland. But that misconceived plan was now cancelled, due to the unhappy Lufthansa pilots. This turn of fortune forced the booking of a much faster (and more expensive) connection through London: two hours less time in the air and just enough time in Heathrow to grab breakfast. So we arrived in Edinburgh only very tired instead of totally exhausted. But all that was forgotten the moment our groggy eyes peered up at the television monitors over the baggage carousels and saw images of our home, the National Arts Centre, and the War Memorial immediately in front of it, surrounded by cordons of police and flashing red lights and general emergency mayhem. During our short flight from London, there had been an act of terrorism virtually on our doorstep and all of downtown Ottawa was under lockdown. Data limits were thrown to the winds as cell phones were grabbed from pockets and carry-ons to frantically phone families back home. A journalist in Ottawa was talking to our director of communications as she waited for her luggage. Her face was as white as the paper you're looking at.

The National War Memorial in downtown Ottawa is a tall, imposing granite monument in the centre of Confederation Square. It's the most important ceremonial public space in the country, placed literally in the shadow of the Parliament Buildings and, looking the other way, in the shadow of the National Arts Centre. The memorial was originally dedicated to Canadians who lost their lives serving in the First World War, but was later rededicated to commemorate Canadians whose lives were sacrificed in all conflicts, since "the war to end all wars" so obviously wasn't.

Facing the memorial is the Tomb of the Unknown Soldier, a low, stone monument surrounded by a great open space, the solemn site for national observances on Remembrance Day. The Canadian military takes this commemoration seriously by posting uniformed sentries at the memorial seven days a week during daylight hours from May to November. States the Government of Canada:

> The National Sentry Program reinforces Canada's commitment to remember and honour Canadians who served in the twentieth century's major wars . . . . On October 22, 2014, Corporal Nathan Cirillo was tragically killed while on sentry duty. Sentry duty at the Tomb of the Unknown Soldier now holds an even deeper meaning for both the Canadian Armed Forces and the Canadian public.

October 22, 2014, is when we landed in Edinburgh.

On pleasant days, most tourists stop for a moment, take a picture of the sentries and move on. But once in a while someone stops and does not take a picture. They just stand quietly with respect, hat removed, and let the mortal gravity of the place sink in. I wish there were more like that.

While we were in the air from Heathrow, a terrorist had walked up to the memorial with a rifle and shot Corporal Cirillo three times in the back.

While shocked onlookers rushed to help the mortally wounded soldier, the gunman ran and hijacked a car, crashed through the security checkpoints at the main door to the Parliament Buildings, and forced his way inside looking for the prime minister, who, it turned out, was in a meeting just down the hallway. But before the gunman could get that far, he was shot by the Sergeant-at-Arms of the House of Commons, RCMP veteran Kevin Vickers, and RCMP Constable Curtis Barrett. Their actions were heroic and they were appropriately recognized. When the details came out, it was not like a movie. It was real, chaotic and horrible. The whole downtown of Canada's capital went on lockdown for fear there might be other terrorists at large. There weren't, but rumours were flying and it took hours to make sure.

The next day in Edinburgh we ran up more data charges reading the news and getting updates from home. People were especially alarmed because it was the second attack on a member of the Canadian military within a week. The first was a targeted hit-and-run in Saint-Jean-sur-Richelieu that cost the life of Warrant Officer Patrice Vincent. Now Corporal Cirillo. Would there be a third? It was a sobering, frightening time.

But for us on the other side of the Atlantic, it was time to get to work. Our performance at Edinburgh's Usher Hall was long-planned to honour members of the Canadian Armed Forces who had made the ultimate sacrifice, but now the tour would also commemorate two mortal sacrifices made just days before. We are often billed as Canada's national orchestra, which is accurate enough I suppose, since we're located in the national capital, perform at the National Arts Centre and have significant funding from Parliament. But suddenly we were responsible for representing Canada to honour the loss of two Canadian soldiers with names and faces who had been alive and with their families while we were packing our suitcases. There is no way to prepare for such a responsibility. One must simply accept it, and with honour.

With such events back home weighing on our hearts, here we were in the great historical city of Edinburgh. Our schedule gave us a day to get over our jet lag, so people went wherever they felt they needed to go. For me, that was St Giles' Cathedral, the only cathedral in the Presbyterian Church and that only by virtue of being Anglican for about five minutes four hundred years ago. Anyway, it seemed appropriate.

I ended up spending the whole day in this beautiful, ancient, occasionally creepy building. Tourists came and went, but there was one person, sitting alone in the back row, who had been there for hours. I took her example and sat quietly for a long time, just thinking and trying to absorb a little of the inspiring, sometimes frightening history of the place.

When Charles I attended a service in St Giles' in 1633, he didn't like the Calvinist service so he had his own chaplains take over. This caused people to basically go ballistic. He wanted to make the Edinburgh services more like the way they were done in, ahem, England. He also set up an Anglican diocese in Edinburgh, which is how St Giles' became a cathedral.

Worse, a few years later Charles I insisted that St Giles' use a prayer book based on the Anglican *Book of Common Prayer*. When the dean began reading from the new prayer book, an enraged parishioner named Janet Geddes picked up a wooden stool and threw it at him. At least that's the very popular legend. This incident, or whatever really happened, triggered a cascade of events that led eventually to the English Civil War, the execution of Charles I, and the establishment of the Commonwealth and the Protectorate under Oliver Cromwell. It all started in St Giles'. Probably right over there.

A bronze plaque, modestly positioned on a side column, commemorates James Hannay, Dean of St Giles' at that time. It reads, succinctly, "He was the first and the last to read from the Service Book in this church. This memorial is erected in happier times by his descendant." Another plaque nearby reads, "Protestant oral tradition affirms that near this spot a brave Scotch woman Janet Geddes on July 23, 1637 struck the first blow in the great struggle for freedom of conscience which after a conflict of half a century ended in the establishment of civil and religious liberty."

After reading all this, it was good that St Giles' of the scary history also has a good cafeteria in the basement. Or maybe it was the crypt. In any case, the ham and cheese was excellent.

In addition to the cafeteria. the nine-hundred-year-old St Giles' building has been brought into our time by a number of other upgrades. To control the constant stream of visitors, there's now an automatic sliding entrance door of strikingly contemporary design, which means it's both functional and beautiful but looks like it belongs on a museum of modern art. There's also a super-high-tech lighting system that changes the colour and intensity of the lighting depending on the time of day, and a magnificent new pipe organ, its imposing, brilliantly polished pipes presiding over what would have been called the transept if it had been Anglican long enough. St Giles' also has a highly accomplished choir of thirty adult singers which has made many recordings. You can buy their CDs in the gift shop.

Yes, I make light, but the tragedy back home just the day before was never far from our minds. Despite being a focal point for historic religious upheavals, St Giles' is also a profoundly spiritual place. So I followed the example of my unknown friend in the back and just sat quietly until I could hear, or at least imagined I could hear, the stern but not unkind Scottish voice of this holy place. As with my unknown companion, I imagine, it's what was needed to collect unsettling thoughts and hand them over to a higher authority for a while.

Remembrance Day

Churches are best for prayer that have least light.

—John Donne

"IF ONE THOUGHT ABOUT IT, one could become quite depressed. But I think it's less important why people come here and more important what they find when they get here."

This brave effort at deflection from the Dean of King's College, Cambridge was his reply when asked how he felt about the thousands of tourists wandering through the exquisite fifteenth-century chapel of King's College each year, snapping selfies. It's the same in any of the world's great sacred spaces that feature in guided tours, historical novels of varying quality, and innumerable bucket lists.

Yet the entirety of King's College chapel, including "the noblest stone ceiling in existence," could easily fit inside the immense eight-hundred-year-old cathedral of the Diocese of Salisbury, over centuries home to countless people of faith, the oldest working clock in the world, the highest spire in the United Kingdom, and one of the few original copies of Magna Carta. And beautiful new washrooms, but that's for later.

And it was in October 2014, within these lofty stone walls built by workers climbing hundred-foot-high wooden scaffolds eight centuries before workers' compensation, that the Canadian Broadcasting Corporation built a temporary stage at the east end of the nave, set up television lights, hung HD video cameras on huge, counterbalanced cranes, and curtained off changing areas beneath the Prisoners of Conscience stained glass window. All this for the musicians of the National Arts Centre Orchestra, preparing to perform a concert that evening (what they find when they get here) to commemorate the one-hundredth anniversary of the arrival of thousands of Canadian troops to train on nearby Salisbury Plain. That, and the obscenely accidental start of the war in which so many perished—the Great War, as it was then called, with no number, since after its unspeakable carnage there surely could never be another.

Dear friends had driven for two hours up the narrow, winding roads from Dorset, just for the occasion. One of them was a canon of the cathedral, no less, that august honorific carrying with it a designated seat in the cathedral's ancient oak stalls in the quire, a position of eminence in the diocesan hierarchy and, not least, recognition of the kind of spiritual achievement that is a priceless blessing at hospice bedsides. She is one in a million.

On that chilly October afternoon, the great cathedral was crowded with video technicians, electricians, musicians, stagehands, producers, major donors fresh from a historical lecture by Margaret MacMillan, and a throng of tourists craning their necks at the vaulted ceilings and reading the kind of descriptive signs that begin, "In 1224 . . ."

Out of nowhere, a kind, soft voice, but authoritative (quite the trick, and helped by a good sound system) welcomed all those present to Salisbury Cathedral and wished all an enjoyable visit. And just a gentle reminder, this is a house of God, sanctified over eight centuries as a holy place. Let us take just a moment for a few words of prayer.

Prayer? This crowd?

But a hush came over the great space, a transformation. People stood quietly and respectfully and listened to a dignified, non-denominational prayer, read by the soft but authoritative voice. The prayer was generic but it meant business. It was as if the cathedral had noticed the bustling, noisy crowd and felt it necessary to gently remind us that we were, in fact, guests in a great house to which we had been admitted only by virtue of grace. "Surely the LORD is in this place; and I knew it not."

Then there were the chairs.

One of the many things audiences shouldn't know is that the comfy-looking folding chairs you always get in unusual concert venues, like eight-hundred-year-old cathedrals, were designed for snoozing during boring committee meetings. They were not designed for straight-backed manual labour, which is one incomplete but accurate way to describe playing in an orchestra. The folding chairs of Salisbury Cathedral were, not to put too fine a point on it, torture.

First, they were low. Playing a classical instrument at an international level is a full-contact sport. It requires freedom of motion, muscular support, and strategic distribution of weight, none of which are possible from boring committee meeting posture. Second, the chairs were angled back, which throws your balance all to hell. Third . . . oh, it doesn't matter. They looked nice but they felt miserable. On the other hand, we were there to commemorate the hundreds of thousands of Canadian soldiers who went off to fight in the trenches, many of whom, of course, never came back. So we didn't complain about the chairs.

As our rehearsal began, the cathedral was still full of light. The crowds of tourists and technicians and friends and major donors were still wandering around reading about what happened in 1224. But the compelling sound of the Vaughan Williams *Fantasia on a Theme by Thomas*

Tallis made things get real in a hurry. Great music sanctifies whatever space it's made in. The great cathedral had already been sanctified for eight hundred years. It was as if the music and the cathedral joined hands. Another transformation.

But after the rehearsal, our concerns became strictly secular. Where were the wardrobe trunks with our concert clothes? Under the Prisoners of Conscience stained glass window, of course—a curtained-off *de facto* dressing room, complete with coat racks already hanging with street clothes and the occasional unmentionable. Was this a safe place to leave our instruments? Security is never taken for granted, even here. And, most important, where were the beautiful new washrooms we'd been told about? What? Way out *there*?

With television cameras on cranes, technical equipment all over the place, huge storage trunks for an entourage of over a hundred people, and miles of wiring, it was like a benign military invasion. We had taken over.

But the cathedral had other ideas.

A modest notice posted near the entrance read: "Evensong 4:00." Like the prayer on the sound system, another gentle but authoritative reminder that this huge, bustling, famous place was also a working church. And Evensong, no less, that kindest, most inviting service in the whole Anglican liturgy. I write about this beautiful service in "When Will You Pay Me?" Say the Bells of Old Bailey. Right on cue, the gentle, authoritative voice echoed through the huge space, "The service of Evensong will begin at four o'clock. The cathedral is now closed except for those attending the service." Nothing could have emptied the place faster. Soon the sounds of chairs scraping and rapid footsteps and doors closing faded as the last of the afternoon crowd fled the building.

Only fifteen people stayed behind and found their way to the ancient oak stalls on either side of the quire, the special space directly beneath the organ and the towering pillars of Purbeck marble that support the tallest spire in the United Kingdom. The guidebooks say that the polished stone columns are visibly bent by the immense weight they carry, and so they were. Hmm, one thinks, looking up. They've been like that for centuries, it's pretty unlikely they'll finally give way this afternoon at four o'clock. But then there was that unsettling book by William Golding, *The Spire*: "There was one August gale from the southwest that set the spire swaying like a mast; but though the pillars were bent, they did not break."

"In sure and certain hope . . ." took on new meaning.

The sun went down. The darkening interior of the cathedral loomed larger as the shadows lengthened, until only the ancient oak stalls with fifteen people in them could be dimly seen, illuminated only by candlelight. John Donne said, "Churches are best for prayer that have least light." He was onto something.

Some people think Anglican services are too theatrical—all those kneelers and robes and incense—but I can't agree. Anglican liturgies like Evensong are based on centuries of faith, wisdom, and tradition, and find expressive power in every word and gesture. As James Wood says in his introduction to the Penguin Classics edition of the *Book of Common Prayer*:

> And so begins a service whose roots stretch as far back as the tenth century, and whose liturgy has been in almost continuous use since 1549 . . . one of the great, abiding works of English literature, what the historian Diarmaid MacCulloch calls "one of a handful of texts to have decided the future of a world language."

He means the *Book of Common Prayer*, the *King James Bible* and Shakespeare.

A small choir began the service, singing one of Anton Bruckner's most beautiful motets, "Locus iste."

> Locus iste a Deo factus est, inaestimabile sacramentum: irreprehensibilis est.
> (This place was made by God, an inestimable mystery, flawless and sanctified.)

And then the opening words of Evensong, as spoken for centuries:

> Priest: LORD, open thou our lips; and our mouth shall shew forth thy praise.
> Answer: O God, make speed to save us; O Lord, make haste to help us.

This, as an earthy, priestly friend once said to me, is where the rubber hits the road.

Half an hour ago, the cathedral was a bright, bustling, noisy public place, full of busy people, busy with, well, busyness. Now it had transformed into what it always was, and is, and always shall be: a place of peace, a place of sacred silence, a place, in the words of Dylan Thomas, of close and holy darkness.

The pianist and writer (and Roman Catholic) Stephen Hough described Anglican Evensong in these lovely words:

> It is a service into which all can stumble without censure—a rambling old house where everyone can find some corner to sit and think.

So for an hour we sat and thought, and listened to beautiful words and beautiful music in this peaceful, holy place. Being Evensong, there was no expectation that we would do anything, no standing or kneeling, though I wouldn't be surprised if there were, perhaps, somewhere in the darkness, a prayer or two, even, perhaps especially, by people who don't normally think of themselves as prayerful. That's the beauty of Evensong, the threshold. Another transformation.

Then the service was over. The lights came up, we could see the high stone walls again and we realized that it was getting on to dinnertime. Wake up, the day isn't done, not by a long shot. We still have a concert to play and we need food.

My Dorset friends and I walked into downtown Salisbury to a Waitrose to get some takeout. Walking back to the cathedral offices to find a room where we could sit down, we passed by a bench that would become infamous a few years later as the place where Sergei and Yulia Skripal were found unconscious after being poisoned with Novichok. Even in a place like Salisbury, the distance between sacred and profane can be pretty short.

We could already see the audience lining up outside the east door. How many can Salisbury Cathedral actually hold, we wondered. Inside at the far end, seemingly a mile away, I found the wardrobe trunks and changed into my concert clothes (we still wore formal tails then), thinking it a little odd to be standing there in my underwear looking up at the Prisoners of Conscience stained glass window. But really, it was not so incongruous. Earlier, the cathedral had transformed from a tourist destination and temporary television studio into its true self for Evensong. We, in our way, were now transforming into our true selves. We were about to play great music as well as any orchestra in the world could play it, a well-practiced professional transformation that is not as easy as we make it look.

It's always a bit unsettling to be in the presence of a transformation—the sounds of the rehearsal, the unexpected public prayer, the service of Evensong, shopping for dinner in a supermarket, and now, finally, the real reason we were here.

The cathedral darkened again, but now full of people as far as you could see. But no prayerful, contemplative silence for us. We had to perform, we had to be a great orchestra, playing great music, sitting on uncomfortable chairs, far from the washrooms. But then great music did what great music always does. The music of Vaughan Williams filled the cathedral with beauty and sadness beyond words. We could not speak for the sixty-six thousand Canadians who lost their lives in the Great War we were there to commemorate, nor for the many thousands of Canadians who have given their lives in conflicts since, nor for Corporal Cirillo or Warrant Officer Vincent who gave their lives a week ago. But the music could.

When the unavoidable applause was over and people got up for intermission, I noticed one of our most generous supporters—a distinguished lawyer, former chair of the NAC Foundation and, as of this writing, chair of the National Arts Centre Board of Trustees—standing by his seat near the front, unembarrassed as tears streamed down his face. Without thinking, I stepped down from the stage, walked over to him and, given permission I suppose by the occasion and by this great sacred space, put my arms around him and wept with him.

O God, make speed to save us; O Lord, make haste to help us.

Epilogue

The Life It Brings

I LIKE THE TITLE OF this book. It's descriptive, it's a little breezy, and it's accurate. But there's an even better title I'd like to steal. The physicist Jeremy Bernstein wrote an excellent book (four and a half stars on Amazon) about his life working with the great minds in his field, giants like Oppenheimer, Fermi, Bohr, Einstein—their immense intellects, of course, but also their culture, their love of everything to do with scientific discovery, and their kindness. His book was basically one long expression of gratitude for being where he was, when he was, to experience, as I recall, "the infinite astonishments of physics."

Well, I've spent a lifetime experiencing the infinite astonishments of music. The title of Bernstein's book is *The Life It Brings*. That phrase is actually from a letter by Robert Oppenheimer to his beloved younger brother Frank, who was studying at Cambridge. Oppenheimer writes, "I take it that . . . physics has gotten now very much under your skin, physics and the obvious excellences of the life it brings."

The Life It Brings would have been the title of this book, if someone even more grateful than I am hadn't already thought of it. So I acknowledge it here, along with Bernstein's astonishments and Oppenheimer's obvious excellences. Why not? Music is basically physics, and physics, in its more subtle manifestations, is music. And both disciplines look up at the stars, wondering . . . what the hell?

Acknowledgements

I MUST GIVE SPECIAL THANKS to my publisher, Sutherland House and its president Ken Whyte. I've been a writer of some kind all my life, but only when a publisher accepts your work and puts you through the mandatory initiation to forge your stuff into something professional do you become an author. It's quite a ride.

If the wonderful staff of Sutherland House have one thing in common, it's endless patience. Assistant Publisher and Managing Editor Shalomi Ranasinghe, Editor Leah Ciani, Director of Publicity Sarah Miniaci, and the estimable Ken Whyte displayed that virtue with me countless times.

And to Paul Wells, chapeau. This is all your fault.

A decade ago, a journalist whom I greatly admire published her first book, called *Drift: The Unmooring of American Military Power*. It was a successful, highly readable book on an important subject, but she said, "I'm never going through this again." She has since written three more, but it took a while.

The people who encourage an author, especially a first-time author, and patiently read through early drafts full of howling misjudgments yet look on the bright side, are the rarest of friends. I said to one of them, "Writing a book is like giving birth." Giving me a cold look, she said,

"No, it's not." But she acknowledged the point. Without these dear people whom I gratefully acknowledge here, this book, for better or worse, would not be in your hands.

Having to start the personal acknowledgements somewhere, I'll start on the couch by thanking my imperious, demanding, loving, unassailable British father. It was tough for a kid growing up in Detroit to have a father who was born during the reign of Queen Victoria. He wrote in an elevated style with just a touch of earthiness that made me think, as a worshipful young son, that my father was more cultured and better educated than anybody else's father. Turned out I was right. For most of his life he maintained a voluminous correspondence with family, friends, and business associates, and kept carbon copies of everything. I read it all.

As a child, I also developed a strange addiction to *Reader's Digest*. My impressionable young mind loved its signature stories that always began "George was delayed in traffic and missed his flight. Good thing, since his plane disappeared off the radar an hour after takeoff and was never heard from again." I loved those. Despite its formulas, *Reader's Digest* provided a young reader with excellent examples of clear, concise writing, always keeping it short. Obviously, I didn't learn anything.

And I have to thank my high-school sweetheart, a blindingly beautiful, take-no-prisoners redhead who was much smarter and more talented than I was. She was also two years older, so when she left for university a thousand miles away, I learned to type in a hurry. When she started dating a fourth-year pre-med student (later of the Mayo Clinic), I was still in my second year of high school. The agonies that caused were like a Russian novel.

Many lifetimes later, my writing took up arms, so to speak, when the National Arts Centre Orchestra's founding concertmaster, Walter Prystawski, and I found ourselves using words to defend our jobs, our colleagues, and our beloved ensemble against the forces of darkness. That's not just a colourful metaphor. Together, we wrote position papers, Q&As, speaking points, press releases (no internet then, - 30 -) and, our *chef-d'œuvre*, a commercially printed tract detailing the financial, political, and artistic history of the National Arts Centre Orchestra, how it was created out of nothing, and how its home had turned against us. Walter wrote, I deleted half of it. Given how much we both cared about our beloved orchestra—and our writing—it was an acid test of a friendship that has lasted now for close to forty years. Hence the dedication.

Then my writerly ego was given a boost when the great pianist Angela Hewitt unexpectedly found herself needing program notes for her summer festival in Italy and asked me if I could write some. Yesterday, if possible. I learned that I could write on a deadline and people seemed to like the result, so I thought, "Hey, I should do more of this." Later, I wrote program notes for a festival in Prince Edward County presented by several of my esteemed NACO colleagues, then I was asked by the National Arts Centre (no longer the enemy) to write a piece for the fiftieth anniversary of the orchestra, a gratifying assignment. None of that made me rich and famous, but it was nice to be asked.

Of course, writing a book has been, as they say, a whole different thing. This is completely the fault of one of Canada's finest political writers, Paul Wells. He read my blog during the COVID lockdown and, as I said in the introduction, liked it enough to suggest I send it to Ken Whyte, publisher of Sutherland House. The continuing encouragement of these professionals made me wake up in the middle of the night realizing that this might actually happen.

Years ago, Christine Hanssens, a wise European of many languages, told me I should write a book and never gave up encouraging me. Hana Kinsman, native of Prague which she misses twenty-five hours a day and granddaughter of Václav Talich, was such a fan of my daily posts that she'd become concerned if I let it get too late before posting something. Evelyn Greenberg, present at the very first rehearsal of the NAC Orchestra because she accompanied the original auditions, left me a glowing voicemail from Italy that I still have. Colleagues David Marks, Jessica Linnebach, Carissa Klopoushak, and Julia MacLaine left me glowing emails from Prince Edward County that I still have. Victoria Hathaway, Elizabeth Burbidge, Martha Nixon, Gloria Fox, Deb Norman, and Dr. David Gillies read all or parts of the manuscript in its various awkward stages and were unfailingly critical, in the nicest way.

Tom Annand, Wesley Warren, Geneviève Baldassare, Maria Calderisi, Margaret Floyd, Nora Shulman, Dr. Felix Tyndel, Sylvia Gazsi Gill, Dr. Edward Krul, Mary Lockhart, Janet Smith, Freda Ross, and Ambassador Vernon Turner gave invaluable advice, mostly about parts that confused them.

Finally, I must thank again my best friend, former colleague, superlative orchestra leader, and occasional comrade-in-arms, Walter Prystawski. Without his daily advice, encouragement, and the occasional kick in the pants, this book absolutely would never have happened. As John le Carré has Toby Esterhase lovingly say to George Smiley in *Smiley's People*, ". . . we had a lot of times together, stole some horses."